Law and Philosophy Library

Volume 112

AF181668

Series editors
Francisco J. Laporta
Department of Law, Autonomous University of Madrid, Madrid, Spain

Frederick Schauer
School of Law, University of Virginia, Charlottesville, Virginia, USA

Torben Spaak
Department of Law, Stockholm University, Stockholm, Sweden

The Law and Philosophy Library, which has been in existence since 1985, aims to publish cutting edge works in the philosophy of law, and has a special history of publishing books that focus on legal reasoning and argumentation, including those that may involve somewhat formal methodologies. The series has published numerous important books on law and logic, law and artificial intelligence, law and language, and law and rhetoric. While continuing to stress these areas, the series has more recently expanded to include books on the intersection between law and the Continental philosophical tradition, consistent with the traditional openness of the series to books in the Continental jurisprudential tradition. The series is proud of the geographic diversity of its authors, and many have come from Latin America, Spain, Italy, the Netherlands, Germany, and Eastern Europe, as well, more obviously for an English-language series, from the United Kingdom, the United States, Australia, and Canada.

More information about this series at http://www.springer.com/series/6210

Thomas Bustamante • Christian Dahlman
Editors

Argument Types and Fallacies in Legal Argumentation

Springer

Editors
Thomas Bustamante
Faculdade de Direito
Universidade Federal de Minas Gerais
Belo Horizonte, Minas Gerais, Brazil

Christian Dahlman
Faculty of Law
Lund University
Lund, Sweden

ISSN 1572-4395 ISSN 2215-0315 (electronic)
Law and Philosophy Library
ISBN 978-3-319-35487-3 ISBN 978-3-319-16148-8 (eBook)
DOI 10.1007/978-3-319-16148-8

Springer Cham Heidelberg New York Dordrecht London
© Springer International Publishing Switzerland 2015
Softcover reprint of the hardcover 1st edition 2015
This work is subject to copyright. All rights are reserved by the Publisher, whether the whole or part of the material is concerned, specifically the rights of translation, reprinting, reuse of illustrations, recitation, broadcasting, reproduction on microfilms or in any other physical way, and transmission or information storage and retrieval, electronic adaptation, computer software, or by similar or dissimilar methodology now known or hereafter developed.
The use of general descriptive names, registered names, trademarks, service marks, etc. in this publication does not imply, even in the absence of a specific statement, that such names are exempt from the relevant protective laws and regulations and therefore free for general use.
The publisher, the authors and the editors are safe to assume that the advice and information in this book are believed to be true and accurate at the date of publication. Neither the publisher nor the authors or the editors give a warranty, express or implied, with respect to the material contained herein or for any errors or omissions that may have been made.

Printed on acid-free paper

Springer International Publishing AG Switzerland is part of Springer Science+Business Media (www.springer.com)

Contents

About the Authors

Michał Araszkiewicz is an adjunct lecturer in the Department of Legal Theory of Jagiellonian University (Kraków, Poland). His areas of research interest include theories of legal argumentation, application of AI tools to legal reasoning and general methodology of jurisprudence. He is a co-editor of several contributed volumes, including *Coherence: Insights from Philosophy, Jurisprudence and Artificial Intelligence* (with J. Šavelka), Law and Philosophy Library vol. 107, Springer 2013, as well as author of numerous papers published in monographs, journals and reviewed conference proceedings.

Thomas Bustamante is Associate Professor of Legal Philosophy and Legal Theory at the Federal University of Minas Gerais, in Brazil, and has previously taught at the University of Aberdeen, in the UK, where he still has an Honorary Appointment, and at the Federal University of Juiz de Fora, where he still contributes to the Program of Graduate Research Studies in Law. His publications include the books *Teoria do Precedente Judicial* (2012), *Teoria do Direito e Decisão Racional* (2008) and *Argumentação Contra Legem* (2005), as well as several articles in Portuguese, English, Spanish and French and the edited books *On the Philosophy of Precedent* (2012, co-edited by Carlos Bernal Pulido), *Global Harmony and the Rule of Law* (2012, co-edited by Oche Onazi) and *Human Rights, Language and Law* (2012, co-edited by Oche Onazi).

Pierluigi Chiassoni is Professor of Jurisprudence of the University of Genova. He graduated in law at the University of Genova (*Università di Genova*), has a Master's Degree from Cornell University, in the USA, and a Doctorate in Legal Philosophy from the University of Milan (*Università di Milano*). His academic scholarships include the books *Law and Economics: L'analisi economica del diritto negli Stati Uniti* (1992), *La giurisprudenz civile: Metodi d'interpretazione e techniche interpretative* (1999), *L'utopia della ragione analitica* (2005), *L'interpretazione delle norme giuridiche* (2006), *Tecnica dell'interpretazione* *giuridica* (Italian Edition 2007, Spanish edition 2011), *Diritti umani, sentenze elusive, clausole ineffabili. Saggi di realismo militante* (2011) and *Desencantos para abogados realistas* (2012).

Christian Dahlman is a Professor in Jurisprudence at Lund University (Sweden), specializing in legal argumentation and the theory of legal evidence.

Bernardo Gonçalves Fernandes studied law at the Federal University of Minas Gerais (*Universidade Federal de Minas Gerais*) in Brazil, where he graduated and obtained his M.Phil. and his Ph.D. He has permanent positions of Associate Professor of Constitutional Theory and Constitutional Law at the Federal University of Minas Gerais and Associate Professor of Constitutional Theory and Constitutional Law at the Pontifical Catholic University of Minas Gerais. His publications include: *Curso de Direito Constitucional*, now on the 6th Edition (2014) and one of the best-selling textbooks of Law in Brazil, with an average of 10,000 copies per year, and the books *Interpretação Constitucional: Reflexões sobre a (nova) Hermenêutica Constitucional* (2010), *Remédios Constitucionais* (2009) and *Poder Judiciário e(m) Crise* (2008). He has also edited the books *Estudos de Direito Constitucional e Teoria da Constituição, Volume 1* (2011) and *Estudos de Direito Constitucional e Teoria da Constituição, Volume 2* (2011).

Eveline T. Feteris is an Associate Professor at the Department of Speech Communication, Argumentation Theory and Rhetoric and a member of the research programme Argumentation and Discourse and the research school of the International Learned Institute of Argumentation Studies (ILIAS). She is director of the research master's programme Text and Communication. She is a member of the editorial board of the journal *Argumentation*, the journal *Argumentation in Context* and the journal *Language, Law and Interdisciplinary Practice*. She is a member of the editorial board of the series Argumentation in Context of John Benjamins. She has been a visiting professor at the University of Lethbridge and the University of Lund. She received her Ph.D. in Humanities in 1989 at the University of Amsterdam with the dissertation *Discussieregels in het recht* (Discussion rules in law). Feteris is author of several books, academic volumes and many publications in international journals. Among Feteris key publications are *Fundamentals of Legal Argumentation: A Survey of Theories of Justification of Judicial Decisions*, Dordrecht: Springer Netherlands 1999 (also translated into Chinese, Spanish and Turkish); E.T. Feteris, H. Kloosterhuis, H.J. Plug, *Argumentation and the application of legal rules*, Amsterdam: Sic Sat, 2009; C. Dahlman & E.T. Feteris (Eds.), *Legal argumentation theory: Cross-Disciplinary perspectives*. Dordrecht etc: Springer (2012).

Harm Kloosterhuis studied Argumentation Theory (M.A. and Ph.D.) and Law (LLM). He is Lecturer and researcher at the Erasmus School of Law Rotterdam and Lecturer at the University of Aruba. His main areas of research are legal argumentation theory, legal theory and speech act theory. His publications include: *Reconstructing Interpretative Argumentation in Legal Decisions* (2006) and

Argumentation and the Application of Legal Rules (2009, co-edited with E.T. Feteris and H.J. Plug). His articles on legal theory and argumentation theory have been published in *Argumentation*, *Ratio Juris* and *Artificial Intelligence and Law*.

José Juan Moreso is Professor of Legal Philosophy at the Universitat Pompeu Fabra, where he was also the Rector from 2005 until 2013. He is also a member of the Adjunct Faculty at the Universidad Diego Portales (Santiago de Chile). He took a Law Degree (with honors) from the Universitat Autònoma de Barcelona in 1983 and a Doctorate in Law (with honors) from the same University in 1988. He has taught at the Universitat Autònoma de Barcelona (1988–1995), Universitat de Girona (1996–2000) and Universitat Pompeu Fabra de Barcelona (2000–2005). Moreso has fundamentally worked in legal theory, with special attention to the structure and the dynamics of legal systems, using the contributions of deontic logic. Now he is working in the philosophical foundations of the constitution, in a broad area where coincides metaethics, philosophy of language, theory of legal interpretation and argumentation, political philosophy and democratic theory. He was Visiting Scholar in the University of Buenos Aires, University of Oxford and University of Genoa and Visiting Professor in some European Universities. He is also editor of the review *Doxa*, Associate Editor of *Ratio Juris* and the collection *Law and Philosophy of Marcial Pons*, member of the Advisory Board of several publications as *Ragion Pratica, Toeria Politica*, *Isonomia*, *Law, Ethics and Philosohy.* In 2010 he was nominated as Doctor Honoris Causa by the University of Valparaíso (Chile) and in 2014 by the University Antenor Orrego of Trujillo (Perú). He is author of several books and a good number of papers in International Journals of Philosophy. Among them: *Legal Indeterminacy and Constitutional Interpretation,* English version of R. Zimmerling, (Dordrecht: Kluwer, 1998) and *La Constitución: modelo para armar* (Madrid: Marcial Pons 2009).

Giovanni Battista Ratti is Lecturer in Legal Philosophy in the Department of Law of the University of Genoa (Italy) and Visiting Lecturer in Legal Argumentation in the School of Law of Bocconi University (Italy). He has been Government of Canada Research Scholar (University of Toronto, 2004–2005), Government of Spain "Juan de la Cierva" Fellow in Law (University of Girona, 2008–2011), and Visiting Professor at the Universities of Girona (Spain, 2006–2008), Pompeu Fabra (Spain, 2008–2009), and Nacional de Mar del Plata (Argentina, 2011). Amongst his main books are: Studi sulla logica del diritto e della scienza giuridica, Madrid, 2013; El gobierno de las normas, Madrid, 2013; The Logic of Legal Requirements, Oxford, 2012 (w/Jordi Ferrer Beltrán); Norme, principi e logica, Rome, 2009; Sistema giuridico e sistemazione del diritto, Turin, 2008.

Janice Schuetz is Professor Emerita of Communication from the University of New Mexico in the United States. Her specialties are political and legal argumentation and civil and criminal trial court communication. She has experience working as a consultant with US trial courts. Her publications include nine books, more than 80 articles and book chapters, and more than 100 conference papers. Her most recent book is *Communicating the Law: Lessons from Landmark Legal Cases.*

Giovanni Tuzet studied law and philosophy in Turin and Paris and wrote his Ph.D. thesis on Peirce's theory of inference. Formerly post-doc researcher at the universities of Lausanne, Switzerland, and Ferrara, Italy, he presently teaches Economic Analysis of Law and Legal Hermeneutics at Bocconi University in Milan, Italy. His areas of interest include epistemology, pragmatism, argumentation theory, philosophy of law and economic analysis of law. His publications include *La prima inferenza. L'abduzione di C.S. Peirce fra scienza e diritto* (2006), *Dover decidere. Diritto, incertezza e ragionamento* (2010), *La pratica dei valori. Nodi fra conoscenza e azione* (2012), *Filosofia della prova giuridica* (2013) and *The Planning Theory of Law. A Critical Reading* (2013, co-edited with D. Canale).

Lena Wahlberg is an Assistant Professor in Jurisprudence at Lund University (Sweden), specializing in medical law. Previous publications by Dahlman and Wahlberg as co-authors include *Fallacies in* Ad Hominem *Arguments*, *Cogency*, 2011.

Audrey Yap is an Associate Professor at the University of Victoria, in Canada. She works in the history and philosophy of mathematics, in dynamic epistemic logic and in the intersection between feminist philosophy and philosophy of logic.

Introduction

The aim of this book is to provide theoretical tools for evaluating the soundness of arguments in the context of legal argumentation. The book deals with a number of general argument types and their particular use in legal argumentation. It provides detailed analysis of argument from authority, argument *ad hominem*, argument from ignorance, slippery slope argument and other general argument types.

It is the case for each of these argument types that they can be used to construct arguments that are sound as well as arguments that are unsound. There are, for example, some arguments from authority that are sound and some arguments from authority that are unsound, where the latter arguments commit an argument fallacy known as the *ad verecundiam* fallacy. To evaluate an argument correctly one must, therefore, be able to distinguish the sound instances of a certain argument type from its unsound instances. The essays in this book are dedicated to the development of theoretical tools for this task.

Whether an argument is sound or unsound depends to a large extent on the context in which the argument is made. There are arguments that are unsound when they occur in legal argumentation, in spite of the fact that they would be sound in other contexts. This is, for example, the case with certain arguments *ad hominem* that are considered unacceptable in the law. And there are arguments where the legal context makes a difference in the opposite direction, making the argument sound in a legal context, in spite of the fact that it would be considered unsound in other context. This is, for example, the case with certain arguments from authority and certain arguments from ignorance. The fact that the legal context makes an important difference in this respect explains the need for literature on argumentation specifically aimed at the evaluation of arguments in a legal context.

The present book should be of great interest to scholars of legal theory and argumentation theory, as well as judges and practicing lawyers, looking for useful tools that can be applied in the evaluation of legal arguments.

The book is divided in two parts. The first part deals with the use of argument types generally perceived by scholars, logicians and jurists as "suspicious", if not entirely fallacious. Contrary to the popular and often unchallenged assumption that these forms of argument are always and necessarily a fallacy, the first four chapters offer a more detailed analysis of these argument types and explain how they may be used legitimately in legal reasoning.

The second part, in turn, focuses on argument types that are generally deployed in the specific context of legal interpretation, which is understood as a subset of legal reasoning in general, in the sense that it is concerned specifically with the meaning of controversial sentences and normative utterances. The essays attempt, therefore, to connect legal interpretation and argumentation, with a view to providing a normative framework to evaluate an interpretive reasoning.

Let us briefly summarize the arguments that the reader finds in the book.

In the first chapter, Christian Dahlman and Lena Wahlberg offer a Bayesian model for evaluating expert testimony in the court room. Statements from a putative expert are difficult for a legal decision maker to assess, as the legal decision maker must try to distinguish between experts that are highly reliable and experts that are less reliable, in spite of the fact that the legal decision maker lacks expert knowledge on the subject issue. A methodology for the assessment of the expert testimony has been suggested previously, in the works of Walton and Goldman, and the authors develop this methodology further, using a Bayesian approach to reliability assessment. The reliability of an expert can be questioned on different grounds (lack of competence, bias and lack of motivation), and the authors clarify different effects on the expert's reliability. Lack of competence typically lowers the expert's reliability by decreasing P(E|H), the probability that the expert would make the statement given that the statement is true, and increasing P(E|-H), the probability that the expert would make the statement given that the statement is false. The effect of bias differs greatly between the situation where the expert is biased in favor of the state of affairs that she testifies to be true and the situation where the expert is biased against the state of affairs that she testifies to be true. In the first case (bias towards H), bias typically lowers the expert's reliability by increasing P(E|-H) more than P(E|H). In the second case (bias towards -H), it increases the expert's reliability by decreasing P(E|-H) more than P(E|H). Lack of motivation has the same effect as lack of competence. It lowers the expert's reliability by decreasing P(E|H) and increasing P(E|-H).

In the second chapter, on the other hand, Audrey Yap adopts a less optimistic view on the use of the argument *ad hominem*, which is identified as a fallacy or an 'error in logical reasoning in which an interlocutor attacks a person making an argument rather than the argument being made'. The focus of the chapter, however, is narrower, since the author is worried about one specific variant of this fallacy, consisting on attacks that draw on 'false-identity stereotypes'. This type of fallacy is regarded as 'context-dependent', in the sense that 'what counts as an *ad hominen* attack in one context will not count as such in another context'. Still, it is possible to develop a general account of the reliance on stereotypes as a basis of an epistemic injustice. Such general account is particularly serious because the fallacious reliance on implicit bias may lead not only to epistemic injustice made by the author of the fallacy, but also to a phenomenon called by Steele and Aruson 'stereotype thread', which happens when 'negative stereotype about a group to which an individual belongs can cause that individual to perform below his or her actual ability'. After identifying these fallacies, Yap offers a few examples that illustrate this fallacy and discusses whether there are appropriate means for alleviating the pernicious effects of these argumentative vices.

In the third chapter, Giovanni Tuzet is worried about a possible legitimate use of the argument from absence of evidence in legal reasoning. Though the author is aware of the fallacious uses of the argument from ignorance, he believes that it is possible to justify its uses in legal reasoning, depending on the 'background knowledge', the 'relevant information' and the 'theory of fallacies relied upon'. The crucial aspects to 'redeem' the argument from ignorance are, according to the argument developed in the chapter, the 'nature' of the evidence at stake (whether it is a negative evidence or merely the absence of evidence) and the regulation of the 'burden of proof' in the case under consideration. The chapter presents, therefore, a normative account which understands the argument from ignorance as a 'practical argument', which is 'decision-oriented' and requires a 'presumptive rule' about some burden of proof.

In the fourth chapter, José Juan Moreso undertakes an analysis of the slippery slope argument in the context of legal (but also moral or political) reasoning. The slippery slope is understood as a *practical* argument that faces the so-called Sorites Paradox. To be sure, the 'core' of the slippery slope argument is the 'sorites argument', which seems to lead to fallacious or unacceptable consequences. To pick up a classical example referred to in the text, one would be able to claim that if Michael, who has $ 1 Billion, is rich, then, Mary, who has $ 1 Billion minus $ 1 is also rich. The repetitive application of the second premise would obviously be objectionable, for it would end up in asserting that John, who has only $ 1, must be also considered a rich person. Nonetheless, one can see that there is nothing in the logical structure of the Slippery Slope that makes it inherently inconsistent from the logical point of view. The Slippery Slope Argument, according to Moreso, is a 'suspicious argument', but 'not in virtue of their logical validity', since the second premise of the argument is not universally true. In fact either it is false or it has a limited application.

In the fifth chapter, Harm Kloosterhuis undertakes an analysis of institutional constraints on topical strategic manoeuvring in legal argumentation, with specific reference to the case of *insulting*. After classifying the types of strategic manoeuvring in three types of strategic behaviour – topical selection, audience-directed framing and presentational devices – the author deals both with the legal constraints, which can be found in statutory regulations and in normative legal practices developed in the case-law, and with the communicative or linguistic constraints that regard the language use and the "logic of conversational implicatures". Though it is uncontroversial that insulting is normally a gross fallacy in legal argumentation, it is argued that this structural account provides important criteria for the reader to identify such type of fallacy in legal reasoning and to determine the limits of legitimate criticism and use of *ad hominen* arguments in legal discourse.

Finally, in the sixth and final chapter of the first part, Janice Schuetz deals with the potentially fallacious use of one-sided argumentation, which is exemplified with the United States Supreme Court case *United States v. Windsor* (2013, Case 12–307), where the main issue was whether the traditional concept of "marriage" developed in the Defense of Marriage Act 2006 should be admitted as an excuse for not granting a pension to a homosexual partner in a long term relationship. By analyzing the arguments presented by the parties and the *amici curiae* briefs in the case, the author provides a sound framework for understanding the most typical argumentative strategies found in one-sided arguments, and how these strategies help in reinforcing one's biases and prejudices in favour of a particular position.

Opening the second part of the book, in Chap. 7, Thomas Bustamante revisits a meta-interpretive debate about the role of philosophy in choosing a theory of legal interpretation. Legal theorists disagree, as it is argued in the beginning of the chapter, not only about the interpretation of a particular legal provision, but also about the procedure or the interpretive attitude that lawyers should adopt while interpreting statutes and other legal materials. Some of these theorists, in a paradoxical way, hold that theory and philosophy have nothing to offer jurists and play a very limited role in the justification of a legal decision. Posner, for instance, is famous for saying that no moral theory can ever provide a solid basis for moral and legal judgments. This is, as the author puts it, the core of the "Anti-Theoretical Claim". Nonetheless, in spite of the appeal of this anti-theoretical movement, the author holds that the claim is fallacious and self-contradictory, and that the choice of a theory of legal interpretation must be based on moral and political values. This conclusion is valid even for the moderate variants of the Anti-Theoretical Claim, which hold that lawyers may bracket their theoretical disagreements on the basis of an incompletely theorized agreement.

In the eighth chapter, Pierluigi Chiassoni deals with the problem of uncertainty in legal interpretation. He discusses two alternative theoretical accounts of the nature of legal interpretation, which offer different views about legal interpretation, written-law norms and interpretive argumentation. The first is the so-called "the Frames of Interpretation Theory", which is an interpretive legal theory within analytical Kelsenian realism. The second, in turn, is the "Container-Retrieval view of Interpretation". While the former acknowledges a wide degree of discretion in legal interpretation, along the lines of Kelsen's view on legal interpretation, the latter sees each authoritative legal sentence as "containing" a set of legal norms. Legal interpretation, therefore, is merely the activity of "retrieving" the norms expressed or contained in its text. The paper provides, under this scenario, a defence of the "Frames of Interpretation View" that purports to evaluate these theoretical conceptions in the light of their ability to make sense of conventional concepts usually deployed by analytical jurists.

Michał Araszkiewicz's contribution, in Chap. 9, deals with another aspect of interpretation, which refers to the role of balancing in statutory interpretation. His analysis focuses on ordinary statutes, instead of the usual approach to balancing in the realm of abstract constitutional principles. The point of the chapter is to develop a descriptive model of interpretation that incorporates the structure of balancing in the areas of formulation of interpretive statements, generation of arguments that support or demote the interpretive statements and comparison of arguments supporting incompatible interpretive statements. If this account is sufficiently developed, one can build a descriptive system of the "thresholds" that "activate" certain types of interpretation and determine the result of a given interpretive debate. The chapter includes, also, a case study to illustrate this possibility.

In Chap. 10, Giovanni Ratti offers an analysis of some of the most typical techniques used by scholars and lawyers in order to "systematize the law". According to the theoretical framework developed by the author, the systematization of law comprises 11 juridical operations: "(1) identification of a 'relevant' normative problem (Ahcourrón and Bulygin); (2) identification of the legal sentences forming a 'sentential basis'; (3) validation of the sentences which belong to the sentential basis; (4) interpretation of each of the sentences belonging to the sentential basis (the product thereof being a normative basis); (5) argumentation of the interpretations that have been provided; (6) development of the normative basis, by means of either logical rules of inference (*stricto sensu* logical development), or of different rules of inference commonly used by jurists (e.g., argument *a simili*), in order to infer implicit norms that cannot be derived by the simple interpretation of the sentential basis; (7) analysis of some possible defects of the normative basis: in particular, gaps and inconsistencies; (8) conservative reformulation of the normative basis, by means of generalizing methods (so-called 'legal induction'), which allows one to eliminate the possible redundancies; (9) removal of inconsistencies; (10) filling of gaps; (11) ordering the normative material according to a certain scheme". In the chapter presented in this book, the author offers a careful analysis of operations 7–11 in this theoretical framework, which helps lawyers and legal scholars to understand the structure of legal construction, with particular emphasis on continental scholarship in legal theory.

Already approaching the end of the book, Eveline Fetteris provides a comprehensive analysis of the standard of reasonableness in legal reasoning, which is ordinarily used as a ground for carving exceptions to legal norms in the context of adjudication. According to her analysis, in spite of its rhetorical success and general use, the standard of reasonableness lacks an adequate theoretical stance for determining *what* counts as an adequate justification for its use and what in reality it amounts to. The main purpose of the chapter, as it appears in section 3, is to offer a normative model for the "rational reconstruction of legal arguments from reasonableness", as well as to test this model in the two final sections of the chapter, which refer to an application of this standard in Dutch Civil law.

In the final chapter, in turn, Bernardo Fernandes attempts to unveil the connections between legal argumentation theories and the debates among U.S. legal scholars concerning the interpretation of constitutions. He revisits John Hart Ely's distinction between "interpretivism" and "non-interpretivism" in constitutional adjudication, and analyses three theoretical conceptions of constitutional interpretation that depart from this dichotomy and provide a normative model for applying the constitution. These three conceptions are Cass Sunstein's minimalism, Richard Posner's anti-theoretical pragmatism and Ronald Dworkin's model of "Law as Integrity". After expounding the key claims of these accounts about legal interpretation, the author takes a stand in this debate and offers a set of arguments in favour of the latter view about constitutional argumentation.

All the chapters in the book, therefore, have a similar point. Even though legal theorists have been largely concerned with general theories of legal argumentation, such theories lack a specific analysis of the *argument types* that one can find in the book. These argument types are particularly important to legal reasoning, and one of the tasks of legal argumentation studies is to offer a rational framework for dealing with these argument structures. We hope that the book helps filling this gap.

Faculdade de Direito
Universidade Federal de Minas Gerais
Belo Horizonte, Minas Gerais, Brazil
Thomas Bustamante

Faculty of Law
Lund University
Lund, Sweden
Christian Dahlman

Part I
Argument Types or Fallacies?

Chapter 1
Appeal to Expert Testimony – A Bayesian Approach

Christian Dahlman and Lena Wahlberg

Abstract In this chapter, we offer a Bayesian model for evaluating expert testimony in the court room. Statements from a putative expert are difficult for a legal decision maker to assess, as the legal decision maker – who lacks expert knowledge on the subject issue – must distinguish between experts that are highly reliable and experts that are less reliable. A methodology for the assessment of the expert testimony has been suggested previously, in the works of Walton and Goldman, and we develop this methodology further, using a Bayesian approach to reliability assessment. The reliability of an expert can be questioned on different grounds (lack of competence, bias and lack of motivation), and we clarify different effects that these grounds can have on the expert's reliability.

1.1 Introduction

Scientific information plays a pivotal role in today's courtrooms. Testimonies of scientific experts have determined the outcome in countless rulings on murder and manslaughter, as well as cases on medical malpractice, product liability, compulsory mental care and other legal issues. Judges and juries often lack adequate scientific knowledge, and must hence to some extent rely on the experts' opinions. However, their trust should not be blind. There are both empirical and theoretical reasons to take seriously the risk that an expert witness goes wrong (see e.g. Huber 1993; Meester et al. 2006; Dwyer 2008; Wahlberg 2010; Råstam 2012). Moreover, blind trust does not provide any guidance in the common situation where two experts disagree. Consequently, it is important to devise tools that allow legal decision makers to evaluate experts' opinions. This article discusses the notorious difficulties that surround this task and explores some promising, but hitherto largely

C. Dahlman (✉)
Faculty of Law, Lund University, Lund, Sweden
e-mail: christian.dahlman@jur.lu.se

L. Wahlberg
Lund University, Lund, Sweden
e-mail: lena.wahlberg@jur.lu.se

© Springer International Publishing Switzerland 2015

T. Bustamante, C. Dahlman (eds.), *Argument Types and Fallacies in Legal Argumentation*, Law and Philosophy Library 112,
DOI 10.1007/978-3-319-16148-8_1

neglected strategies to avoid them. More precisely, it shows how a straightforward application of Bayes' theorem can provide valuable insights into the mechanisms of reliability, and thereby cast doubt on the categorical approaches to appeal to expert opinion that presently dominate argumentation theory. These and similar findings suggest that courts' assessments of scientific information could be improved by relatively simple means, and they provide an incentive to elaborate a special method, an 'expertology', to guide non-experts' assessments of expert testimony.

1.2 The Problem with Trust

The tricky thing with experts is how to determine who should be trusted and who should not be trusted. It would be foolish to trust every self-proclaimed expert, so a person who seeks help from an expert must be able to distinguish real experts from fake experts and experts that are highly reliable from experts that are less reliable. This is no easy business. The criteria for distinguishing the reliable from the unreliable must be criteria that can be applied without expert knowledge, since a person in search of a reliable expert does not possess such knowledge. If he had expert knowledge himself he would not need an expert. In this article we will identify some of these criteria and discuss how they can be applied successfully.

It should be mentioned that there are authors who claim that the problem we are addressing is unsolvable. According to these authors it is downright impossible for a non-expert to assess if a person is reliable as an expert or not. Only a person with expertise on the subject issue can assess if someone else is an expert on the issue. It follows from this view that the whole idea of trusting experts is paradoxical. Only a non-expert has the need to trust an expert, but only an expert can assess if someone is trustworthy as an expert. This means that every argument that appeals to authority is fallacious. An argument that appeals to authority claims that we have good reason to trust someone as an expert, but if trust in experts is paradoxical in the way just stated, it can never be the case that we have good reasons to trust someone. If we are non-experts we can never know if the person in question is trustworthy, and if we are experts we have no reason to trust someone other than ourselves.

In a famous article by the judge Learned Hand, published in *Harvard Law Review* 1901, Hand employed this paradox to criticize the use of expert witnesses. According to Hand, the jury is placed in an impossible position when the prosecution and the defense calls expert witnesses that make contradictory statements and the jury has to assess which expert to trust.

> … how can the jury judge between two statements each founded upon an experience confessedly foreign in kind to their own? It is just because they are incompetent for such a task that the expert is necessary at all. […]
>
> Knowledge of such general laws can be acquired only from a specialized experience such as the ordinary man does not possess […] The jury by hypothesis have no such experience directly, it being of a kind not possessed by ordinary men […] Therefore, when any conflict between really contradictory propositions arises, or any reconciliation between seemingly contradictory propositions is necessary, the jury is not a competent tribunal. […] [the jury] will do no better with the so-called testimony of experts than without, except where it is unanimous. (Hand 1901, 54–56)

To solve the paradox Hand proposed that juries should be composed of experts. For every trial, the procedure for selecting the jury should make sure that the jurors are picked among people with expertise in the field of the dispute. In a case of murder by poisoning, the jury should be composed of people with expert knowledge in toxicology, in a case of murder by arson the jury should be composed of people with special knowledge on fires, and so on. In such a system, expert witnesses would no longer be necessary. Evidently, Hand's proposition was never adopted by the American legal system. Criminal defendants are still judged by a jury of their peers, not by a jury of experts. And the use of expert witnesses has not ceased. On the contrary, it has increased tremendously (Graham 1977, 35).

In our view, it is not the case that the idea of trusting experts is inherently paradoxical. As many authors have pointed out, we can have good reasons for trusting someone as an expert, even if we do not possess the relevant expert knowledge ourselves (Salmon 1963, 63; Hamblin 1970, 42; Dwyer 2008, 108; Govier 2010, 121). Arguments that appeal to authority are not necessarily fallacious, but we need to acknowledge the difficulties that undeniably are associated with appeals to expert opinion, and develop tools that can be used to overcome them. In this article, we will show how Bayes' theorem can be used to assess the reliability of a putative expert.

1.3 Expertology and *Ad Hominem* Arguments

This investigation is a contribution to a research area that we will refer to as 'expertology', where the assessment of experts and expert testimony is studied, and methods for such assessments are developed. Philosophers and lawyers have discussed expertology for quite some time, albeit not under this name. For example, judges and legislators have developed criteria for the admissibility of expert testimony in court. Some of these criteria are straightforward demarcation criteria, which are meant to distinguish admissible 'true science' from inadmissible 'pseudo-science'. A well-known example is the so-called *general acceptance test* which was first laid down in *Frye v. United States 293 F. 1013, D.C. Circ., 1923*. The Court in *Frye* held that in order to be admissible, expert testimony must be based on scientific principles and discoveries that are "sufficiently established to have gained general acceptance in the particular field" (at 1024). Another example is *Daubert v. Merrell Dow Pharmaceuticals 509 U.S. 579 (1993)*, where the court referred to the works of Karl Popper and Carl G Hempel and identified testability, peer review, error rate and general acceptance as criteria for determining the reliability of expert testimony.

In philosophy, Douglas Walton, Alvin Goldman and others have contributed to the development of expertology. Walton has devised a list of critical questions that non-experts can use to challenge an argument from expert opinion. The list includes questions regarding the alleged expert's education, experience and personal reliability:

1. *Expertise* question: How credible is E as an expert source?
2. *Field* question: Is E an expert in the field that A is in?
3. *Opinion* question: What did E assert that implies A?
4. *Trustworthiness* question: Is E personally reliable as a source?
5. *Consistency* question: Is A consistent with what other experts assert?
6. *Backup evidence* question: Is A's assertion based on evidence?
(Walton 1997, 223, 2006, 750; Gooden and Walton 2006, 278–279)

Similarly, Goldman has identified and discussed five sources of evidence that a non-expert can use in determining the reliability of expert testimony: "arguments presented by contending experts", "agreement from additional putative experts", "appraisal by 'meta-experts' of the expert's expertise", "evidence of the expert's interests and biases" and "past track records" (Goldman 2001, 93).

These methods build on assessment criteria that can be used by a person who lacks special knowledge on the subject issue. In contrast to what is the case in a dialogue among peers, a layman's argument for/against a statement by a putative expert is rarely an argument *ad rem* (on the subject issue of the statement), it is typically an argument *ad hominem* (on the person making the statement) (Hardwig 1985, 342). It is an argument about the reliability of the putative expert. More precisely, the argument *ad hominem* points to a specific attribute of the person in question and claims that the attribute has a certain effect on the person's reliability (Walton 1998, 273–278; Dahlman et al. 2011, 109; Yap 2013, 102). The effect can be positive or negative. A positive *ad hominem* argument claims that the attribute makes the person more reliable. A negative *ad hominem* argument claims that the attribute makes the person less reliable (Dahlman et al. 2011, 211–212). Thus, an argument that appeals to authority is a positive *ad hominem* argument. The argument that Jane is reliable as an expert on medical issues because she has a university degree in medicine is an example of a positive *ad hominem* argument. The argument that she is unreliable as an expert on the side effects of a certain drug, because she is employed by the pharmaceutical company that manufactures the drug, is a negative *ad hominem* argument. In expertology, positive *ad hominem* arguments can refer to diplomas and job titles, while negative *ad hominem* arguments can point to bias or a poor track-record. Some *ad hominem* arguments are sound, while others are fallacious (Brinton 1995, 215; Walton 1998, 125; Dahlman et al. 2011, 107). An argument *ad hominem* is sound if it is true that the indicated attribute really has the effect on reliability claimed by the argument. It is fallacious if the attribute does not have this effect. An argument *ad hominem* is fallacious in cases where the attribute is irrelevant for the person's reliability as well as in cases where the attribute is relevant, but its effect on the person's reliability is exaggerated (Dahlman et al. 2011, 113).

1.4 Competence and Motivation

As we have seen, an argument about the reliability of an expert claims that the fact that the expert has a certain attribute affects the expert's reliability. Reliability is currently often conceived of as having both epistemic/cognitive and moral/motivational components (Hardwig 1991, 700; Solomon 1992, 452). Correspondingly, attributes that appear in *ad hominem* arguments can roughly be divided into two main categories: those that relate to competence and those that relate to motivation. Attributes that relate to competence can refer to the expert's education, employment and experience, whereas attributes that relate to motivation refer to the objectivity and dedication of the expert. A typical example of a positive *ad hominem* argument that relates to education is the argument that someone with a PhD in medicine is reliable as a medical expert. The argument that the expert has worked at a hospital as a doctor for 20 years is an example of a positive argument relating to employment and experience. A negative *ad hominem* argument about competence is an argument to the effect that the knowledge of the alleged expert on the subject issue is inadequate. Some negative arguments make the rather aggressive claim that the alleged expert is actually no expert at all, and seek to expose the expert as a fraud. More often, negative arguments take a softer line and acknowledge that the expert has genuine expertise, within a certain field, but claim that the testimony deals with a subject issue outside that field. The latter is very common in the courtroom, for example when the testimony of a doctor is challenged with the argument that the doctor is not a specialist within the branch of medicine that the testimony concerns.

Arguments about motivation relate to objectivity and dedication. That an expert is objective means that he or she is unbiased with regard to the hypothesis. The expert has nothing to gain from making one statement rather than the other. That an expert is dedicated means that the expert is motivated to do a good job. A dedicated expert is committed to the truth and investigates the facts thoroughly. Positive *ad hominem* arguments about motivation often relate to the expert's reputation. That the expert has published scientific articles that are frequently quoted by other experts is often taken as a sign of objectivity and dedication. Negative *ad hominem* arguments about motivation often point to a circumstance that suggests bias. The expert has something to gain from testifying in a certain way. A typical case of bias is the situation where the interest of a big corporation is at stake and the expert is on the corporation's payroll. A TV commercial where a doctor endorses a pharmaceutical product is an everyday example. In the courtroom, this kind of situation arises every time an expert who has been commissioned by one of the parties takes the stand. The expert is also biased if the testimony is linked to the expert's personal prestige and standing as an expert (Dwyer 2008, 171). This is the case, for example, when the expert is a scientist whose publications create a commitment to a certain scientific theory or tradition. An example can be taken from the infamous *Thomas Quick Case*, a Swedish case where a mental patient confessed that he was a serial killer. Quick confessed to 39 killings, and was convicted for murder in eight cases. At the trials, Quick said that he had realized in therapy that he was a serial killer. He did not know that he was a killer when the therapy sessions started, as he did not have any memory of killing anyone, but when he was given facts and details about the killings, he experienced memory flashes of the murders. Professor of Psychology Sven Å. Christianson testified as an expert witness, and told the court that repression and recovery of repressed memories had been his main research topic for many years, and that he was absolutely certain that Quick's memories were genuine.

In 2006, 7 years after the last trial, Quick withdrew all of his confessions, and claimed that his therapists had induced him to fabricate them. The case was reopened and Quick was acquitted on all charges. The Quick Case is generally considered to be the biggest scandal in Swedish legal history. The judges that convicted Quick of murder have been heavily criticized for putting too much trust in the expert testimony of Professor Christianson. Critics have argued that Professor Christianson was biased, since Quick's 'recovered memories' supported a theory that had built Professor Christianson's own scientific career (Råstam 2012; Josefsson 2013).

It has been suggested that interest-based objections to expert testimony are useless in argumentation. According to Frank Zenker, such objections cannot be assessed by people who lack expert knowledge on the subject issue and are not needed by people who have expert knowledge (Zenker 2011, 366–368). This is a variation of judge Hand's argument (discussed above) that there is something paradoxical about trusting experts. In Zenker's version, it is not aimed at arguments that appeal to authority. It is aimed at arguments that raise interest-based objections to arguments that appeal to authority.

As we have argued above, this kind of paradox can be solved by expertology. The *ad hominem* argument attacks an expert's *person* and can therefore be leveled by someone who lacks scientific expertise. This is what makes it such a central component of the expertological toolbox. However, if the argument is fallacious, it will hamper, rather than contribute to, a sound assessment of the expert's testimony. To develop an adequate expertology, we must therefore carefully study where and when these arguments go wrong. This is in part a task for argumentation theory. Thus, we saw above that according to the taxonomy in (Dahlman et al. 2011) arguments *ad hominem* are fallacious when the cited attribute is entirely irrelevant for reliability or when the argument exaggerates the attribute's effect. Empirical studies can provide information on when, how and to what extent attributes relating to competence and motivation indeed affect reliability. For example, it has been shown that financial interests tend to affect what conclusion the scientist draws, and what drug the physician prescribes (Barnes and Florenico 2002). However, there is also a mathematical side to the question of how attributes like these affect reliability. In the following sections, we shall see that already a basic acquaintance with the laws of probability can enhance our understanding of this matter. More precisely, we shall see how Bayes' theorem can be of service here.

1.5 Bayes' Theorem and Arguments from Authority

There are many versions of the argument from authority (Salmon 1963, 2013; Hamblin 1970; Walton 1989, 1997; Bachman 1995; Coleman 1995; Copi et al. 2010). These versions differ somewhat in how they represent the argument's premises and conclusion, but most of them incorporate a claim to the effect that *the fact that an expert makes a certain statement confers a high degree of probability onto the statement*. In order to assess if an argument from authority is sound, it is essential to critically evaluate the expertise that this claim presumes. We saw above that Walton has formulated a set of critical questions that are meant to serve as guidelines in this respect. On Walton's account, the disqualification of an alleged expert's reliability has the effect that the argument from expert opinion must be discarded: "If a respondent asks any of the six basic critical questions [...] appropriate for the appeal to expert opinion, the proponent must either give a satisfactory answer to the question asked, or else give up the appeal to the expert opinion argument" (Walton 2006, 750). This rather categorical approach to expertise has the apparent benefit of making it relatively easy to decide whether to trust the alleged expert: if he or she does not pass the critical questions' test, the argument from expert opinion must go. However, it is important to observe that evaluations of expertise likewise have a *quantitative* dimension in that they require us to decide whether the "expert" is *sufficiently reliable* to qualify as a real expert. To do so, we must assess *how* reliable he or she is. This quantitative dimension of expertise is present in Walton's account too and reflected, for example, in the question "*how* credible is the expert as a source?" (our italics). Hence, if we want to assess the reliability of an alleged expert, it is not sufficient to identify factors that affect reliability, we also need to identify tools that can help us to assess *to what extent* these factors affect reliability.

Bayes' theorem derives from basic axioms of probability and can be used to calculate conditional probabilities. Its most common version looks like this.

$$P(H|E) = \frac{P(H)P(E|H)}{P(H)P(E|H) + P(\neg H)P(E|\neg H)}$$

By the aid of Bayes' theorem, we can calculate the probability (P) of a hypothesis (H) given some evidence (E). We can therefore use the formula to update our belief in a hypothesis after considering new evidence. The usefulness of the formula is today widely acknowledged. In the argumentation context, it has proven capable of accounting for several informal fallacies (Korb 2003; Bender et al. 2007) and promises to be a generally useful tool for the analysis of argumentation, including source reliability and appeal to expert opinion (Schum 1975; Goldman 2001; Hahn et al. 2009, 2013).

In this article, we will use Bayes' theorem to assess how the probability of a hypothesis (H) is influenced by the fact that an expert claims that the hypothesis is true. In our analysis, the evidence (E) consists in the expert's testimony that H is true, and the left-hand side of the formula, P(H|E), is the probability that the hypothesis is true given that the expert says so. To calculate this probability with Bayes' theorem we need to know three things:

1. P(H), *The probability that the hypothesis is true before considering the expert's testimony*. This probability is referred to as the *prior probability*.[1] From here, we can derive the prior probability that the hypothesis is false $P(\neg H)$, which also appears in the formula, by applying the negation rule, $P(H) = 1 - P(\neg H)$,
2. $P(E|H)$, *The probability that the expert would testify that the hypothesis is true, given that it is true*. This is the probability of a *true* positive.
3. $P(E|\neg H)$, *The probability that the expert would testify that the hypothesis is true, given that the hypothesis is actually false*. This is the probability of a *false* positive.

In the theorem's terminology, the evidence (the expert's testimony that the hypothesis is true) increases the probability that the hypothesis is true when $P(H|E) > P(H)$. This situation occurs if it is more probable that the expert testifies that the hypothesis is true when it is true, than when it is false, i.e. when $P(E|H) > P(E|\neg H)$. By convention, these two probabilities, $P(E|H)$ and $P(E \mid \neg H)$, are referred to as *likelihoods*. How much the probability $P(H|E)$ increases depends on how large the difference between the two likelihoods is, as well as on the size of the prior probability P(H). If, on the other hand, $P(E|H) = P(E|\neg H)$, the probability of the hypothesis is unaffected by the expert's testimony. The strength of the evidence is therefore measured as the *likelihood ratio* (LR), in the following way:

$$LR = \frac{P(E|H)}{P(E|\neg H)}$$

If $LR > 1$ the expert testimony increases the probability that the hypothesis is true. The higher the *likelihood ratio*, the more it raises the probability. If $LR = 1$, the expert testimony has no effect on the probability. And, in the strange but not impossible case that $LR < 1$ the expert testimony lowers the probability that the hypothesis is true. The *likelihood ratio* is hence a measure of the diagnosticity of the expert testimony.

In the next section we will discuss how factors that relate directly to the expert's reliability affect the *likelihood ratio*, and thereby the probability that a hypothesis is true, given that an expert says so. With the aid of Bayes' theorem, we can clarify how important these factors are, and to what extent they should affect our decision to trust, or not trust, an expert. It is interesting to note that many experts and other scientists make similar evaluations of their own diagnostic tools. For example, a physician who wants to calculate the probability that a person with a positive biopsy suffers from cancer needs to consider the probabilities of true and false positive test results as well as the prior probability of the disease. Just like the physician uses

[1]A much discussed problem is how to calculate the probability that a statement is true when there is no evidence whatsoever. We will not try to solve this problem here but submit that, in a legal context, legal norms can be useful to solve this problem. For example, in a criminal case, the presumption of innocence requires us to set the prior probability close to zero.

medical knowledge and Bayes' theorem to arrive at her conclusion, the layman can use expertology and Bayes' theorem to evaluate the reliability of the expert's conclusion. In this way, expertology and Bayes' theorem allow us to assess the diagnosticity of expert testimony as an instrument in a way that complements the expert's evaluation of her own instruments.

1.6 Assessing Arguments that Question the Expert's Reliability

As we have seen, an appeal to expert testimony can be met by counter arguments that cast doubt on the expert's competence or motivation. It goes without saying that deficiency in competence or motivation should decrease our trust in an expert's testimony. It is less obvious by what mechanisms changes relating to these factors affect the evidentiary value of the testimony, to what extent they do so, and how these changes should influence our actions. The answers to these questions are in part empirical, but also have a mathematical dimension, which must not be neglected. In this section, we will discuss some of the insights that Bayes' theorem can give us to these questions.

As we have seen, the evidentiary value of the expert testimony is reflected by the *likelihood ratio*, $P(E|H)/P(E|\neg H)$. If the expert has *insufficient competence*, the *likelihood ratio* will decrease. The magnitude of the decrease, and the mechanisms underlying it, depend on the expert's awareness that her competence is insufficient, as well as on her cautiousness to avoid incorrect statements. For example, lack of competence in combination with lack of awareness/cautiousness will strongly increase the probability that the expert erroneously claims that the hypothesis is true, $P(E|\neg H)$. Insufficient competence in combination with awareness and cautiousness, on the other hand, will normally not have this strong effect on $P(E|\neg H)$, since the expert who realizes that her competence is insufficient will be inclined to say that she is unable to judge whether the hypothesis is true or false. If the expert is *extremely* cautious, insufficient competence could, theoretically, decrease both $P(E|H)$ and $P(E|\neg H)$ but the combined effect remains a decrease in evidentiary value, as long as $P(E|H)$ decreases more than $P(E|\neg H)$. How people react when they have insufficient competence is an empirical question. Here, we will make the assumption that extreme awareness/cautiousness or unawareness/incautiousness are rare and that insufficient competence therefore typically makes the expert more prone to say that H is true when it is false and less prone to say that H is true when it is true. In other words, we will assume that insufficient competence typically increases $P(E|\neg H)$ and decreases $P(E|H)$. Since the numerator of the *likelihood ratio* (LR) in this situation decreases and the denominator increases, LR will decrease accordingly.

Table 1.1 Insufficient competence

	$P(E\|H)$	$P(E\|\neg H)$	LR	$P(H\|E)$
Competence	0.90	0.02	$0.90/0.02=45$	$(0.5*0.90)/(0.5*0.90+0.5*0.02)\approx 0.98$
Insufficient competence	0.80	0.20	$0.80/0.20=4$	$(0.5*0.80)/(0.5*0.80+0.5*0.20)\approx 0.80$

To illustrate, let us consider a case where we initially perceive the expert to be highly competent and estimate $P(E|H)$ at 0.90 and $P(E|\neg H)$ at 0.02. Under these circumstances $LR=45$. What this means for $P(H|E)$ depends, of course, on the prior probability P(H). Let us assume as an example, that $P(H)=0.50$ (given the evidence that we had taken into count prior to the expert's testimony). In this case, the probability that the hypothesis is true given that the expert says so is approximately 0.98. Now, suppose that we learn that the expert is less competent than we first thought. It turns out that the expert lacks practical experience. Due to the expert's insufficient competence, we find it reasonable to adjust $P(E|H)$ from 0.90 to 0.80 and $P(E|\neg H)$ from 0.02 to 0.20. With these modified likelihoods, the *likelihood ratio* drops from 45 to 4, and the probability that the hypothesis is true, given that the expert claims that it is true, drops from 0.98 to 0.80. The new information has significantly lowered the evidential value of the expert's testimony (Table 1.1).

However, it should be observed that the testimony of the fairly competent expert still increases the probability of the hypothesis from 0.50 to 0.80. The expert's testimony is hence not worthless. How, then, should the information about the expert's insufficient competence affect our actions? On Walton's account, failure to give a satisfactory answer to a critical question pertaining to, for example, practical experience implies that we must give up the appeal to expert opinion. But if the new information leads us to discard the expert's statement entirely, we will in effect ignore relevant evidence and, as it were, throw the baby out with the bathwater. Simply lowering the threshold to include likelihood ratios of, say, 4 would not suffice to avoid this problem, since any threshold that exceeds 1 means that relevant evidence is ignored. Moreover, lowering the threshold for expertise comes with the obvious and high price of trusting too much. Hence, Bayes' theorem exhibits the oversights involved in ignoring the testimony of experts that are not considered to be sufficiently reliable, while reminding us of the risk of blindly trusting those that are.

Above, we saw that insufficient competence can reduce the evidentiary value of expert testimony in different ways and assumed that it, for many experts, decreases $P(E|H)$ and increases $P(E|\neg H)$. The effect of *bias* is different. Let us return to the example with the competent expert above, where $P(E|H)$ was estimated at 0.90 and $P(E|-H)$ at 0.02. If this expert turns out to have a bias in favor of H, the probability increases that the expert will claim H when H is false. However, in contrast to insufficient competence, the bias likewise increases the probability that the expert will claim H when H is true. Unlike insufficient

Table 1.2 Bias towards H

	$P(E\|H)$	$P(E\|\neg H)$	LR	$P(H\|E)$
Non-biased	0.90	0.02	$0.90/0.02 = 45$	$(0.5*0.90)/(0.5*0.90+0.5*0.02) \approx 0.98$
Biased towards H	0.99	0.25	$0.99/0.25 \approx 4$	$(0.5*0.99)/(0.5*0.99+0.5*0.25) \approx 0.80$

competence, bias typically increases $P(E|\neg H)$ *as well as* $P(E|H)$, but nevertheless decreases the *likelihood ratio*, provided that the relative increase in $P(E|\neg H)$ exceeds the relative increase in $P(E|H)$. For example, if we adjust the biased expert's $P(E|H)$ from 0.90 to 0.99, and $P(E|\neg H)$ from 0.02 to 0.25, the likelihood ratio will drop from 45 to 4, and the probability that the hypothesis is true given the expert's statement will drop from 0.98 to 0.80 (Table 1.2).

Again, the testimony will retain *some* evidential value as long as $LR > 1$, i.e. unless the expert is *equally likely* to claim H when H is false as when H is true. We would assume that it is very unusual that bias affects the likelihood ratio to the radical degree that $P(E|H)$ equals $P(E|\neg H)$. The rather common argument that a biased expert's opinion should be discarded is hence normally not convincing.

However, because bias, unlike insufficient competence, tends to increase both $P(E|\neg H)$ and $P(E|H)$, it will also have the counterintuitive effect of *increasing* the evidential value of some expert testimony. This happens when an expert who testifies that H is true is biased in favor of *the negation* of H. A bias towards ¬H decreases the probability that the expert will say that H is true if H is false. Let us, for example, assume that we are dealing with an expert witness with $P(E|H) = 0.80$ and $P(E|\neg H) = 0.20$ (like the expert with insufficient competence in the example above), and that we learn that the expert has a bias in favor of ¬H. This would give us reason to adjust $P(E|H)$ from 0.80 to, say, 0.60. At the same time, we would adjust $P(E|\neg H)$ from 0.20 to, at least, 0.02, since it is unlikely that an expert who is biased in favor of ¬H would testify in favor of H in a case where H is actually false. These adjustments would increase the *likelihood ratio* from 4 to 30, and increases $P(H|E)$ from 0.80 to 0.97 (Table 1.3).

Another problem pertaining to motivation is *insufficient motivation*. An expert can, for example, lack motivation if she is badly paid and therefore does not bother too much about doing a good job. Like insufficient competence and bias, insufficient motivation tends to decrease the likelihood ratio, $P(E|H)/P(E|\neg H)$, and thereby decrease the evidentiary value of the expert's testimony that H is true. The mechanisms underlying the decrease resemble those at work when the expert's competence is insufficient. For example, the behavior of an expert who is unmotivated, but reluctant to give an incorrect statement is similar to the behavior of the expert who is incompetent but aware of her own incompetence and cautious to avoid incorrect statements: in both cases, it can be expected that the expert will be inclined to say that she is unable to judge whether the hypothesis is true or false. Consequently,

Table 1.3 Bias towards ¬H

	$P(E\|H)$	$P(E\|\neg H)$	LR	$P(H\|E)$
Non-biased	0.80	0.20	$0.80/0.20 = 4$	$(0.5*0.80)/(0.5*0.80+0.5*0.20) = 0.80$
Biased towards ¬H	0.60	0.02	$0.60/0.02 = 30$	$(0.5*0.60)/(0.5*0.60+0.5*0.02) \approx 0.97$

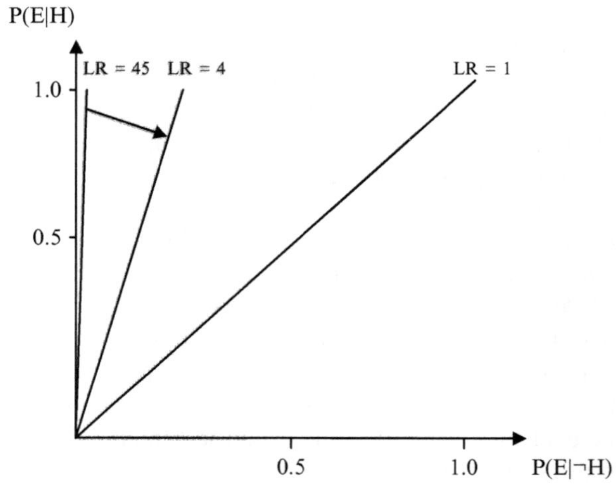

Fig. 1.1 Insufficient competence/Insufficient motivation

the unmotivated but cautious expert will be less likely to say that H is true when H is true, but not necessarily more likely to say that H is true when H is false. On the other hand, if the unmotivated expert does not care too much about whether what she says is correct or not, insufficient motivation can, just like insufficient competence, be expected to decrease $P(E|H)$ and increase $P(E|\neg H)$. This means that insufficient motivation and bias – two factors that are both related to motivation – affect the likelihood ratio differently: as seen above, bias in favor of H typically increases *both* $P(E|H)$ and $P(E|\neg H)$. Because of this difference, the observation that bias increases the evidentiary value of some expert testimony does not generalize to problems of motivation that consist in insufficient motivation. In this perspective, insufficient motivation appears to have more in common with insufficient competence than it has with bias.

As we have seen, insufficient competence, bias towards H, bias towards ¬H and insufficient motivation have different effects on the evidentiary value of expert testimony. The differences, as they have been discussed in our examples are illustrated below in Figs. 1.1, 1.2 and 1.3, where each line represents a certain *likelihood ratio* (LR). A change in $P(E|H)$ and $P(E|\neg H)$ is marked with an arrow that describes the result of the change. A change in $P(E|H)$ and $P(E|\neg H)$ where the arrow goes from a point that lies on a line with one *likelihood ratio* to a point on a line with a lower *likelihood ratio* means that the evidentiary value of the expert's testimony has

Fig. 1.2 Bias towards H

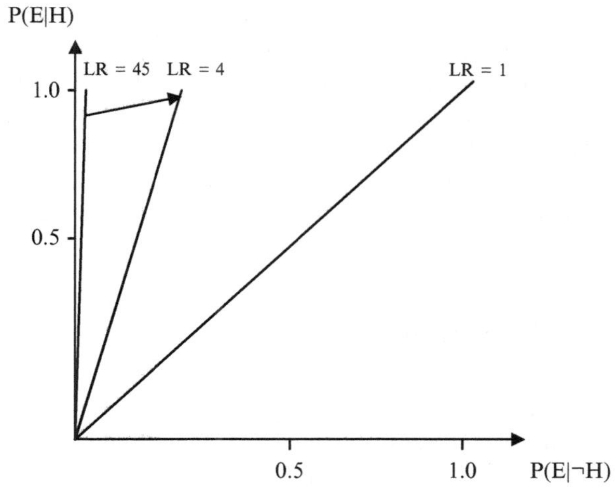

Fig. 1.3 Bias towards ¬H

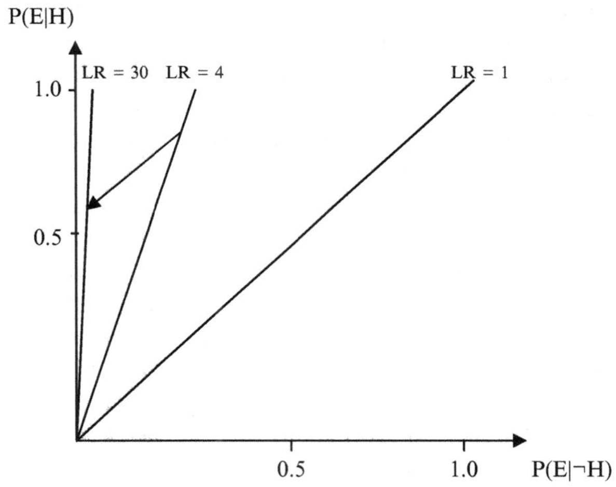

decreased. A change where the arrow goes to a point on a line with a higher ratio means that the evidentiary value has increased. We have assumed that insufficient competence or motivation typically leads to a decrease in $P(E|H)$ and an increase in $P(E|\neg H)$. The result of these changes is illustrated in Fig. 1.1. As we can see, the result is a change to a line with a lower *likelihood ratio*.

The effect of bias towards H is an increase in $P(E|H)$ as well as $P(E|\neg H)$, where the increase in $P(E|\neg H)$ is relatively greater than the increase in $P(E|H)$. The result of this kind of change is illustrated in Fig. 1.2. Even though $P(E|H)$ increases, the result of the bias is a change from a point on a line with a higher *likelihood ratio* to a point on a line with a lower *likelihood ratio*.

The difference between insufficient competence and bias towards H is illustrated by Fig. 1.1 compared with Fig. 1.2. $P(E|H)$ decreases with insufficient competence and increases with bias towards H, but the *likelihood ratio* decreases in both cases, due to a significant increase in $P(E|\neg H)$. In situations where the expert is biased towards ¬H there is a decrease in $P(E|H)$ as well as $P(E|\neg H)$, and the decrease in $P(E|\neg H)$ is relatively greater than the decrease in $P(E|H)$. Figure 1.3 shows how this results in a change to a point on a line with a higher *likelihood ratio*.

1.7 Conclusions

This article has discussed ways in which a person who does not possess expert knowledge can assess the reliability of an expert and the evidentiary value of expert testimony. The discussion belongs to a research area that we have referred to as 'expertology'. Expertology studies the mechanisms underlying the reliability of experts and develops methods for lay assessments of expert testimony by exploiting criteria that can be assessed without expert knowledge. In this way, expertology can be used to evaluate the diagnosticity of an expert's testimony in a manner similar to the way that the expert evaluates her own instruments. This makes expertology highly relevant to legal argumentation, where it can be used to assess legal arguments that appeal to expert testimony as well as counter arguments that question the reliability of an expert witness.

In this article, we have discussed the relevance of assessment criteria that pertain to the expert's person and that can be used in *ad hominem* arguments against the expert. More precisely, we have discussed how and to what extent *insufficient competence*, *bias* and *insufficient motivation* affect the reliability of an expert's testimony. This – partly empirical – question has an important mathematical dimension, which can be clarified by the aid of Bayes' theorem. Using a Bayesian approach, we have seen that all these factors tend to reduce the reliability of the expert's testimony, but that they do so in different ways, triggering different mechanisms. Whereas the effects of insufficient motivation and insufficient competence are similar, bias affects reliability in a different manner and can, as we have discussed, in fact *increase* the reliability of some expert testimony.

More generally, our analysis has made clear that although insufficient competence, insufficient motivation and bias all tend to reduce the evidentiary value of the expert's testimony, the testimony normally retains *some* evidentiary value despite the presence of these factors. When an argument that appeals to expert testimony is met by a counter argument pointing out that the expert's knowledge is inadequate or that the expert is biased, it is therefore, *pace* Walton, seldom the case that the appeal to expert testimony is defeated completely.

Acknowledgments Research financed by the Swedish Research Council (Vetenskapsrådet) and Ragnar Söderbergs Stiftelse. Thanks to Thomas Bustamte, Roberta Colonna Dahlman, Ulrike Hahn, Farhan Sarwar and Frank Zenker.

References

Bachman, James. 1995. Appeal to authority. In *Fallacies – Classical and contemporary readings*, ed. Hans V. Hansen and Robert C. Pinto. University Park: Pennsylvania State University Press.

Barnes, Mark, and Patrik S. Florenico. 2002. Financial conflicts of interest in human subjects research: The problem of institutional conflicts. *Journal of Law, Medicine and Ethics* 20(3): 390–402.

Bender, Rolf, Armin Nack, and Wolf-Dieter Treuer. 2007. *Tatsachenfeststellung vor Gericht*, 3rd ed. München: Verlag C.H. Beck.

Brinton, Alan. 1995. The *Ad Hominem*. In *Fallacies – Classical and contemporary readings*, ed. Hans V. Hansen and Robert C. Pinto. University Park: Pennsylvania State University Press.

Coleman, Edwin. 1995. There is no fallacy of arguing from authority. *Informal Logic* 17(3): 365–384.

Copi, Irving, Carl Cohen, and Kenneth McMahon. 2010. *Introduction to logic*, 14th ed. Boston: Pearson.

Dahlman, Christian, David Reidhav, and Lena Wahlberg. 2011. Fallacies in *Ad Hominem* arguments. *Cogency* 3(2): 107–126.

Dwyer, Déirdre. 2008. *Judicial assessment of expert evidence*. Cambridge: Cambridge University Press.

Goldman, Alvin. 2001. Experts: Which ones should you trust? *Philosophy and Phenomenological Research* 63(1): 85–109.

Gooden, David M., and Douglas Walton. 2006. Argument from expert opinion as legal evidence: Critical questions and admissibility criteria of expert testimony in the American legal system. *Ratio Juris* 19(3): 261–286.

Govier, Trudy. 2010. *A practical study of argument*, 7th ed. Belmont: Wadsworth.

Graham, Michael H. 1977. Impeaching the professional expert witness by showing financial interest. *Indiana Law Review* 53: 85–110.

Hahn, Ulrike, Adam J.L. Harris, and Adam Corner. 2009. Argument content and argument source: An exploration. *Informal Logic* 29(4): 337–367.

Hahn, Ulrike, Mike Oaksford, and Adam Harris. 2013. Testimony and argument: A Bayesian perspective. In *Bayesian argumentation: The practical side of probability*, ed. F. Zenker. Dordrecht: Springer.

Hamblin, C.L. 1970. *Fallacies*. London: Methuen.

Hand, Learned. 1901. Historical and practical considerations regarding expert testimony. *Harvard Law Review* 15(1): 40–58.

Hardwig, John. 1985. Epistemic dependence. *The Journal of Philosophy* 82: 335–349.

Hardwig, John. 1991. The role of trust in knowledge. *The Journal of Philosophy* 88: 693–708.

Huber, Peter. 1993. *Galileo's revenge: Junk science in the courtroom*. New York: Basic Books.

Josefsson, Dan. 2013. *Mannen som slutade ljuga – Berättelsen om Sture Bergwall och kvinnan som skapade Thomas Quick*. Stockholm: Lind & Co.

Korb, Kevin. 2003. Bayesian informal logic and fallacy. *Informal Logic* 23(2): 41–70.

Meester, Ronald, Mareike Collings, Richard Gill, and Michiel van Lambalgen. 2006. On the (ab) Use of statistics in the legal case against Nurse Lucia de B. *Law, Probability and Risk* 5(3–4): 251–254.

Råstam, Hannes. 2012. *Fallet Thomas Quick – Att skapa en seriemördare*. Stockholm: Ordfront.

Salmon, Wesley. 1963. *Logic*. Englewood Cliffs: Prentice-Hall.

Salmon, Merrilee. 2013. *Introduction to logic and critical thinking*, 6th ed. Boston: Cengage.

Schum, David A. 1975. The weighing of testimony in judicial proceedings from sources having reduced credibility. *Human Factors* 17(2): 172–182.

Solomon, Miriam. 1992. Scientific rationality and human reasoning. *Philosophy of Science* 59: 439–454.

Wahlberg, Lena. 2010. *Legal questions and scientific answers: Ontological differences and epistemic gaps in the assessment of causal relations*. Lund: Lund University Mediatryck.

Walton, Douglas. 1989. Rezoned use of expertise in argumentation. *Argumentation* 3: 139–159.
Walton, Douglas. 1997. *Appeal to expert opinion.* University Park: Pennsylvania State University Press.
Walton, Douglas. 1998. *Ad Hominem arguments.* Tuscaloosa: University of Alabama Press.
Walton, Douglas. 2006. Examination dialogue. *Journal of Pragmatics* 6: 3–26.
Yap, Audrey. 2013. Ad Hominem fallacies, bias and testimony. *Argumentation* 27(2): 97.
Zenker, Frank. 2011. Expert and bias: When is the interest-based objection to expert argumentation sound? *Argumentation* 25: 355–370.

Chapter 2
Ad Hominem Fallacies and Epistemic Credibility

Audrey Yap

Abstract An ad hominem fallacy is an error in logical reasoning in which an interlocutor attacks the person making the argument rather than the argument itself. There are many different ways in which this can take place, and many different effects this can have on the direction of the argument itself. This paper will consider ways in which an ad hominem fallacy can lead to an interlocutor acquiring less status as a knower, even if the fallacy itself is recognized. The decrease in status can occur in the eyes of the interlocutor herself, as seen in cases of *stereotype threat*, or in the eyes of others in the epistemic community, as in the case of *implicit bias*. Both of these will be discussed as ways in which an ad hominem fallacy can constitute an *epistemic injustice*.

2.1 Introduction

An ad hominem fallacy is an error in reasoning in which an interlocutor attacks a person making an argument rather than the argument being made. These attacks address an irrelevant aspect of the person's character or circumstances rather than the argument the person herself makes, but purport to undermine the argument nevertheless. A wide variety of character traits and circumstances can constitute an ad hominem attack, but we will focus on attacks that draw on false identity-prejudicial stereotypes. This is so we can consider in more detail the effect that ad hominem fallacies can have when we consider the broader context in which such a fallacy is committed. At least in textbook treatments of informal logic, the focus tends to be on the identification of fallacies, many of which are presented in short paragraphs without any discussion of the context in which the dispute might be taking place. But in actual application, a fallacy is generally committed within a longer dialogue, which itself is occurring in a social context. They are also committed by individuals who have their own distinct backgrounds and character traits, and may occupy very

A. Yap (✉)
Department of Philosophy, University of Victoria, Victoria, BC, Canada
e-mail: ayap@uvic.ca

© Springer International Publishing Switzerland 2015

T. Bustamante, C. Dahlman (eds.), *Argument Types and Fallacies in Legal Argumentation*, Law and Philosophy Library 112,
DOI 10.1007/978-3-319-16148-8_2

different places in society. When we pay attention to the bigger picture instead of looking only at a single passage in which a fallacy is committed, we can see more clearly the connections between fallacies and societal prejudices.

First, we should highlight several aspects of ad hominem fallacies that will be assumed in this paper, stemming from the idea that these fallacies are context-dependent. This means that what counts as an ad hominem attack in one context will not count as such in another context. Branding someone as a "liberal academic" and therefore incapable of understanding everyday experience would be an ad hominem attack given a politically conservative audience. But it would seem like a strange criticism of, say, a speaker at a philosophy conference. This is because an ad hominem attack will bring up something negative about an interlocutor, but what counts as a negative trait may vary depending on factors such as the parties' respective backgrounds and the topic under discussion. Similarly, ad hominem fallacies are classified as fallacies of relevance, in which something irrelevant to the quality of the interlocutor's argument is cited; but what counts as relevant to the argument will vary with context. For example, saying that a person lacks a university education is irrelevant if they are making an argument about how you should best fix your car, since university education typically does not address automotive repair. On the other hand, it is relevant if they are making a scientific argument, since scientists generally do generally need formal university education to be credible.

One account of ad hominem fallacies which accounts for this context-dependence, adapted from Yap (2013), is that ad hominem fallacies are situations in which a speaker's argument is illegitimately treated as an instance of testimony. And the believability of an individual's testimony is also context-dependent. We count people as knowledgeable testifiers in some areas (such as areas in which they have expertise), but not others. Similarly, we count people as trustworthy testifiers in some areas (such as areas in which they do not have a personal stake), but not others. These assumptions can easily overlap, but they do illustrate the importance of paying attention to the context of an argument. Many of them can be addressed by paying attention to the topic of the argument, but we will see that enlarging our scope and paying attention to further features of the context is also useful.

Once we situate informal fallacies in a larger context, a wide range of topics in argumentation opens up, although this paper will maintain a relatively narrow focus, looking only at ad hominem fallacies that attack people in ways that evoke identity prejudice. This perspective allows us to focus on the significant disruption they can cause to the dialogue as a whole, regardless of whether the fallacy is recognized as having been committed. This disruption may vary in degree and reparability. In most cases, the fallacy will do the most harm to the person against whom it is committed, but it can also have negative effects on others. Our examples will also focus principally on stereotypes prevalent in mainstream Western society, though different examples could certainly illustrate the same phenomena in societies with other sets of biases and stigmas.

The discussion of the effects of ad hominem fallacies will use several related concepts from psychology that have been getting increased attention in the philosophy literature, particularly *stereotype threat* and *implicit bias*. The following section will give a brief outline of these concepts and show how they can impact individuals in the course of their everyday lives. We will then discuss the philosophical concept of epistemic injustice from Fricker (2007), and show how certain ad hominem fallacies can constitute an epistemic injustice. This will help showcase two ways in which deploying problematic stereotypes in the course of an argument can adversely affect its course. First, highlighting an individual's membership in a group that has false identity-prejudicial stereotypes associated with it can affect her self-perception in a way that is very difficult to counteract. This is the case in which epistemic injustice causes underperformance associated with stereotype threat, and may cause the individual to make her point less effectively than she might otherwise have been able to do. Second, it can also affect the way in which others in the broader epistemic community perceive her. This is the case in which epistemic injustice intersects with implicit bias. This is particularly relevant for situations in which an ad hominem fallacy is committed in the course of a public discussion. In these cases, the perceptions of individuals who are not direct participants in the argument may be important. And the occurrence of an ad hominem fallacy in a public discussion might, in the eyes of those observing the argument, diminish the epistemic credibility of one of its participants.

2.2 Stereotype Threat and Implicit Bias

Stereotype threat is a phenomenon described in Steele and Aronson (1995), in which invoking a negative stereotype about a group to which an individual belongs can cause that individual to perform below his or her actual ability. Calling attention to the fact that an individual belongs to a group stereotypically less skilled at a particular task can cause that person to perform more poorly at it. The original study considers African-Americans' performance on standard aptitude tests, but many other studies have been conducted since then. Other studies have considered negative stereotypes about women's mathematical aptitude and related them to women and girls' performance on math tests (Spencer et al. 1999; Ambady et al. 2001). In general, what such studies have found is that negative stereotypes, particularly when highlighted, can become self-confirming.

We can put this in terms of ability by considering several stereotypes about different groups and their capacities. For instance, women are often stereotyped as being worse at math, the elderly as being worse drivers, and African-Americans as being worse academically. When a member of one of these groups finds themselves faced with a task associated with a negative stereotype, their performance risks being evaluated in terms of that stereotype. More specifically, if a woman does poorly in a math class, some might simply explain this in terms of her gender's lower ability, rather than her personal circumstances or even just her *individual* ability, independent of gender. But the pressure from this threat might be what leads to her poor performance, or even her choosing not to take the class in the first place.

However, several points about stereotype threat ought to be highlighted. First, one does not have to endorse the negative stereotype to be affected by it, so long as it is a recognizable stereotype in one's culture. Women who do not believe that gender affects mathematical ability can nevertheless underperform as a result of stereotype threat. It is less a matter of our own self-conception than of our perception of the way in which others might see us. Being labeled as an individual who is rationally inferior, or less skilled in argumentation, can become self-confirming for an individual previously confident in her own abilities.

Second, many people belong to several different groups to which stereotypes are associated, some of which may conflict with each other. What makes a study such as Ambady et al. (2001) particularly interesting is their investigation into exactly this phenomenon, which looks at mathematical performance among Asian-American girls. Asians are typically stereotyped as being good at math, while girls are typically stereotyped as being bad at it. The girls in the study were first asked to color a randomly selected picture before taking a standardized math test. The three pictures girls could have received to color were intended to activate their female identity (a girl holding a doll), their Asian identity (two Asian children eating from rice bowls), or neither (a landscape). For most age groups, the best performances were among the girls whose ethnic identity was activated, and the lowest among girls whose gender identity was activated, with the control group intermediate between the two.[1] So due to the complex nature of many people's identity, it is possible to affect performance on certain tasks by activating one stereotype or another about a group to which they belong.

The second psychological concept we will discuss is *implicit bias*. Where stereotype threat has largely to do with a person's views about how she will be perceived, implicit bias has to do with the way in which others actually do see her. We will look primarily at ways in which implicit bias can affect others' judgments of credibility about an individual. Now, judgments of credibility are not always conscious, and especially when unconscious, may be affected by negative stereotypes having to do with a person's identity. For example, studies of implicit bias have shown that factors such as race and gender can affect even well-meaning individuals' assessment of job candidates. One study found that fictitious resumes of identical quality sent out to employers were much more likely to receive callbacks if they were attached to a traditionally white name than if they were attached to a traditionally African-American name. This was even the case among employers who explicitly state that they are equal opportunity (Bertrand and Mullainathan 2004). Another similar study looked at the effects of gender, by sending identical CVs to various academic psychologists for evaluation, but varying the name. Some were given typically male names and others, typically female names. In general, the finding was that the CVs with male names were evaluated more highly than their identical counterparts with female names attached. Also important is that there was no significant difference between men and women's evaluations of the CVs – both had a tendency to rank the male candidates more highly (Steinpreis et al. 1999). So judgements made by

[1] There was admittedly one age group in which this order was reversed.

members of marginalized groups may still be affected by negative stereotypes, even when those are stereotypes about a group to which they belong.

This last fact may seem counterintuitive, but an important aspect of this type of bias is that it tends to manifest itself in ways that the biased person is typically unaware of. What makes it a particularly difficult thing to combat, or even mitigate, is that people who do have implicit biases do not generally see themselves as being influenced by bias. For instance, the *bias blind spot* is the commonly held (but mistaken) belief that one's own judgments are less susceptible to bias than the judgments of others (Pronin et al. 2002; Ehrlinger et al. 2005). This means that even under very good conditions, in which we have a well-meaning person who does not harbor conscious prejudice, and is even aware of biases to which she might be susceptible, we still see the effects of implicit bias. Now, in order to articulate some of the harms that can result from these psychological phenomena, we will turn to the concept of *epistemic injustice*.

2.3 Epistemic Injustice

Epistemic injustice, as discussed in Fricker (2007) in particular, is a kind of epistemic wrong done to an individual, in her capacity as a knower, as a result of systemic injustice. Her main focus is on testimonial injustice, which stems from our often unconscious assessments of a speaker's credibility. Literature on the epistemology of testimony does not give a uniform account of the manner in which we come to accept testimonial evidence, but it is acknowledged that some judgment on our part, whether explicit or implicit, of the testifier's credibility plays a role. Put simply, we are less likely to accept a claim if we do not see the person making it as credible. And prejudice can result in a person's being assigned a lower degree of credibility solely on the basis of a negative stereotype about a group to which she belongs. There are many ways in which this can actually happen – probably as many as there are factors involved the assessment of credibility. However, trustworthiness and competence can be singled out as important dimensions of credibility assessment, and both can be negatively impacted by prejudice. African-American males in North America are often unfairly criminalized, and this negative stereotype can affect assessments of trustworthiness. In different situations, members of racial groups who have negative stereotypes assorted with business practices might be assessed as less trustworthy than people who are not members of those groups. Similarly, there are negative stereotypes about competence at particular tasks. We have already mentioned negative stereotypes about women and math performance, but we will shortly discuss problematic stereotypes about gender and rationality that can cause women to be negatively evaluated. Fricker, in her book, makes use of an example from the screenplay from the film *The Talented Mr Ripley*, in which a woman is told "Marge, there's female intuition, and then there are facts." (Fricker 2007, p. 88) Fricker discusses this instance of testimonial injustice in more detail than will be covered here, but it illustrates the point, at least, that identity prejudice can seriously affect the reception of a person's claims. In this case, Marge, despite intimate knowledge of the subject in question, is dismissed because of her gender, and her views are discounted.

There has been some work done in adapting this idea to arguments, and developing a concept of *argumentative injustice* (Bondy 2010). This is an analogous concept to Fricker's in that it involves harm done to an individual due to false identity-prejudicial stereotypes. However, instead of harming someone as a knower, it harms her as a reasoner, or someone capable of drawing conclusions from premises. While Bondy does cite some disanalogies between his concept and Fricker's, the issues under discussion in this paper could easily be discussed in terms of either or both.[2] Particularly when we consider the close relationship between ad hominem fallacies and testimony, it ought not matter too much which term we use to talk about the injustice being done – whether it is a wrong to the person as an arguer or as a source of good information. So at least in this particular case, testimonial injustice and argumentative injustice intersect. As such, we will continue to use the original term "epistemic injustice," recognizing that our examples fall into both categories.

2.4 Fallacies in Dialogue: Bill and Sue

Some treatments of fallacies do consider their effect on dialogues in general. One particularly good treatment is Woods and Walton (1982), in which we see disagreements between two agents in a romantic relationship: Bill and Sue. Woods and Walton use these characters as part of a running example in order to illustrate different ways in which agents might disagree. For instance, they provide examples of their disagreeing about the facts, such as what Bill might have said on a particular occasion. They also provide examples of their drawing different conclusions from the same facts. The former is called premissory instability, and the latter, conclusional instability. These concepts are used to show when an argument becomes a *quarrel*, which is often what the word "argument" is taken to mean in ordinary language contexts. Quarrels, however, are typically unproductive and unpleasant.

> If, as in the case of premissory instability, we cannot even get started on the road to agreement, then frustration, accusation, and hurt feelings are bound to occur. References will tend to become personal and disagreeable. Sue might eventually complain that if Bill can't recall what he said last Friday, then he is a simpleton; Bill might retort that Sue is a hysterical shrew. Before you know it, things will have taken another nasty turn. Similarly, having got the discussion nicely under way with some basic premissory agreement, things might come grinding to a halt owing to a lack of common conclusions. Then the same personal disruptions could occur. Bill might contend that Sue shows herself to be a "typical woman" in having no capacity to reason beyond her nose, or to perceive what follows from what. And Sue may earnestly offer to slap Bill's moronic face (and perhaps be forgiven for it.) (Woods and Walton 1982, p. 4)

[2] One exception is that Bondy allows for argumentative injustice to involve credibility excesses rather than just credibility deficits, which is something I will not address. In this work, I will only consider cases of credibility deficit as a result of injustice.

The Bill and Sue example also serves the purpose of illustrating some fallacies that can occur in the course of an argument, particularly when it becomes a quarrel. Obviously, threatening to slap someone's face is an appeal to force, and a poor argumentative move. However, we also see several cases of personal insults, or ad hominem attacks. These are also fairly obvious, especially when we are primed to look for such things. For example, "simpleton" and "hysterical shrew" are both given as examples of insulting phrases that are irrelevant to the quality of someone's argument. But we might want to think again before simply accepting them as examples of ad hominem fallacies and moving on. And what about the accusation of being a typical woman? There is some initial difficulty in seeing this as a proper ad hominem attack, because at least according to the criteria we set out above, being a woman has to be seen as a negative trait in this context. But what is problematic is the characterization of a typical woman, not the fact of Sue's being a woman. There is more to be said about this case than simply the fact that fallacies are being committed, and tempers are being lost. We will take the three reasoning errors individually.

First, there is the accusation that Bill is a simpleton for not being able to recall what he said at an earlier time. This is clearly an insult, but is it relevant to the quality of his argument? In the context of this argument, perhaps not, but a minor modification could make it seem relevant. In this particular case, Bill's being a simpleton is a consequence of Sue's belief that he is simply wrong about what he said on Friday. So the insult is predicated on his having said something false, and only further demonstrates the fact that the two interlocutors are disagreeing about the truth of the premises of an argument: what it was that Bill actually said. As such, it does not perfectly fit the model of an ad hominem attack. In a typical ad hominem attack, someone's argument is discredited on the basis of an irrelevant negative characteristic that he is said to possess. But if Sue's claim had been that, since Bill is a simpleton, he is probably misremembering what he said last Friday, the deficiency is relevant to the argument. It would, of course, have been better if instead of accusing Bill of being a simpleton, Sue had more specifically accused him of having a terrible memory. If it is in fact true that Bill's memory is bad, this is bound to have a lasting effect on his credibility in future discourse, assuming that his testimony or the truth of his premises is based on his memory of the facts. But despite the lasting effects and Bill's likely credibility deficit, this is not a real case of epistemic injustice in Fricker's sense, even if the claim is false. Even though this does harm Bill in his capacity as a knower, the wrong is not based on any kind of structural injustice. No negative stereotypes have been invoked, and there is nothing about Bill's identity that is connected to the claim that he is less than intelligent.

Now we turn to the attacks on Sue, which are connected in that both evoke problematic stereotypes about women and rationality. The first is Bill's retort that Sue is a hysterical shrew. While it does not explicitly raise the issue of gender, there is a gendered quality to the label "hysterical shrew" that is not really present in calling someone a simpleton.[3] Both men and women could be simpletons, but it seems that

[3] Though the label "simpleton" arguably brings up problematic stereotypes about disability, making a more intersectional analysis desirable, for the sake of simplicity here, we will suppose that neither Bill nor Sue is cognitively disabled.

only women are called shrews, and it is rare to say that a man is being hysterical. Even though the fallacy in the accusation is obvious, it still renders gender salient to the dispute in a way that it might not have been before.

The last ad hominem attack of the passage state that Sue is a typical woman, and is therefore incapable of reasoning properly. There are at least two features of this attack that distinguish it from the previous two. First, being a woman is not an obviously negative trait (or at least should not be!), where a simpleton or a hysterical shrew is easily recognizable as something we would not want to be. While being incapable of reasoning properly is clearly something negative, note that it is supposed to follow from a trait (gender) that we do not obviously recognize as being negative. Second, if women were less capable of proper reasoning, this would not really be an ad hominem fallacy, since it would be very relevant to the argument. Pointing out that one's argumentative opponent is somehow lacking in their ability to reason and think through consequences is actually relevant to whether or not they should be taken seriously. As an illustration of this, note that if one was engaged in an argument with someone (of any gender) and said, "Look, you've had a lot of alcohol tonight, and so you're being totally irrational," this would not count as an ad hominem fallacy. There are plenty of things that could impair someone's ability to reason, such as drugs, alcohol, injury, or illness, and bringing them up as a reason to take that person's argument less seriously does not seem properly fallacious. But of course what makes this case different from dismissing someone because they've had too much to drink is that the latter case allows for the possibility of revisiting the discussion later, when the person has sobered up. It is not common for someone to change genders, and I suspect that people who say things like Bill did in this argument would not also be thinking of revisiting the argument after such a change.

So this needs to be further broken down. Here we have a case of an accusation that is in part true, since Sue is a woman, and would be relevant if entirely true, since someone's ability to reason is relevant to the quality of their argument. An alternative diagnosis of the problem is that we do not have an ad hominem fallacy, but a false claim built in to the accusation in the first place, namely that women are poor reasoners. This really depends on how we treat the characterization of a "typical woman." If we take it as part of the attack, then the charge against Sue is just false, since the characterization of women that it depends on is just false. On the other hand, if we take it as a background assumption, then we can see it as an ad hominem fallacy, since being a woman is irrelevant to one's ability to reason, though Bill is falsely treating it as a relevant factor. Also, this is a case of epistemic and argumentative injustice, generally wronging Sue in her capacity as a participant in this dialogue. The reason why the authors are able to use this as an example of an ad hominem fallacy in the first place is that the stereotype of women as being less rational is a recognizable one, even if we do not endorse it. If Bill had said that Sue is a typical brown-eyed person and therefore unable to reason properly, it would not have done a particularly good pedagogical job, since there are no common stereotypes about brown-eyed people being poor reasoners.

Further, given the literature on stereotype threat, we might worry that calling attention to a negative stereotype about women and rationality might have a negative effect on the female participant in the discussion. But we need to be careful about just how we characterize this phenomenon, particularly since the causal mechanism that results in underperformance is not quite understood at this point. Still, note that what happens in next in the story is both plausible and in some sense a confirmation of the stereotype, namely an appeal to force. In making this move, Sue gives up on rational argument, and threatens to slap Bill. It is telling that the person against whom a stereotype about rationality is deployed immediately resorts to an irrational response. Of course this is just a story, but it could easily have been an actual interaction.

Another thing to talk about, then, is what an alternative next part of the story could have been instead of a slap. Walton and Woods use this as an example of a way in which tensions can escalate in a quarrel, but what, if anything, could salvage this argument? Bill could show that his memory is perfectly good, and Sue might be able to show herself to be calm and collected, but how could she show that the last ad hominem attack is unjustified? In the previous two cases, it was possible to show that the negative trait ascribed was inapplicable, but in this case, Sue certainly is a woman. What is false is the assumption that her being a woman makes her less capable of producing a proper argument. It seems very unlikely that anything Sue could do would conclusively show the falseness of the stereotype generally, and it does not seem much more likely that she would even be able to combat it in this individual instance.

The problem is that once her rationality has been undermined, Sue's prospects for rationally defending herself obviously diminish. There is now an easy way to dismiss any further counterargument that she gives as a further manifestation of her irrationality, and thus not worth considering as a serious point in a debate. This is largely because what she has to argue against is the view that women are irrational. No easy demonstration is available to show that typical women are perfectly good reasoners. So her principal argumentative resource has been removed, and Sue may easily find herself appealing to force or emotion, or committing some other kind of fallacy, because it has become the only way for her to make a point heard. Notice, though, that this is a potential mechanism for the underperformance effect of stereotype threat. When a person's capacity to engage as a rational agent has been undermined by deploying a stereotype, they may find themselves confirming that stereotype because they are no longer accepted in the discourse as a rational agent. More simply, underperformance in this particular way may be their only way to stay in the conversation because of the epistemic injustice that has been done.

If Sue's prospects for defending herself using only her own resources are poor, what if Bill apologizes for the sexist remark, or he is called out by a third party? Can this correct the epistemic injustice? Does it neutralize the problem, and allow Sue back into the dialogue as an equal participant? Not necessarily. Bill can certainly take back what he said, either because he regrets it or because of someone else's intervention, but issues of gender and rationality have now been rendered salient to the argument. Is there then any way for someone hearing their argument to see Sue just as a reasoner, and not as a female reasoner? This is the place where issues of implicit bias become relevant, as we see just how difficult it is for people, even those people who express a commitment to treating men and women equally, to really do so. This may have been the case even before gender was explicitly introduced, but is certainly so at this point in the argument. Implicit bias, by its very nature, is extremely difficult to switch off. And we have already seen that there are negative stereotypes about women and rationality. Once a woman has been labeled as an irrational female in an argument, the threat of the label remains for her. These features of the situation are what really make it an injustice in Fricker's sense – something that does epistemic harm to Sue.

It might be arguable that any case of an ad hominem attack does some epistemic harm to an interlocutor. I would be happy to grant this point, but nevertheless would maintain that there is a real difference between this last case and the others due to the irreparability of the damage done to the discourse as a whole. Suppose Bill had claimed instead that she was revealing herself to be a typical brown-eyed person and therefore a bad reasoner. This is an *incidental*, rather than *systematic* case of testimonial injustice. A prejudice against the reasoning powers of brown-eyed people is unusual, and though it might cause significant problems for Sue in the course of this argument, its effects will most likely be quite localized to her interactions with Bill. On the other hand, a prejudice related to women and rationality will likely affect Sue in many areas of her life:

> Systematic testimonial injustices, then, are produced not by prejudice *simpliciter*, but specifically by those prejudices that track the subject through different dimensions of social activity – economic, educational, professional, sexual, legal, political, religious, and so on. Being subject to a tracker prejudice renders one susceptible not only to testimonial injustice but to a gamut of different injustices, and so when such a prejudice generates a testimonial injustice, that injustice is systematically connected with other kinds of actual or potential injustice (Fricker 2007, p. 27).

The fact that a testimonial injustice is systematic is significant for two main reasons. First, we are also concerned with the effects of the fallacy on outside participants to the dialogue. A prejudice against brown-eyed people is unlikely to be shared by a wide segment of the population, whereas prejudices about gender are common (though in many cases unconscious). So a brown-eyed person is unlikely to be affected by implicit bias against brown-eyed people, but a woman is likely to be affected by implicit sexism. Second, the confidence-eroding effects of testimonial injustice are much more significant when a person has been consistently subject to it. Even if Bill has not expressed sentiments like this in the past, if Sue has found herself being discounted, or treated as less rational, because of her gender, an attack such as this will contribute to an already substantial harm. Even though this paper is focusing primarily on instances of one-off testimonial injustices, or at least injustices committed in the course of a single dialogue, the line between long-term injustice and one-off injustice can become blurry in many situations. And even in a one-off situation, Fricker writes that "the recipient of a one-off testimonial injustice may lose confidence in his belief, or in his justification for it, so that he ceases to satisfy the conditions for knowledge" (Fricker 2007, p. 47). This means that the (perhaps cumulative) epistemic harm might render things such that Sue is no longer capable of acting as a rational participant in the dialogue – hence the appeal to force.

Thus far, we have only looked at a single case of epistemic injustice and looked at its problematic effects, but the comments about the case of Bill and Sue certainly generalize to many other situations. There are certain fallacies whose negative effects on an argument may be counteracted. Someone may be able to show that a negative stereotype is inapplicable to them, because they do not actually belong to the group being stereotyped. However, if the problem is one of showing that the stereotype is inaccurate, this is a problem that requires much more than a single exchange. We can also talk more generally about ways in which ad hominem attacks might constitute an epistemic injustice against a participant in a discussion. As we alluded to earlier, there are two main problematic effects of ad hominem attacks that invoke identity-prejudicial stereotypes. First, there is the epistemic harm done to the individual who is being attacked. Stereotype threat and the cumulative effects of epistemic injustice can cause a person to become a worse participant in the dialogue. This may result in her becoming less sure of her beliefs, ultimately failing to satisfy the conditions for knowledge, or may leave her with too few resources with which to engage as a legitimate participant in the discussion. Second, there is the potential for implicit bias in outside observers, once the negative stereotype has been rendered salient to the discussion.

Even if people do attempt to discount stereotypes, they may nevertheless have significant effects in their assessment of the situation, and of the merits of each individual's arguments. The anchoring effect is a phenomenon in which people, when primed with certain pre-established categories or amounts, tend to produce estimates which are closer to those categories or amounts than those who are not primed (Slovic 1967; Tversky and Kahneman 1974). For instance, Desmarais and Bruce (2010) found that sports commentary that invokes stereotypes influences viewers' interpretation of the game being played. It seems entirely plausible that stereotypes could influence observers' interpretation of an argument taking place in front of them without their being aware of this influence.

Regardless of whether the effects on Sue are visible to the other participants, we can at least acknowledge that she now bears a burden in the debate that Bill does not. She has to be more careful than he does to be even-tempered and rational, lest she be seen as a hysterical woman. This is a burden that has been unfairly placed upon her in the debate due to her gender. More specifically, the fact that Bill's ad hominem attack has made her gender salient to the argument they are having. She may admittedly choose not to try to take up this challenge, and continue to argue as before, but for all involved parties (including most likely herself) she is at risk of being evaluated more harshly if she fails to meet it. What this means practically speaking is that Bill may be permitted to make an appeal to emotion in the course of their argument and have that be considered a relatively acceptable, if not optimal, argumentative move. However, Sue's making the same emotional appeal would likely result in her being viewed negatively, as being overly emotional and possibly hysterical. This effect might become obvious to observers if both Bill and Sue were to make an identical appeal, but such a situation seems unlikely to arise in the course of any real life argument.

2.5 The Credibility of Female Attorneys

Epistemic injustice can arise in the course of ordinary dialogue, as in the previous section, but it can also have significant effects in legal contexts as well. A case study of tactics used by attorneys in the courtroom showed a variety of credibility lessening tactics used against opposing counsels. One particular dimension of this study looked at the ways in which these credibility attacks were gendered. Based on gender bias reports as well as anecdotal evidence, Ubel (2008) conducted a survey of Kansas attorneys asking about credibility lessening tactics, described as "any tactic in which an attorney uses speech or actions to negatively impact the credibility of another attorney in court." While the participants were only asked to describe situations in which such tactics had been used, the analysis classified them into eight categories that they identified. The two most relevant to our purposes are Experience and Reference Gender, since they specifically attack aspects of the opposing counsel's identity: age and gender, respectively. We will focus on the latter.

Anecdotal evidence and earlier studies mention sexist remarks, derogatory treatment, inappropriate forms of address, references to female stereotypes, foul language, cute names, and making references to physical appearance (Ubel 2008, p. 44). Some of these appeared in Ubel's study. As examples of responses that were coded as Reference Gender, (Ubel 2008, p. 47) gives the following:

- Sometimes older (much older) male attorneys will call you "honey" or "lady lawyer"
- Referring to me as "little lady," "young lady"
- When picking my first felony jury, the prosecutor announced to the jury I was 5 months pregnant. He asked the jury if this would influence their decisions.

Ubel found that while 15 % of the tactics that female respondents reported were classified as Reference Gender, no males reported their gender being referenced in order to lessen their credibility. Further, no one mentioned using this tactic against another attorney (Ubel 2008, p. 49). This study did have its limitations, however. While the gender breakdown of respondents was similar to that of Kansas attorneys, the study was obviously geographically constrained and self-reported. Further, the extent to which these tactics were successful was impossible to measure. It may have been that in some cases, the credibility of the attacker was lessened more than the credibility of the one under attack.

However, in light of stereotypes about the gendered nature of rationality, and about women being more emotionally governed, it seems very plausible that many of the Reference Gender attacks would have had very much the desired effect, and further, because of the unconscious nature of implicit bias, listeners may not have been aware that they were affected. These are real cases in which some of the hypothetical tactics outlined in the previous section against Sue have been used to commit an epistemic injustice. The next section, however, will turn to situations in which issues of credibility and identity are much more complex and difficult to untangle.

2.6 "Authentic" Victims and Credibility

In cases of sexual assault, perceived credibility of victims is an extremely salient issue. While the gender of an attorney is irrelevant to the quality of her arguments, aspects of an individual's identity can be more easily seen as relevant to her credibility. So this section will look at ways in which attacks against an individual evoking aspects of their identity can result in unfair credibility deficits and in such a way constitute epistemic injustice. In a well-known Canadian case in which a man was accused of sexually assaulting a young woman who he was interviewing for a job. Justice McClung remarked that the 17-year old complainant did not present herself to the accused in "a bonnet and crinolines" – a statement duly criticized by another Supreme Court judge, Justice L'Heureux-Dubé (R v. Ewanchuk 1999). While the accused, Ewanchuk, was acquitted, and the acquittal upheld on appeal as per the views of Justice McClung, the appeal was later overturned. The trial ruling as well as McClung's ruling, were based on the idea of "implied consent," that the complainant's behaviour and lack of resistance to some of the accused's advances could objectively be construed as consent.

The judges who overturned McClung's ruling did so on several grounds – some on the more purely legal grounds that there was no implied consent defence, and that the accused's behaviour made it clear that he understood that his advances were unwanted. However, L'Heureux-Dubé's remarks pointed out instances in which McClung's remarks about the complainant's character were problematic, and that we can recognize as cases of ad hominem attacks that contribute to epistemic injustice. These create tension with the fact that the trial judges initially did find the complainant to be a credible witness. In addition to McClung's remarks about the lack of "bonnet and crinolines," he also pointed out that she was the mother of a 6-month-old baby, and shared an apartment with her boyfriend and another couple. In response to this, L'Heureux-Dubé wrote:

> Even though McClung J.A. asserted that he had no intention of denigrating the complainant, one might wonder why he felt necessary to point out these aspects of the trial record. Could it be to express that the complainant is not a virgin? Or that she is a person of questionable moral character because she is not married and lives with her boyfriend and another couple? These comments made by an appellate judge help reinforce the myth that under such circumstances, either the complainant is less worthy of belief, she invited the sexual assault, or her sexual experience signals probable consent to further sexual activity. Based on those attributed assumptions, the implication is that if the complainant articulates her lack of consent by saying "no", she really does not mean it and even if she does, her refusal cannot be taken as seriously as if she were a girl of "good" moral character. (R v. Ewanchuk 1999)

Based on what we have seen thus far about the pervasiveness of stereotypes, even if someone claims that these are not being pointed out in order to reduce the complainant's credibility, they can still very easily have that effect, and L'Heureux-Dubé is quite right to connect them to the myth that, on some occasions, "no" might mean "yes." Since this case, some research has been done on the concept of the "ideal victim" in sexual assault cases, and the extent to which assertions about a complainant's character can affect assessments of her credibility, even if they are not framed as such (and even if, as in Ewanchuk's case, credibility has supposedly already been established.)

In some aspects of sexual assault cases, credibility judgments are explicit, for instance in police assessments of the believability of rape reports. Randall (2010) discusses several situations in which police disbelieved several women's rape reports on account of their demeanor. We will focus more on credibility attacks in trial contexts, however, in which aspects of a woman's background can be raised in order to discredit her. One egregious example of this is the view that sex workers, by the nature of their work, cannot be raped. This is in part due to a credibility deficit due to their identity; but women who are in a relationship with their assailant will also be discredited along similar lines, due to "the (mistaken) assumption of 'continuous' or 'implied' consent given by women in these situations" (Randall 2010, p. 409). However, there are other ways in which women's credibility can be attacked that have little or nothing to do with the idea of implied consent. Women who are already socially marginalized (perhaps because they are sex workers, but also perhaps due to issues of race or class) can often be seen as less "authentic" victims of rape. Randall cites an Australian study (discussed in more detail in Cossins (2003)) investigating the way in which adult female sexual assault victims are treated in the courtroom, with a particular focus on the treatment of black and Aboriginal women:

> The analysis showed that the credibility testing of the victims was compounded by cultural and language problems for Aboriginal women, who were subjected to a significantly greater and more intense amount of defence questioning their drinking, drug use, lying, and the levels of casual sexual relations in their communities. The more hostile and racist the credibility assaults, the more distressing and traumatizing the trial process is for rape complainants, creating a vicious circle such that their very distress undermines their ability to "hold up" under legal interrogation in a way that is seen to be credible. (Randall 2010, p. 410–1)

This study raises clear worries of both stereotype threat and implicit (perhaps not even implicit) bias. The way in which victims often broke down under hostile and racist questioning is even more extreme than the usual underperformance effect described in studies of stereotype threat. Further, the questions drinking and drug use clearly invoke certain problematic stereotypes and render them salient to listeners at the trial. The study even notes that a Crown Prosecutor remarked to the judge, "these are not educated people," in reference to the Aboriginal woman who was the complainant (Cossins 2003, p. 80). The fact that these stereotypes are even invoked by the prosecution is striking, since it shows us the extent to which they are seen as relevant to the decision. Had this been a remark by the defence, it could easily have been labeled an ad hominem attack. After all, a woman's level of education is likely irrelevant to her ability to provide accurate testimony about personal events, but could prejudice listeners against her regardless.

Now it may seem difficult to separate ad hominem attacks from truly relevant concerns in sexual assault cases, since personal testimony about events plays such a significant part in the evaluation of what in fact happened. However, the asymmetry with which different groups face credibility attacks makes it very likely that something problematic is happening. Indeed, the very concept of the "ideal victim" makes it clear that some victims of sexual assault will find it harder to make their cases than others in ways that have nothing to do with the facts of the situation, merely their social identity.

2.7 Conclusion

The story thus far has been primarily a pessimistic one, about the fact that negative stereotypes and the epistemic injustice associated with their use in arguments, cannot simply be ignored. Once they have come into play in an argument, they render certain features of a participant salient to the discourse in question. We have also seen that there is very little that an individual herself can do once being subjected to an epistemic injustice, to correct or even improve her argumentative situation. Further, the psychology literature is both extensive and mixed when it comes to the possibility of becoming unbiased individuals, or successfully correcting for biases that we know we might possess. Some articles are extremely pessimistic about the possibility of bias correction (Wilson and Brekke 1994; Wegner 1994; Sanna et al. 2002). But despite this, certain biases do have certain strategies that work to some degree (Anderson and Sechler 1986; Pettigrew 1998). However, since different biases are mitigated by different strategies, there cannot be an across-the-board solution that could be implemented for cases in which identity prejudicial stereotypes can interfere with the course of an argument. There is no clear way in which an individual can defend herself against an epistemic harm done to her. We might just be lucky in some cases, and people outside of the dialogue might accord less credibility to the person making the prejudicial ad hominem attack, which could help balance out the issues of bias.

Surprisingly, one of the few sources of hope for defending oneself against ad hominem attacks on credibility can be found in the literature on "ideal" victims of sexual assault. While much of this literature focuses on issues of identity, Larcombe (2002) provides a different perspective, in which a victim's ability to demonstrate resistance during the trial process itself might enhance her credibility rather than damage it. We have already discussed ways in which defence lawyers in trials can frequently, and in a hostile fashion, attempt to discredit a witness. However, if she is able to resist the underperformance effects of stereotype threat, she may be able to turn the situation to her advantage:

> if she can hold up under the pressure, if she can withstand the defence counsel's seductive and/or aggressive attempts to impose an alternative/normative account, if she can resist their attempts to take control and determine the course of events; if she can stick with her version of what happened and is clear about what she said, felt, and wanted – all in the face of explicit and calculated attempts to trip her up – she will have represented herself not only as a persuasive and credible witness but, more importantly, as a victimized yet resistant female subject. (Larcombe 2002, p. 142)

The reason this works, Larcombe reasons, is that this allows the jury to observe a scenario of the victim's firm non-consent, which makes it easier for them to picture an analogous scenario as having taken place in the past. This can make her account of non-consent to the accused's advances more plausible. But of course, while there be an upside to credibility attacks in this specific situation, turning it to her advantage still requires a tremendous effort on the part of the victim of these attacks. However, Larcombe does also mention one situation in which a judge intervened on behalf of a victim who was being examined in a particularly aggressive fashion, and rebuked the defence lawyer for his conduct. Perhaps it can be in the power of authoritative outside parties to ameliorate the negative effects of ad hominem attacks and reduce the epistemic harms being done. Those who already have been accorded significant credibility would do well to speak up on the part of those who may be likely to suffer an epistemic injustice; this may be the best solution we have so far.

References

Ambady, N., M. Shih, A. Kim, and T.L. Pittinsky. 2001. Stereotype susceptibility in children: Effects of identity activation on quantitative performance. *Psychological Science* 12(5): 385–390.

Anderson, C.A., and E.S. Sechler. 1986. Effects of explanation and counterexplanation on the development and use of social theories. *Journal of Personality and Social Psychology* 50(1): 24–34.

Bertrand, M., and S. Mullainathan. 2004. Are Emily and Greg more employable than Lakisha and Jamal? A field experiment on labor market discrimination. *American Economic Review* 94(4): 991–1013.

Bondy, P. 2010. Argumentative injustice. *Informal Logic* 30(3): 263–278.

Cossins, A. 2003. Saints, sluts, and sexual assault: Rethinking the relationship between sex, race and gender. *Social and Legal Studies* 12(1): 77–103.

Desmarais, F., and T. Bruce. 2010. The power of stereotypes: Anchoring images through language in live sports broadcasts. *Journal of Language and Social Psychology* 29(3): 338–362.

Ehrlinger, J., T. Gilovich, and L. Ross. 2005. Peering into the bias blind spot: People's assessments of bias in themselves and others. *Personality and Social Psychology Bulletin* 31(5): 680–692.

Ewanchuk, R. v. 1999. 1 SCR 330. Retrieved from the Supreme Court of Canada website: http://scc-csc.lexum.com/decisia-scc-csc/scc-csc/scc-csc/en/item/1684/index.do.

Fricker, M. 2007. *Epistemic injustice: Power and the ethics of knowing*. New York: Oxford University Press.

Larcombe, W. 2002. The 'ideal' victim v successful rape complaints: Not what you might expect. *Feminist Legal Studies* 10: 131–148.

Pettigrew, T.F. 1998. Intergroup contact theory. *Annual Review of Psychology* 49(1): 65–85.

Pronin, E., D.Y. Lin, and L. Ross. 2002. The bias blind spot: Perceptions of bias in self versus others. *Personality and Social Psychology Bulletin* 28(3): 369–381.

Randall, M. 2010. Sexual assault law, credibility, and "ideal victims": Consent, resistance, and victim blaming. *Canadian Journal of Women and the Law* 22(2): 397–434.

Sanna, L.J., N. Schwarz, and S.L. Stocker. 2002. When debiasing backfires: Accessible content and accessibility experiences in debiasing hindsight. *Journal of Experimental Psychology: Learning, Memory, and Cognition* 28(3): 497–502.

Slovic, P. 1967. The relative influence of probabilities and payoffs upon perceived risk of a gamble. *Psychonomic Science* 9(4): 223–224.

Spencer, S.J., C.M. Steele, and D.M. Quinn. 1999. Stereotype threat and women's math performance. *Journal of Experimental Social Psychology* 35: 4–28.

Steele, C.M., and J. Aronson. 1995. Stereotype threat and the intellectual test performance of African Americans. *Journal of Personality and Social Psychology* 69(5): 797–811.

Steinpreis, R.E., K.A. Anders, and D. Ritzke. 1999. The impact of gender on the review of the curricula vitae of job applicants and tenure candidates: A national empirical study. *Sex Roles* 41(7–8): 509–528.

Tversky, A., and D. Kahneman. 1974. Judgment under uncertainty: Heuristics and biases. *Science* 185(4157): 1124–1131.

Ubel, S. 2008. Credibility lessening tactics utilized in the courtroom by male and female attorneys. *Communication Law Review* 42(2): 42–51.

Wegner, D.M. 1994. Ironic processes of mental control. *Psychological Review* 101(1): 34–52.

Wilson, T.D., and N. Brekke. 1994. Mental contamination and mental correction: Unwanted influences on judgments and evaluations. *Psychological Bulletin* 116(1): 117–142.

Woods, J. And, and D. Walton. 1982. *Argument: The logic of the fallacies*. Toronto: McGraw-Hill Ryerson.

Yap, A. 2013. Ad hominem fallacies, bias, and testimony. *Argumentation* 27(2): 97–109.

Chapter 3
On the Absence of Evidence

Giovanni Tuzet

Now faith is the substance of things hoped for, the evidence of things not seen.

(Hebrews 11: 1, King James Version)

Abstract In this paper, I intend to show that the absence of evidence about a claim is not inferentially inert in legal argumentation. Arguing from ignorance is usually taken to be a fallacy, but it can yield two sorts of justified conclusions in a trial: epistemic ones concerning what is plausibly true, and normative ones concerning what should be taken as true. In the former, the absence of evidence generates an argument from ignorance justified by non-deductive standards. In the latter, the absence of evidence triggers a normative presumption. I also show that in both we should not conflate the absence of evidence with the negative evidence provided by some test or research. Arguments from ignorance depend on the absence of certain evidentiary items, not on the evidence of an absence, even though also the lack of evidence is sometimes probative.

3.1 Introduction

In this paper, I intend to show that the absence of evidence about a claim is not inferentially inert in legal argumentation. Arguing from ignorance is usually taken to be a fallacy, but it can yield two sorts of justified conclusions in a trial: epistemic ones concerning what is plausibly true, and normative ones concerning what should be taken as true. In the former, the absence of evidence generates an argument from ignorance justified by non-deductive standards. In the latter, the absence of evidence triggers a normative presumption. I also show that in both we should not conflate the absence of evidence with the negative evidence provided by some test or research. Arguments from ignorance depend on the absence of certain evidentiary items, not

G. Tuzet (✉)
Bocconi University, Milan, Italy
e-mail: giovanni.tuzet@unibocconi.it

© Springer International Publishing Switzerland 2015
T. Bustamante, C. Dahlman (eds.), *Argument Types and Fallacies in Legal Argumentation*, Law and Philosophy Library 112,
DOI 10.1007/978-3-319-16148-8_3

on the evidence of an absence, even though also the lack of evidence is sometimes probative.

In our ordinary life it is not unusual to infer the truth-value of a claim from the absence of evidence about it. But that is a fallacy. This fallacy is called "argument from ignorance" (*argumentum ad ignorantiam*)[1] and it basically exists in two different versions: first, inferring the truth of a claim from the absence of evidence against it; second, inferring the falsity of a claim from the absence of evidence in favor of it. We might call the two versions *affirmative* and *negative* respectively. Here is an instance of the affirmative:

(A) There is no scientific proof that silicone breast implants are unsafe; therefore, they are safe.

And here is an instance of the negative version:

(N) There is no scientific proof that silicone breast implants are safe; therefore, they are unsafe.

Put as such, both (A) and (N) are fallacious. What kind of fallacy is it? It can be argued that this fallacy belongs to the category of relevance fallacies. The premises are not relevant to the conclusions, because the truth-value of a claim is independent from the evidence about it (and from the absence of evidence also). But don't we ordinarily argue from evidence to truth-values? And don't we often argue from absence of evidence too? I think it is possible to defend some version of the argument from ignorance. And I think that the possibility of justifying at least some instances of it depends on the background knowledge, on the relevant information and on the theory of fallacies agreed upon. However, the present work doesn't aim at upholding an overall theory of fallacies. The only question it deals with is whether the argument from ignorance – as defined here – has a legitimate role in legal argumentation, and when.[2]

I will proceed as follows: after some remarks on absence of evidence and argumentation theory (§2), I will address the saying that absence of evidence is not evidence of absence (§3) and I will finally consider the effect of the legal burdens of proof on the absence of evidence (§4). My main claims will be that, first, we have to distinguish deductive from non-deductive accounts of fallacies; second, we have to distinguish absence of evidence (e.g. not knowing whether there are footsteps in the snow) from negative evidence (knowing there are no footsteps in the snow); and third, we have to distinguish in the field of legal argumentation the uses of the argument that are epistemically justified in virtue of the background knowledge and the relevant information and the uses of it that are practically justified by the relevant presumptions and burdens of proof. Given these distinctions, it happens that absence of evidence *is* evidence of absence; but this only concerns the epistemic uses of the

[1] See Robinson (1971) for several varieties and examples of the argument. Cf. e.g. Walton (1999b, 368, 2008, 57).

[2] To be precise, I focus on its role in adjudication. I leave aside the role it has in legislative debates and political argumentation, where it is often connected to the so-called Precaution Principle.

argument from ignorance, for the practical uses of it do not say what is true or false but, rather, what should be treated as true or false.

3.2 Absence of Evidence and Argumentation Theory

The argument from ignorance is a fallacy from a deductive point of view. This means that, if "inferring" is understood as *deductively inferring*, the inference from the absence of evidence to the truth of a claim (in the affirmative version of the argument), or to the falsity of it (in the negative version), is an invalid one. For the truth or the falsity of a claim is not logically implied by the absence of evidence against or in favor of it.

However, if "inferring" is read as meaning *inductively* or *abductively inferring*, that argumentative move is not necessarily a fallacy.[3] This is common sense. There are cases in which it is reasonable to infer the truth of a claim from the absence of evidence against it, and cases in which it is reasonable to infer the falsity of a claim from the absence of evidence in favor of it. So, if we move from the class of deductive fallacies to that of non-deductive ones, the question we face is how to distinguish the cases in which it is reasonable to draw some non-deductive inferences from ignorance, from those in which it is not. In short, we have to determine when and why that argumentative move is not fallacious any longer.

Now an argument is an inductive fallacy when a weak conclusion is presented as strong, or vice versa. (Here for simplicity I skip considerations on abductive fallacies, which are similar to inductive ones).[4] To put it in a more abstract way, such a fallacy occurs when contrary to appearances the inductive justification standards are not met. That happens when the inductive support given by the premises to the conclusion is disguised, misconstrued, or altered in some significant way.

That could be cast in different terms according to the theory of fallacies and argumentation agreed upon. Locke was apparently the first to use the name *argumentum ad ignorantiam*.[5] Today the argument is usually included in the list of fallacies that theories of argumentation try to cast and explain. Let us consider the pragma-dialectical theory of argumentation, which regards a fallacy as a deficient move in an argumentative discourse or text (not just as an error of reasoning, i.e. not only a violation of logical standards of validity).[6] The authors who support this theory claim that a pragma-dialectical treatment of fallacies provides a more systematic account of them (including in the picture the so-called informal fallacies) than the standard, logical treatment. For, according to the pragma-dialectical

---

[3] Cf. Wreen (1989, 1996).

[4] On abduction and induction see Flach and Kakas (2000).

[5] See Hamblin (1970, 159–162).

[6] Van Eemeren and Grootendorst (2004). See also van Eemeren (2010, 193–196).

approach, a fallacy is a violation of any of the rules for a critical discussion.[7] On the one hand, this view is taken to be broader than the standard conception, and, on the other, it is taken to be more specific:

> Our view is broader because we do not link the fallacies exclusively to one particular discussion stage, which we call the argumentation stage, in which the reasoning of the protagonist is tested for its correctness. It is more specific because it links the fallacies specifically and explicitly with the process of resolving a difference of opinion (van Eemeren and Grootendorst 2004, 162).

This conception captures more fallacies than others and places them at different stages of a critical discussion. Then, what is wrong with the argument from ignorance? In the context of a conversation, or a discussion, or an exchange of reasons in general, what is wrong is the act of making a statement unsupported by evidentiary reasons. This is related to Grice's maxim of quality (1989, 27): "Try to make your contribution one that is true". This maxim is constituted of two more specific maxims, or sub-maxims: (1) Do not say what you believe to be false; (2) Do not say that for which you lack adequate evidence. The second sub-maxim is what interests us here. It says that we are not entitled to assert something we lack evidence for. Then, from the absence of evidence about *p*, we cannot conclude to the truth of *p* nor to its falsity. Frans van Eemeren and Rob Grootendorst (2004, 76–77) rephrase the point claiming that we must not perform any speech acts that are "insincere" (or for which we cannot accept responsibility).[8]

But arguments from ignorance are not always wrong. Douglas Walton has remarked, from the standpoint of a different but similar theory of argumentation,[9] that some uses of that kind of argument are not fallacious. The problem is "how to determine, by some clear and useful method, which are the fallacious and which are the nonfallacious cases" (Walton 1999a, 53). He basically uses the notion of *plausible inference* and applies it to the absence of a certain kind of evidence in given situations. For instance: "if it were raining now I would know it (by the noise); but I do not know it; therefore, it is not raining now" (Walton 1996, 1).[10] If the premises are plausible, the conclusion is plausible as well. Moreover Walton claims that some instances of the argument can be reconstructed as applications of *modus tollens* that provide plausible conclusions; but this is puzzling given that *modus tollens* provides deductive conclusions. In fact, Walton adds, it is not really *modus tollens*, but a kind of abductive argument (Walton 1999a, 57–58). He refines this idea saying that there

[7] "Every violation of any of the rules of the discussion procedure for conducting a critical discussion (by whichever party and at whatever stage in the discussion) is a fallacy" (van Eemeren and Grootendorst 2004, 175). Fallacies are "argumentative moves whose wrongness consists in the fact that they are a hindrance or impediment to the resolution of opinion on the merits" (van Eemeren 2010, 193).

[8] See van Eemeren and Grootendorst (2004, 187ff.). Cf. Walton (1999a) and van Eemeren and Grootendorst (1992, 187–194).

[9] Similar in that it is focused on the pragmatic and dialectical aspects of arguing. See e.g. Walton (1996, 1999a, b).

[10] Note that "I do not know it" is ambiguous between: (1) I have no evidence about it and (2) I have evidence it is not raining. This will be relevant for the discussion below.

is a "plausibilistic *modus tollens* form characteristic of typical *ad ignorantiam* arguments: 'if *A* then one would normally expect *B*; not *B*; therefore (plausibly) not *A*'" (Walton 1999a, 60). Some *prima facie* examples of this are the dog that did not bark, the snow without footsteps outside the house, and similar cases from which a set of plausible conclusions can be drawn.[11] So, the argument from ignorance "is a plausible inference that makes the conclusion plausible, on the assumption that the premises are plausible" (Walton 1999a, 64); and often such arguments are defeasible bases for practical deliberation (Walton 1999a, 59).

Walton also notices that the argument from ignorance is usually construed as related to non-ordinary things such as aliens and ghosts:

> it is characteristic of many of the fallacious arguments from ignorance cited in the logic textbooks that they tend to be about UFO's, the existence of God, ghosts, the paranormal, and so forth – all subjects in which there is a verifiability problem in the sense that it would be hard to know what counts exactly as evidence either for or against the claim (Walton 1999b, 369).

Besides, there are the non-fallacious uses of the argument. But Walton (1999b, 369) conceives of them as the cases where the argument is a "presumptive guide to action", which is a misleading account insofar as it misses the distinction between epistemic and practical considerations.[12] One thing is to have a set of epistemic reasons to uphold a (presumptive or plausible) belief, and quite another is to form a plan of action based on (i) that belief and (ii) a practical attitude such as a desire. The crucial aspects one must insist upon in order to redeem the argument from ignorance from easy criticism are (a) the nature of the evidence at stake and (b) the regulation of the burden of proof. As to (a), we have to distinguish the so-called negative evidence from the mere absence of it: "What is called *negative evidence* in scientific research is the kind of evidence where an outcome is tested for and does not occur".[13] As to (b), we need to observe that in a dialectical exchange "fallacious arguments from ignorance are often connected with first, a reversal of burden of proof, and second, a difficulty in fulfilling that burden, once it has been reversed, especially in cases where genuine evidence is difficult to find" (Walton 1999b, 375–376). (More on both points below).

---

[11] Wreen (1996, 354–356) argues that using *modus tollens* here counts as reconstructing deductively a genuine inductive argument, something he criticizes as artificial and based upon highly disputable premises. In fact, Walton (1999a, 60) qualifies that *modus tollens* as "plausibilistic", and Walton (2006, 323) qualifies it as "presumptive".

[12] At most, I would say that practical interests influence epistemic justification. See Stanley (2005) and Tuzet (2008). That idea was already in Carnap (1936, 426): "Suppose a sentence S is given, some test-observations for it have been made, and S is confirmed by them in a certain degree. Then it is a matter of practical decision whether we will consider that degree as high enough for our acceptance of S, or as low enough for our rejection of S, or as intermediate between these so that we neither accept nor reject S until further evidence will be available."

[13] Walton (1999b, 372). Note that this is evidence of absence, not absence of evidence; the absence of evidence would be the absence of testing, which is different from a testing with a negative outcome.

In later works Walton has stressed, on the one hand, the importance of that dialectical dimension to assess what he now calls "lack of knowledge inferences"[14] and, on the other hand, the importance of the epistemic distinction between negative evidence and absence of evidence. Let me focus on the latter point for the moment. If a search is scrupulous and nothing sought for is found, it is plausible to infer that what was sought for is not there. The inference is not a deductive one and the argument is not fallacious if we admit of inductive or abductive standards. "The argument from ignorance can become weak or erroneous where it is taken as a stronger form of argument than the evidence warrants" (Walton 2008, 58).

Revisiting our introductory example, with respect to (A), if the background knowledge suggests that silicone implants are safe and the relevant information is that several tests have been made and they don't prove that such breast implants are unsafe, then by an inductive or abductive standard we can infer that silicone breast implants are safe. If, on the contrary, with respect to (B), the background knowledge suggests that silicone implants are unsafe and the relevant information is that several tests have been made and they don't prove that such breast implants are safe, then by an inductive or abductive standard we can infer that silicone breast implants are unsafe. But these are not arguments from ignorance proper: they are arguments from negative evidence.

Walton et al. (2008, 327) provide this *modus tollens* scheme of the argument:

Major Premise: If *A* were true, then *A* would be known to be true.
Minor Premise: It is not the case that *A* is known to be true.
Conclusion: Therefore, *A* is not true.

The question is in the way we read the major premise.[15] How should we construe that conditional? Does it say that if *A* were true, then *in principle A* would be known to be true after a complete investigation about it? Or that if *A* were true, then *here and now A* would be known to be true as far as we are concerned? Of course the first reading is stronger and is the one that seems to be correct. But that reading transforms the argument into a sort of metaphysical claim, like Peirce's definition of reality as that which would be known at the ideal limit of inquiry.[16] Moreover, it transforms it into an argument from negative evidence; for it (counterfactually) states that a complete investigation was carried out and *A* was not found to be true. In fact, actual uses of the argument from ignorance are in line with the weaker reading. But then the argument is deductively fallacious, for here and now we have no deductive guarantee to know what is the case and what is not.

[14] "Arguments from ignorance presuppose a dialogue that is usually of the information-seeking or inquiry type, in which data are being collected in a knowledge base. How strong the argument is depends on how much data have been collected at the given point in the dialogue where the argument was put forward" (Walton 2006, 323). Cf. Walton (2008, 59) and Walton et al. (2008, 98–100).

[15] On this see also Wreen (1996, 356–358).

[16] Cf. Misak (2004, 5–8) and, for a somewhat different reading, De Waal (2001, 41, 48).

3.3 Absence of Evidence Is Not Evidence of Absence

Logically speaking, the absence of evidence that *p* is not evidence that not-*p*, nor is the absence of evidence that not-*p* evidence that *p*.[17] To put it more simply using the lawyer's saying, "Absence of evidence is not evidence of absence". Is this true? Perhaps it is true in general but not in particular. Or perhaps we have to make some conceptual refinements.

Let me start from a non-legal example (and indeed one of the standard and uninteresting examples that Walton criticizes). We lack evidence of the existence of aliens. What are we entitled to infer from that absence? That aliens do not exist? That they exist? Neither, from a deductive point of view. The absence of evidence about them does not imply anything about their existence. Indeed ignorance is a good ground for suspending judgment, not for taking a side (Robinson 1971, 102). Even Donald Rumsfeld would agree. Once he famously claimed that there are "unknown unknowns" beside the "known unknowns", which meant, in the context of his remark (less silly than it seemed), that the absence of evidence of weapons of mass destruction in Iraq was not evidence of their absence.[18] In logical terms, as we said, that we have no evidence that *p* doesn't mean that we have evidence that not-*p*.

But suppose we get some extraordinarily powerful instruments of observation that make us able to look into every corner of the universe: if we don't find anything about aliens, would it be reasonable to remain agnostic about them? The conclusion that they do not exist would have a much stronger inductive or abductive support than the conclusion that they do. The same holds, *mutatis mutandis*, on weapons of mass destruction. However you could object that in drawing those inferences we would take the absence of evidence as evidence of absence, and that would be incorrect from both an argumentative and a conceptual point of view. Would that be an appropriate objection?

A *thorough, scrupulous and possibly complete search* is the key element here: "lack of confirmation after a hypothesis has been given a fair chance is equivalent to disconfirming it" (Wreen 1989, 310). Note that it is not necessary to use aliens or terrible weapons to build up examples. Imagine that someone asks me to check if Robert is in the room: now I enter the room, look for Robert everywhere (behind the door, under the bed, inside the wardrobe, etc.), but don't find him. Could I say that I have enough evidence that he's not there? Should I rather say that I have no evidence that he's there? This seems to be a typical case of negative evidence, not of mere absence of it. I have a significant amount of negative evidence that he's not in

[17] See e.g. Taruffo (1992, 124ff., 222ff.); Laudan (2006, 93); Haack (2011, 7). In a seminar at Bocconi in March 2013, Hendrik Kaptein pointed out that there is a link between arguments from ignorance and *a contrario* arguments; I cannot elaborate on the point here.

[18] See Stephens (2011, 56–57). Cf. Haack (2011, 1) and Sahlane (2012, 472–473).

the room. A different issue[19] would be to know whether he is in the *next* room; well, in that situation I wouldn't know, for I would have no evidence about it.

That testing procedure is carried out informally in ordinary life and is carefully structured in scientific research and evidentiary legal settings. In these contexts we structure sensible experiments and try to conduct them properly in order to test the hypotheses at stake.

Scientists and lawyers agree that on certain conditions, determined by the characters of the search and of the argumentative exchange, failure to produce evidence is evidence itself. "Our failure to find evidence where we expect to find it or the failure of persons to produce things or provide testimony can in many cases be regarded as a form of evidence" (Anderson et al. 2005, 75). This is related to what we will discuss below under the heading of "negative inferences" triggered by evidentiary "gaps". But missing evidence is different from negative evidence, as the good old saying has it. One thing is the failure to produce evidence where we expect to find it, and the absence of any evidence at all is quite another.

So, what is important here is not only the theory of argumentation you subscribe to, but also the criteria (or standards) of adequacy of search. Once you admit a non-deductive account of argumentative correctness, it seems reasonable to postpone the assessment of an argument from ignorance once the discursive context, the relevant information and the background knowledge have been considered.

Larry Laudan (2006, 93) has said that "failure to prove *X* is never a proof of not-*X*". This is in tune with the idea that absence of evidence is not evidence of absence. But the application of the old saying to the cases in which an experiment doesn't deliver the expected outcome is not persuasive. If we run an experiment expecting to prove *X* and the experiment fails, we have something more than the mere absence of evidence (*a fortiori* if the experiment is crucial for the testing of a hypothesis). Similarly, if we make a thorough, scrupulous and complete search and don't find what we search for, we have something more than the mere absence of evidence. Perhaps the "never" in Laudan's statement is too strong. Or, better, the critical point is the meaning of "proof", which is a success-word and is usually related to a deductive standard. Given such refinements, we could say that, on the one hand, "failure to prove *X* is *never a proof* of not-*X*" and that, on the other, "failure to prove *X* is *often evidence* of not-*X*".[20]

David Kaye has made the point in the context of a discussion about evidence and probability (which is not relevant to the present purpose).[21] He says that gaps in the evidence generate "negative inferences". When we expect to find certain items of

[19] From a pragmatic point of view, one thing is the question ("Is Robert in the room?"), and another is the claim ("Robert is in the room"). When the claim is made, in certain contexts at least there is a presumption of knowledge on the person who makes it. When this is the case, the maxim that is followed is something of this sort: Trust the person and the claim unless there is some reason to have doubts about them.

[20] But one has also to distinguish "failure" as providing no evidence and "failure" as providing negative evidence.

[21] Kaye (1986). On that topic and the absence of evidence cf. Stephens (2011).

evidence, and don't find them, it is natural to draw a "negative inference" about the claim in question. Analogously, when we expect someone to provide us with certain items of evidence, and they do not do so, we generate a "negative inference" about the claim they make. Therefore, gaps in a litigant's evidence make the party's story less believable.

> Any good trial lawyer knows that the jury will expect to hear certain items of evidence in certain cases, and that it may regard the failure to produce such evidence with devastating skepticism (Kaye 1986, 663).

This happens both in civil and criminal cases. Let us consider the example Kaye gives of a gap in civil matters:

> Consider a paternity case in which the plaintiff concedes that two men could have been the father. Suppose the plaintiff compels the defendant to submit to immunogenetic testing, and inexplicably ignores the other man. Even if the genetic tests implicate the defendant, the plaintiff's story is weaker than it would be if both men had been tested and the nonaccused man excluded as a potential father (Kaye 1986, 664).

As a criminal example, consider the case of the defendant who claims to have an alibi and then fails to produce some testimony in this respect. Or the case of the prosecutor who does not produce a crucial testimony.[22]

The same point has been made by Richard Posner discussing the evidentiary virtues of the adversary system and the issue of "evidentiary *lacunae*" (Kaye's gaps):

> The adversarial system [...] facilitates the drawing of reliable inferences from evidentiary *lacunae*. If one party ought to be able to obtain favorable evidence to itself at low cost, then its failure to present such evidence allows the trier of fact to infer that the party is concealing unfavorable evidence and should therefore lose (Posner 1999, 1493).[23]

This kind of examples help us rebut a possible claim generated by the consideration of negative evidence. The claim would be quite radical conceptually speaking and would consist in rejecting the idea of absence of evidence altogether. The argument would consist in claiming that absence of evidence, correctly understood, is always evidence of something else: lack of evidence of footsteps is evidence that there are no footsteps; absence of dog-barking evidence is evidence that the dog did not bark; absence of testimony that *p* is evidence that it is false that *p*; etc. That would be too radical, however. We should not overlook the difference between (*1*) knowing there are no footsteps in the snow, and (*2*) knowing nothing about it, i.e. not knowing whether there are footsteps in the snow or not. Plausibly, cases of type (*2*) are less frequent in legal reasoning and argumentation. Cases are normally of

[22] Of course the case of the prosecutor and that of the defendant are different from the point of view of the burden of proof. More on this below.

[23] This has interesting consequences for the discussion on probabilities and Bayes' theorem applied to legal fact-finding, as far as the critics claim "that Bayes' theorem does not recognize that the weight and *completeness* of the evidence bearing on a hypothesis, and not just the odds that we might give on its correctness if we are betting folk, are important to people's judgments. In fact, weak evidence and *missing* evidence do affect the odds that a person would be willing to give that some hypothesis was correct" (Posner 1999, 1514; my italics).

type (*1*). One of the reasons of this is that legal proceedings do not even start if evidence is completely absent. In any event, more frequent than knowing-nothing cases are gappy-evidence cases, as Kaye's example suggests, or cases with evidentiary *lacunae*, as Posner puts it.

From a logical point of view the same distinction can be drawn in terms of *internal* and *external negation*.[24] External negation corresponds, in this context, to the absence of evidence. Namely, the absence of evidentiary elements. Internal negation corresponds to negative evidence (or, if you prefer, evidence of absence). Namely, evidence of a proposition with a negative content. The dog that did not bark, the window that was not broken, the ground without tracks, the snow without footsteps, my finding that Robert is not in the room, etc. are cases of the latter. They are cases in which there is evidence of a negative propositional content.

Absent and negative evidence risk to be confused. As in the following example:

> The government discovered a substantial marijuana field on Robert Fuesting's property and charged him with possession of marijuana with intent to distribute. At trial, Fuesting attempted to introduce testimony by his banker and attorney that his bank accounts and tax returns showed no large amounts of money. Fuesting argued that, if his finances *had shown* these kinds of transactions, the government would have introduced them to buttress its drug-dealing allegations. The absence of such transactions, Fuesting argued, was equally relevant to suggest that he was *not* engaged in drug dealing.[25]

The judge excluded the evidence, finding that there were too many conceivable (and plausible) explanations for the absence of large funds. But note, apart from the merits, the double aspect of the defendant's argumentation: he claims there is significant absence of evidence in the government's argument (no evidence of his transactions), and he offers evidence of absence (evidence of no transactions of that sort).

So it is true that evidence of absence is not absence of evidence, and some of the cases that are presented as typical instances of absent evidence are actually cases of negative evidence. Beside these, there are the true evidentiary *lacunae* or evidentiary gaps, as genuine cases of absence of evidence. And these are the cases in which ignorance is at stake as a premise for an inference.[26]

---

[24] Internal and external negation can be also used to give an account of the *a contrario* argument. See Canale and Tuzet (2008).

[25] Merritt and Simmons (2012, 64). The case is *U.S. v. Fuesting*, 845 F.2d 664 (7th Cir. 1988). See also Lyon and Koehler (1996, 70ff.) on the lack of physical signs in child sexual abuse cases: attorneys sometimes try to persuade judges to admit testimony about the lack of evidence of *X* on grounds that if *X* were present the judge would admit it for the opposing side; some judges are persuaded by this reasoning, but it is, in general, fallacious; Lyon and Koehler claim that there are special cases in which presence and absence are equally probative (but generally, they are not). Note, however, that a testimony about the lack of signs is *negative evidence*.

[26] Raymundo Gama has pointed out to me that Rescher (2006, 2–3) distinguishes *arguing from ignorance* from *arguing in ignorance*, where the former takes ignorance as a "ground or premise" of the argument itself and the latter is the situation in which we try to build up the best argument we can notwithstanding our ignorance. I am not sure, however, that they do not collapse into one another.

With all this mind, we can actually try to distinguish four versions of the argument from ignorance:

1. strong affirmative (SA): given the absence of evidence against *p*, it is true that *p*;
2. weak affirmative (WA): given the absence of evidence against *p*, it is plausibly true that *p*;
3. strong negative (SN): given the absence of evidence for *p*, it is false that *p*;
4. weak negative (WN): given the absence of evidence for *p*, it is plausibly false that *p*.

Note that (WN) is the use of the argument in which absence of evidence *is* evidence of absence. And observe that the weak versions are in tune with a non-deductive conception of inference and argumentation, while the strong remain fallacious even for inductive and abductive standards.[27] But in a legal perspective the trouble is different. It is not hard to see that *both the affirmative versions of the argument are more worrisome* than the negative from the viewpoint of the due process of law. Consider that the former, namely (SA) and (WA), infer the truth of a claim from the absence of evidence against it, while the latter, namely (SN) and (WN), infer the falsity of a claim from the absence of evidence in favor of it. Now take the claim to be a criminal charge. In a witch-hunt scenario, if you have to disprove a charge made against you and you don't provide evidence against it, you will be convicted. Without the presumption of innocence and without the burden of proof on the prosecution, the affirmative versions of the argument would mean that every person charged with an offence would be convicted unless they were able to present evidence in their favor (with the possible difference that the plausible conclusions of the weak affirmative version may not satisfy the criminal standard of proof). There would be a presumption of guilt indeed. Which means that the argument from ignorance is a worrisome inference, to say the least, in criminal proceedings, but is not necessarily so in civil proceedings, as I will show below with the *McDonnell Douglas* example.

3.4 Absence of Evidence, Burdens of Proof and Presumptions

In this last part of the paper I say something more on the way arguments from ignorance connect with legal burdens of proof and presumptions. The outcome will be that arguments from ignorance determine, on the absence of evidence, normative conclusions where a normative presumption is in play.

Is the absence of evidence as relevant for the defendant as the presence of evidence is for the plaintiff? Is the absence of evidence as relevant for the accused as the presence of evidence is for the prosecutor?

[27] In other words, the strong display the fallacy of "making an absolute of the failure of the defense" (van Eemeren and Grootendorst 1992, 187–191).

Obviously things change according to the burdens of proof. But the issue of legal burdens is quite complex and here cannot be dealt with in detail.[28] Just to nod at it, note that the burden of *persuasion* is different from the burden of *production*, in that the latter consists in the burden of producing enough evidence so that an issue is raised and must be addressed, while the former consists in the burden of proving a claim to some standard of proof. "For the burden of persuasion, there are decision rules that the jury must apply in evaluating the evidence. [...] For the burden of production, the judge applies rules to determine whether a party has produced enough evidence to avoid an adverse judgment" (Allen et al. 2011, 718). And, more importantly here, note that burdens are connected with *presumptions*.[29]

Consider as a significant example the complex intertwining of burden of production, presumption of discrimination and missing evidence in the cases that fall under the *McDonnell Douglas* rule, as presented by Posner (1999, 1503–1504). That rule is mainly applied in employment discrimination cases and it permits the plaintiff, say in cases of racial discrimination in hiring, to establish his *prima facie* case with the only evidence that he were qualified for the job but was passed over in favor of someone of another race.[30] This involves a presumption of discrimination on the basis of a burden of production that is not hard to satisfy. Satisfying this burden of production creates a presumption of discrimination, says Posner, meaning that if the defendant puts in no evidence, the plaintiff is entitled to summary judgment.

> The probability that he lost the job opportunity *because* he was discriminated against might seem not to be very high if the only evidence is as described. But this disregards the evidentiary significance of *missing evidence* [my italics]. If the defendant, who after all made the decision to give the job to someone other than the plaintiff, maintains complete silence about the reason for his action, an inference of discrimination arises. If the reason was otherwise, he should have been able without great difficulty to produce some evidence of that (Posner 1999, 1503–1504).

The presumption shifts the burden of persuasion onto the defendant and if he puts in no evidence he loses. In other words this is an absence of evidence case, in that the failure of the defendant to produce some evidence against the claim of the plaintiff determines a conclusion that is favorable to the plaintiff, given that his claim is supported by a presumption of discrimination triggered by the satisfaction of his burden of production. Posner remarks *inter alia* that the rule has an economic rationale in that, if the defendant's decision was not discriminating, he should have been able to produce some evidence of that without great difficulty, that is, at a low cost. If Posner is right, we could rephrase the point saying that the economic ratio-

---

[28] See e.g. Allen et al. (2011, 718ff.) and Prakken and Sartor (2006). Of course the burden of proof is relevant for argumentation theory too. For instance, van Eemeren (2010, 213) says that the burden of proof is a "procedural concept" required "for dialectical reasons", and van Eemeren and Grootendorst (1992, 123) observe that the argument from ignorance is related to the fallacy of *shifting the burden of proof*. Cf. van Eemeren et al. (2002, 113–116).

[29] Consider also some conceptual questions I must leave aside here: Is there a conceptual dependence relation between burdens and presumptions? Or, are they different sides of the same coin? In the first case, are burdens dependent on presumptions or vice versa?

[30] For a similar rule in Italian law see Taruffo (1992, 481).

nale of the rule rests on an epistemic one, given that the best knowledge of what happened in the hiring decision is on the defendant himself. But things are different in the criminal domain, of course, where the presumption of innocence is in favor of the defendant.

Now some authors say that the presumption of innocence is a justified argument from ignorance: from the absence of evidence of guilt, innocence is inferred.[31] Unfortunately this is a simplistic reading of the presumption. The presumption of innocence is not really an argument from ignorance in the epistemic sense of it. Rather, it is a practical decision upon legal grounds.

> It is a decision to treat the accused henceforth as innocent, rather than an intellectual conclusion that he is innocent. The court does not in fact always conclude that the prisoner is innocent when it declares him not guilty. It concludes rather that he is henceforth to be treated as innocent (Robinson 1971, 106).

This is not surprising if we understand presumptions as inferential and argumentative devices that help us in the process of decision-making. This is in particular the view of Edna Ullmann-Margalit (1983, 155), who takes presumptions to be assumptions for practical deliberation: "they function as a method of extrication, one among several, from unresolved deliberation processes. What they do is supply a procedure for decision by default." Others, who claim that genuine presumptions are beliefs,[32] consider the presumption of innocence as a "rule of inference" or a "methodological principle" applicable in the courtroom.

> Strictly speaking, the presumption of innocence isn't a presumption at all. Presumptions are basically beliefs. The presumption of innocence, on the other hand, is a rule, or [...] a methodological principle, applicable only in the courtroom (Wreen 2003, 374).

This makes it different from an *ad ignorantiam* argument, for the presumption of innocence is rather "on a par with a rule of a game" (Wreen 2003, 375). Therefore, both for the view of presumptions as practical assumptions and for the view of the presumption of innocence as a legal rule of inference, the argument from ignorance is not in this context an epistemic inference purported to draw a conclusion on what is the case: it is instead a practical argument; it is decision-oriented; and it applies a presumptive rule articulated to some burden of proof. The presumption of innocence does not rest on the belief that criminal defendants are usually innocent; in fact "legal innocence" is distinct from "innocence simpliciter", as Wreen (2003, 367) puts it, or, as Laudan (2006, 12) puts it, "probatory innocence" is distinct from "material innocence". In brief the conclusion of this argument from ignorance is *normative*, not epistemic. Because of this, two additional uses of the argument from ignorance must be distinguished:

---

[31] See e.g. Walton et al. (2008, 98). For a more refined view of the presumption, cf. Wreen (1996, 351–353) and Wreen (2003).

[32] This would need a refinement, however. Presumptive beliefs are different from other probabilistic beliefs or degrees of belief in that the former are generated by some prior generalizations or default criteria. See e.g. Lyon and Koehler (1996, 55–57) on the jurors' (false) presumption that a lack of physical signs conclusively disproves child abuse.

5. normative affirmative (NA): given the absence of evidence against *p*, *p* should be treated as true;
6. normative negative (NN): given the absence of evidence for *p*, *p* should be treated as false.[33]

It is easy to see that (NA) is correct when there is a presumption of guilt or some presumption in favor of the plaintiff. Whereas (NN) is correct when there is a presumption of innocence or some civil presumption in favor of the defendant.

To conclude on this point. If in legal argumentation presumptions are rules of inference from some sort of ignorance, they trigger normative conclusions from premises that are in part prescriptive (being made of such rules on burdens and presumptions) and in part descriptive (being made of the statements about a party's failure to satisfy a burden). If the defendant, in our example, does not provide any evidence of the non-discriminatory reasons of his hiring decision, the claim of the plaintiff should be treated as true and a decision should be made in his favor. Then a principled justification of such arguments from ignorance rests on the justification of those burdens and presumptions. And even if epistemic reasons may play a role in it (as in the *McDonnell Douglas* rule),[34] the justification of those burdens and presumptions is essentially practical; for it has to do with the functioning of legal proceedings and, most of all, with the fundamental values protected by the law (individual liberty for the presumption of innocence).

Acknowledgments For helpful comments on a draft of this paper I wish to thank Ron Allen, Christian Dahlman and Jay Koehler in particular. I also thank two anonymous Springer reviewers. And Sarah Robinson for revising my English.

References

Allen, R.J., et al. 2011. *Evidence. Text, problems, and cases*, 5th ed. New York: Wolters Kluwer.
Anderson, T., D. Schum, and W. Twining. 2005. *Analysis of evidence*, 2nd ed. Cambridge: Cambridge University Press.
Canale, D., and G. Tuzet. 2008. On the contrary: Inferential analysis and ontological assumptions of the *a contrario* argument. *Informal Logic* 28: 31–43.
Carnap, R. 1936. Testability and meaning. *Philosophy of Science* 3: 419–471.
De Waal, C. 2001. *On Peirce*. Belmont: Wadsworth-Thomson Learning.
Flach, P.A., and A.C. Kakas (eds.). 2000. *Abduction and induction. Essays on their relation and integration*. Dordrecht: Kluwer Academic Publishers.
Grice, P. 1989. *Studies in the way of words*. Cambridge/London: Harvard University Press.
Haack, S. 2011. *Epistemology: Who needs it?* Typescript.
Hamblin, C.L. 1970. *Fallacies*. London: Methuen.
Kaye, D.H. 1986. Do we need a calculus of weight to understand proof beyond a reasonable doubt? *Boston University Law Review* 66: 657–672.

[33] Things are complicated, however, by the fact that normative considerations (on belief justification in particular) are also in play in epistemic contexts.

[34] Cf. Ullmann-Margalit (1983, 157ff.) on the justification of particular presumptions.

Laudan, L. 2006. *Truth, error, and criminal law*. Cambridge: Cambridge University Press.
Lyon, T.D., and J.J. Koehler. 1996. The relevance ratio: Evaluating the probative value of expert testimony in child sexual abuse cases. *Cornell Law Review* 82: 43–78.
Merritt, D.J., and R. Simmons. 2012. *Learning evidence. From the Federal rules to the courtroom*, 2nd ed. St. Paul: West.
Misak, C. 2004. Charles Sanders Peirce (1839–1914). In *The Cambridge companion to Peirce*, ed. C. Misak, 1–26. Cambridge: Cambridge University Press.
Posner, R. 1999. An economic approach to the law of evidence. *Stanford Law Review* 51: 1477–1546.
Prakken, H., and G. Sartor. 2006. Presumptions and burdens of proof. In *Proceedings of the 19th annual conference on legal knowledge and information systems (Jurix)*, ed. T. Van Engers, 21–30. Amsterdam: Ios Press.
Rescher, N. 2006. *Presumption and the practices of tentative cognition*. Cambridge: Cambridge University Press.
Robinson, R. 1971. Arguing from ignorance. *The Philosophical Quarterly* 21: 97–108.
Sahlane, A. 2012. Argumentation and fallacy in the justification of the 2003 war on Iraq. *Argumentation* 26: 459–488.
Stanley, J. 2005. *Knowledge and practical interests*. Oxford: Clarendon.
Stephens, C. 2011. A Bayesian approach to absent evidence reasoning. *Informal Logic* 31: 56–65.
Taruffo, M. 1992. *La prova dei fatti giuridici*. Milan: Giuffrè.
Tuzet, G. 2008. La justification pragmatique des croyances. *Revue Philosophique* 133: 465–476.
Ullmann-Margalit, E. 1983. On presumption. *The Journal of Philosophy* 80: 143–163.
van Eemeren, F.H. 2010. *Strategic maneuvering in argumentative discourse*. Amsterdam: John Benjamins.
van Eemeren, F.H., and R. Grootendorst. 1992. *Argumentation, communication, and fallacies. A pragma-dialectical perspective*. Hillsdale: Lawrence Erlbaum Associates.
van Eemeren, F.H., and R. Grootendorst. 2004. *A systematic theory of argumentation. The pragma-dialectical approach*. Cambridge: Cambridge University Press.
van Eemeren, F.H., R. Grootendorst, and F. Snoeck Henkemans. 2002. *Argumentation. Analysis, evaluation, presentation*. Mahwah: Lawrence Erlbaum Associates.
Walton, D. 1996. *Arguments from ignorance*. University Park: The Pennsylvania State University Press.
Walton, D. 1999a. Profiles of dialogue for evaluating arguments from ignorance. *Argumentation* 13: 53–71.
Walton, D. 1999b. The appeal to ignorance, or *argumentum ad ignorantiam*. *Argumentation* 13: 367–377.
Walton, D. 2006. *Fundamentals of critical argumentation*. Cambridge: Cambridge University Press.
Walton, D. 2008. *Informal logic. A pragmatic approach*, 2nd ed. Cambridge: Cambridge University Press.
Walton, D., C. Reed, and F. Macagno. 2008. *Argumentation schemes*. Cambridge: Cambridge University Press.
Wreen, M. 1989. Light from darkness, from ignorance knowledge. *Dialectica* 43: 299–314.
Wreen, M. 1996. Most assur'd of what he is most ignorant. *Erkenntnis* 44: 341–368.
Wreen, M. 2003. Arguments from ignorance and the presumption of innocence. *Logique et Analyse* 183–184: 365–382.

Chapter 4
The Uses of Slippery Slope Argument

José Juan Moreso

At vitiosi sunt soritae [...] Quo in numero conticuisti,
si ad eum numerum unum addidero, multane erunt?
Progrediere rursus, quoad videbitur.
Quid plura? Hoc enim fateris, neque ultimum te
paucorum neque primum multorum respondere posse.

Cicero, *Academica II, cxxix, 93.* (Cicero 1993)

Fallacy of Distrust, or, what's at the bottom?
(ad metum): *This argument may be considered as a*
particular modification of the No-Innovation *argument.*

Jeremy Bentham, *The Book of Fallacies*, II.III. (Bentham 1838–1843)

Abstract In this paper, I shall intend to show that the Sorites argument lies at the core of the Slippery Slope Argument and, for this reason, I shall deal with the logical validity of this argument. Once established its logical validity, I shall try to argue that the second premise of the Sorites argument – the premise in accordance with if an individual i has the property P by having n unities of something, then another individual i' which has n-1 unities is also P- in this kind of argument is always false; finally I shall draw some conclusions as to the way to stop the Slippery Slope.

J.J. Moreso (✉)
Pompeu Fabra University, Barcelona, Spain
e-mail: josejuan.moreso@upf.edu

© Springer International Publishing Switzerland 2015

T. Bustamante, C. Dahlman (eds.), *Argument Types and Fallacies in Legal Argumentation*, Law and Philosophy Library 112,
DOI 10.1007/978-3-319-16148-8_4

4.1 Varieties of Slippery Slope Argument[1]

Slippery Slope Arguments are well known and commonly employed in certain areas of inquiry, though mainly in bioethics.[2] There, they have been used to argue against abortion[3]:

> Infanticide is clearly seriously wrong. But there is no morally relevant difference between the neonate and the foetus just before it emerges from the womb. And so, too, for any stage of the developing foetus and the immediately preceding stage, until we slide all the way back to the newly fertilized egg (the zygote).

And against the practice of *in vitro* fertilization[4]:

> IVF [*in vitro* fertilization] gives rise to extra-fertilized ova, and experimentation is at least permitted, and perhaps required, on those ova. The period of time during which such experiments are allowed is limited, but (the argument goes) there is a natural progression to longer and longer such periods being permitted, until we arrive at the horrible result of experimentation on developed embryos.

And, also, against voluntary assisted suicide[5]:

> If assisted suicide is legalized, we will see that what is now considered as a desperate and extraordinary solution for the few will become yet another possible outcome on the care map. My twelve years as a medical social worker convince me that assisted suicide will move at dizzying speed to enter the consciousness of all concerned: patients, doctors, families, and insurers, as an ever-possible 'treatment plan'.

But these arguments are widely appealed to not only in bioethics. In law and in politics too we can find many examples. For instance[6]:

> Take, for example, the common argument against reduction in the size of juries from the traditional twelve, an issue that was presented for criminal cases in *Williams v. Florida* and for civil cases in *Colgrove v. Battin.* In both *Williams* and *Colgrove* it was argued that if jury size could be reduced from twelve to six, then why not to five, or four, or three, with the implicit claim being that there was no real stopping point short of eliminating the jury entirely.

---

[1] The several kinds of Slippery Slope Arguments probably lead to use the metaphor of family resemblance. See Spielthenner (2010), 'A Logical Analysis of Slippery Slope Arguments', *Health Care Analysis*, 18 (2010): 148–163.

[2] See, for instance, Hartogh (2009).

[3] With these words Clement Dore (1989, 279) introduces a version of the argument of conservative people (which he does not share).

[4] The argument as it is presented by Bernard Williams (1995, 213, with no commitment to defend it).

[5] This is part of the text of a letter to the Editors in *The New York Review of Books*, March 29, 1997 by Marjorie Hornik as a response to Dworkin et al. 1997. The NY Review of Books published this text submitted by these philosophers as amici curiae brief to the Supreme Court of US in the cases *Washington v. Glucksberg*, 521 US 702 (1997) and *Vacco v. Quill*, 521 US 793 (1997).

[6] See Schuaer (1985, 379). The cases are *Williams v. Florida* 99 U.S. 78 (1970) *Colgrove v. Battin* and 413 U.S. 149 (1973). In *Ballew v. Georgia*, 435 U.S. 223, 228 (1978), the Court decided that the lesser number of jurors constitutionally admisible was six, drawing in this way the line: six is constitutional and five is unconstitutional. I shall come back on this point.

Another example from politics and law: Senator Rick Santorum declared in an interview by the Associated Press (April 7, 2003)[7]:

> If the Supreme Court says that you have the right to consensual [gay] sex within your home, then you have the right to bigamy, you have the right to polygamy, you have the right to incest, you have the right to adultery. You have the right to anything.

It seems that these five arguments share the idea that accepting a certain practice, prima facie admissible, compels us to accept other practices, which by contrast are clearly impermissible. In this sense it is a practical argument. But what is the nature of that compulsion? Are we logically (conceptually) compelled or are we empirically compelled? While the argument against abortion appears to be conceptual in character, the argument against assisted suicide seems empirical. Indeed, in the relevant literature it is usual to distinguish between two versions of the argument: the logical or conceptual and the empirical or psychological.[8]

The conceptual version, it is commonly argued, is entangled with the sorites paradox. We have notice that Eubulides asked for how many grains of sand we should add to a grain of sand for having a heap, or how many hairs we should cut to a hairy man for getting a bald man.[9] The empirical version is supported by causal mechanisms. Here the question is whether the acquisition of certain beliefs, or the enactment of certain legislation, or the issuing a particular judicial decision, will cause -or probably cause- other undesirable beliefs or legislative enactments or judicial decisions. But, in my view, the peculiarity of this kind of Slippery Slope Argument is given by the participation in the psychological changes of something like a Sorites Argument. If not, it is a consequentialist argument, but not a Slippery Slope one. In the light of this, I strongly agree with Dale Jacquette[10]: 'All slippery slopes can be reduced to a single category of arguments', one kind of Sorites argument.

Consider the case of assisted suicide. The argument against the permission of this practice runs as follows: If adult voluntary and consented assisted suicide is permitted, then our convictions about the wrongness of murder will be weakened, and we could slowly abandon our convictions against homicide, thereby progressively increasing the number of accepted exceptions: not only legitimate defence and other current legal justifications, but also mercy murder of very ill elder people,

---

[7] This was his reaction to the US Supreme Court ruling that struck down the sodomy law in Texas, making same-sex sexual intimacy legally permitted in US and overruling explicitly *Bowers v. Hardwick*, 478 U.S. 186 (1986) in *Lawrence v. Texas*, 539 U.S. 558 (2003). See Cahill (2005).

[8] Govier (1982), van de Burg (1991), Lode (1999), Enoch (2001). Douglas Walton (1992) adds to both kinds of arguments, called by him Sorites and Causal, the two following: Precedent and Full Slippery Slope (which put together the former three). Bernard Williams (1995, 213), in his illuminating contribution, does not follow this path and distinguishes between the Horrible Result Argument (as the argument against IVF) and the Arbitrary Result Argument (as the Argument of the number of jurors admissible constitutionally).

[9] See, for instance, ch. 1 in Williamson (1994).

[10] See Jacquette (1989, 60).

of very handicapped children, and so on. Therefore, something like sorites is presupposed in the empirical kind of Slippery Slope Argument.

Admittedly, knowing the effects of our arguments is important and assessing the way in which certain beliefs generate other beliefs in our societies is a very relevant question.[11] However, I am not interested in that issue here. I am interested in the *rational* value of the Slippery Slope Argument, not in its consequences. Nevertheless, I hope that a clear understanding of the value of this argument will contribute to sharpen our critical attitude vis-à-vis influential, though mistaken, public paths of reasoning.

Sorites arguments have the following structure:

1. Carlos Slim is rich
2. If s, who has n $ is rich; s′, who has n-1 $, is also rich.

Therefore, John Doe, who has only 1 $, is rich.

The reiterated application of premise 2 for a number of times equal Slim's dollars leads us, step of modus ponens by step of modus ponens, to the conclusion. We can substitute in 2, 's' for 'Carlos Slim' and we obtain:

2′. If Carlos Slim, with 73 billion dollars, is rich; then Jane Roe, with 73 billion – 1 $, is rich.

Given that the antecedent of 2′ is true, then it is true the consequent; and the consequent can be the antecedent of other conditionals like 2′ until we achieve the line of John Doe.

In what follows, I shall intend to show that the Sorites argument lies at the core of the Slippery Slope Argument (Sect. 4.2); in Sect. 4.3, I shall deal with the logical validity of this argument; in Sect. 4.4 – once established its logical validity –, I shall try to argue that premise 2 in this kind of argument is always false; finally, in Sect. 4.5, I shall draw some conclusions as to the way to stop the Slippery Slope.

4.2 The Camel's Nose Is in the Sorites Tent[12]

Think of this argument:

1. It is acceptable to punish my daughter to be locked into her room for half an hour.

[11] There are interesting studies about the cognitive origin of our acceptance of Slippery Slope Arguments, for instance Sorensen (2012), studies about the psychological mechanism behind the argument and its consequences: Corner et al. (2011, 2013), about its behaviour in moral reasoning Trianosky (1978), Govier (1982), Woods (2000), LaFollette (2005); about its force as legal argument in the legislative and judicial practice Schauer (1985), Lode (1999), Volokh (2003), Rizzo and Whitman (2003), Codd (2007).

[12] This title is inspired by David Enoch (2001), who defends the view that the Slippery Slope Argument is slippery slope and leads us to a way of self-defeating. However, this argument will not be discussed here.

2. If it is acceptable to punish my daughter to n seconds locked into her room, it is also acceptable to punish her to n + 1 seconds locked into her room,

The reiterated and monotonous application of 2 leads us to an utterly unacceptable conclusion:

Therefore, it is acceptable to punish my daughter to be locked into her room for 5 years.

The paradoxical air of this argument arises from the plausibility of the premises and the logical validity of the reiterated use of modus ponens. The conclusion, however, seems particularly objectionable. The argument, as you can see, is an instance of a sorites argument. I shall claim that the structure of that argument is the core of the conceptual Slippery Slope Argument. And I shall add that in the empirical Slippery Slope Arguments the acceptance of a sorites argument figures among the conditions which cause the final belief in the 'horrible' conclusion.

Logically valid arguments with true premises necessarily produce true conclusions. At least one philosopher, Peter Unger, maintains that Sorites arguments are not paradoxes, and we should accept conclusions like: there are neither heaps nor bald mans.[13] Michael Dummett and Crispin Wright also seem to embrace the paradox and to endorse the conclusion that our ordinary language is inherently inconsistent.[14] In fact, we could imagine a contrary argument to our example of sorites, in which the first premise states something like:

1′ John Doe, who has only 1 $, is not rich,

and the second asserts that for adding 1 $ to a poor person, we cannot convert her in a rich person. Therefore, all of us are rich and not rich at the same time.

We can also change the first premise of our Slippery Slope Argument and put in its place:

1″. It is unacceptable to punish my daughter to be locked into her room for 5 years,

and we can imagine a second premise that one second less to an unacceptable punishment does not make it acceptable. Therefore, all our punishments are acceptable and unacceptable. Other version of the *dictum* everything is permitted (if God does not exist, as claimed Dostoyevsky), even though every action is also forbidden.

Nevertheless, before endorsing this frustrating and pessimistic conclusion, maybe it is worth looking for some way out.

---

[13] See Unger (1979).

[14] See Dummett (1975), Wright (1975). Unger escapes from the inconsistency because he takes as valid and sound arguments that end up concluding that rich or bald persons or heaps do not exist, and unsound (in virtue of the falsity of the first premise), arguments whose conclusion states that every person is rich or bald, or every number of grains of sand is a heap of sand. See, for this point, Sorensen (1989), Hyde (2011).

4.3 The Validity of Modus Ponens

The logical validity of Sorites argument, lying at the core of Slippery Slope Arguments, depends only on the validity of *modus ponens*. Actually a Sorites argument is a chain of modus ponens. The modus ponens is part and parcel of our notion of logical deduction. Without this rule our logic would suffer a paralysis. Admittedly, once in a while theorists happen to cast doubts on the universal validity of the modus ponens or about its logical justification.[15]

Maybe, some pragmatic solutions to the sorites paradox share these doubts about the universal validity of modus ponens; particularly, solutions that arise from the so-called *contextual* logic. As we shall see in the next paragraph, if we want to reject a sorites argument, we must reject either modus ponens or the truth (granting the trivial truth of the first premise) of the second premise. The premise that establishes the *tolerance* of the vague predicate, like 'rich', 'heap' or 'acceptable punishment'.[16] As Haim Gaifman says[17]: 'Tolerance is the insensitivity of predicates to sufficiently small changes in the objects of which they are predicated'. Small differences should not be taken into account and, moreover, it is a part of their meaning that 'small differences should not matter'. Therefore, for Gaifman, the Sorites conditionals are true; it is part of the content of tolerant predicates. However, the context should be able to hedge a certain number of conditionals in order to avoid conclusions like people with 1 $ being rich or one grain of sand being a heap.

I am sceptical about the possibilities of this strategy to avoid the implausible conclusions without begging the question. Saying that the predicate 'rich' can only be used in certain conditionals assumes that there is a precise cut-off point in the conditionals' chain. But if we are able to rule out certain applications of the predicate, then this predicate is not absolutely tolerant.

4.4 The Soundness of the Argument

What warrants the truth of a conclusion in a logical derivation is not only the logical validity of the argument, but also the truth of its premises. In Sorites, and in Slippery Slope Arguments, the *principle of tolerance* is false. We could represent this principle as follows:

$$(PoT)\,\text{For all x : if x is F, then x}'\text{ is also F,}$$

where x′ is the successor in a series of objects which progress gradually, step by step.

---

[15] See McGee (1985) and Schechter and Enoch (2006).

[16] The idea of tolerance of this kind of predicates was introduced in the contemporary debate by Wright (1975, 1976).

[17] Gaifman (2010). See also Shapiro (2006).

PoT seems to be a reasonable principle to hold. In fact it is very similar to the principle of mathematical induction[18]:

The principle of mathematical induction asserts that a predicate applies to every natural number if it applies both to zero and to the successor of every natural number to which it applies.

However, the principle of mathematical induction is not applicable to every predicate. For instance, even if it is true that the number 0 is a small number, it is not true that every successor of a small number will always be a small number. Otherwise the number one billion will be a small number. We can understand the falsity of *PoT* in this case by reflecting on this sentence[19]:

If zero is small, then one billion is small.

We cannot say what is the first number, in the series of natural numbers, which is not small, but we know that one billion is not small.

How can we accommodate both of these intuitions, in tension with each other? The intuition expressed by *PoT* and the intuition that one billion is not small, John Doe is not rich and so on. There are several strategies in the crowded market of philosophical accounts of vagueness.

One account that has surprising consequences is the epistemic theory of vagueness, according to which there is always a precise point that draws the line between the right application of a vague predicate and its complement, even though we are not able to draw that line.[20] *PoT* is always false, even though we are not able to assign truth-values in the penumbra of the predicate.

We have also accounts that reject the excluded middle: many-valued logics, from three-valued logics to infinite valued fuzzy logics.[21] In this case, either some instances of *PoT* have an indefinite truth-value or the reiterated application of the modus ponens diminishes the truth-value of the conditionals until 0, the falsity.

Although this is not the place to discuss these accounts, I would like to suggest two considerations: (a) I never understood what an epistemicist thinks that we should know in order to be able to draw the boundaries of our vague concepts for epistemic accounts and (b) it seems to me that sacrificing the excluded middle, as the many-valued logics would have it, would be too high a cost to bear: for instance, it seems to me that even if Jim was a case of penumbra of the application of rich, the sentence ‘Either Jim is rich or Jim is not rich’ would be necessarily true, because it is a logical truth. However, in many-valued logics this sentence can be not true (indefinite or with a value as ½).

---

[18] See Boolos (1991, 695).

[19] *Ibidem,* at 656.

[20] Without *fear of PoT* (the expression in Sorensen (1989)) we can find Cargile (1969, 1993), Sorensen (1988, 2001) and Williamson (1994).

[21] See, for instance, Łukasiewicz (1970), Körner 1960; Zadeh (1975), Machina (1976), von Wright (1983, 1996). Slightly different is Hilary Putnam (1983) who proposes an intuitionistic logic in which *PoT* (for all x: if x is F, then x′ is F′) is true but it does not entails the negation of “there is an x: x is F and x′ is not F′”.

I prefer an approach that favours the idea that there are 'many permissible boundaries or cut-offs. This runs counter to a familiar tradition, according to which vagueness is characterized as absence of cut-offs'.[22] This is the supervaluation approach and its relatives.

The analysis of vagueness carried out by supervaluationism can throw light on the analysis of the Sorites Paradox.[23] A vague predicate fails to divide things precisely into two sets, its positive and its negative extensions. When this predicate is applied to a borderline case, we will obtain propositions which are neither true nor false. This gap reveals a deficiency in the meaning of a vague predicate. We can remove this deficiency and replace vagueness by precision by stipulating a certain arbitrary boundary between the positive and negative extensions, a boundary within the penumbra of the concept. Thus, we get a *sharpening* or *completion* of this predicate. However, there are not only one, but many possible sharpenings or completions. In accordance with supervaluationism, we should take all of them into account. For supervaluationism, a proposition p -containing a vague concept- is true if and only if it is true for all its completions; it is false if and only if it is false for all its completions; otherwise it has no truth-value -it is indeterminate. A *completion* is a way of converting a vague concept into a precise one. So now we should distinguish two senses of 'true': 'true' according to a particular completion, and 'true' according to all completions, or *supertrue*. If a number x of grains of sand is in the penumbra of the concept of a heap, then it will be true for some completions and false for others that x is a heap and, therefore, it will neither be supertrue nor superfalse.

Completions should meet some constraints. In particular, propositions that are unproblematically true (false) before completion should be true (false) after completion is performed. In this way, supervaluationism retains a great part of classical logic. Thus, for instance, all tautologies of classical logic are valid in a theory of supervaluations, 'x is a heap or x is not a heap' -a token of the law of excluded middle- is valid, because it is true in all completions independently of the truth-value of its disjuncts.

What about Slippery Slope Arguments? Well, *PoT* is, in fact, *superfalse*: in each sharpening there is a precise boundary and, therefore, an x that is F and an x′ that is not-F. But, no vague predicate has only one boundary; all of them have a plurality of boundaries. Many boundaries of the same concept produce the impression that vague concepts are concepts without boundaries, but imprecise boundaries are still boundaries.[24] All sorites arguments, and with it all the Slippery Slope Arguments which have a first premise with a vague predicate, are unsound arguments in virtue of the falsity of the second premise.

---

[22] Mark Sainsbury (2013) claims that his account is different from supervaluationism. His reasons are not transparent to me.

[23] It seems that this theory was formulated for the first time by Mehlberg (1958). Also van Fraassen (1966), Fine (1975), Kamp (1975), Dummett (1978), Przelecki(1979), Lewis (1983), Bencivenga et al. (1986), Williamson (1994), Keefe and Smith (1996), Keefe (2000).

[24] See Sainsbury (2013).

Nonetheless, supervaluational accounts are not without objections. Firstly, it has been argued that these accounts cannot provide a classical notion of logical consequence because they fail to preserve certain rules of inference.[25] Secondly, the definition of supertrue cannot be Tarskian ('p' is true if and only if p) because given that we cannot retain Excluded Middle and Bivalence, we must reject Bivalence.[26] Finally, supervaluationism has problems with the so-called higher order vagueness: (a) given that the same notion of admissible sharpening is vague, there will be not only borderline cases, but also borderline cases of borderline cases and so on,[27] and (b) the introduction of the determinacy operator ('D': 'True in all admissible sharpenings') leads to a contradiction if we assume the normal semantic behaviour of vague predicates.[28]

Even though here I do not intend to reply to these powerful objections, it is worthwhile to note that there are several strategies in the literature to overcome these objections.[29] I would like to emphasize only two aspects: (a) Even if we cannot retain the Tarskian notion of truth, maybe a weaker version is sufficient (from p we can infer 'p' is true, and vice versa),[30] and (b) the clear understanding afforded by the supervaluation theory provides us with an approach to vagueness as a *modal* phenomenon and we need, as usual in modal accounts, to distinguish among several notions of true, not only supertrue.[31]

Despite my preferences for the supervaluationist account, nothing in my argument depends on that. For epistemic accounts and for many-valued logics *PoT* is not universally valid, though this feature of that principle is explained in a variety of ways.[32] And this is, in my view, the point that logic and argumentation theory can contribute to prevent the abuse of Slippery Slope argumentation. The fact that there is no justification to draw the line in a precise place or step does not imply lack of justification to draw the line. We are often justified to draw the line and, in this way, to manage our concepts so as to be able to stop the slippery slope somewhere. In this sense, sometimes the ideal of treating like cases alike is not attainable. It is preferable to sacrifice in some cases such ideal, in order to be able to draw the line.

---

[25] See Machina (1976) and Williamson (1994), ch.4.

[26] See Williamson (1994), ch.4.

[27] See Burns (1991), Sainsbury (1995, ch.2), Williamson (1994, ch, 4), Endicott (2000, ch. 5).

[28] See Wright 1987; Fara 2003.

[29] For instance, Keefe (2000, ch. 7 and 8), Varzi (2007), Ascher et al. (2009).

[30] An idea that it can be found in Van Fraassen (1966, 494): 'To say that these are valid simply means that they preserve truth: when the premise is true, so is the conclusion. This says nothing whatsoever about the truth-value of the conclusion when the premise is not true (that is, when the premise is false or when the premise neither true nor false)'.

[31] Ascher et al. (2009, 931–932).

[32] Contextual logic considers that is universally valid but relative to determined contexts, see Burns (1991) and the criticism of Rosanna Keefe (2000, ch. 6) –and I agree with it- in the sense that pragmatic accounts collapse with supervaluation approach. Intuitonistic Logic considers *PoT* valid, but distinguishing two kinds of negation does not authorize the instantiation of universal quantifier and thus blocks the paradox. See Schwartz (1987) and Horgan (1994).

The impossibility to draw the line is worse, in these cases, than not treating like cases alike.[33]

In brief, the Slippery Slope Arguments are suspicious arguments, not in virtue of their logical validity –they are valid from a logical point of view-, but because they are often *unsound*, since if the first premise of the argument includes a vague predicate, as it is always the case with the Sorites cases, then the second premise incorporating *PoT* is not universally true, in fact either it is false or it has a limited application.

4.5 Conclusion: Preserving Vermeer's Authenticity

In the evocative essay dedicated to Slippery Slope by Bernard Williams, the author remembers and explains the following[34]:

> There is more than one reason why this process is likely to be repeated. It is not merely that, at any given stage, there seems no adequate reason to refuse the next step. In addition, it may well be that when a number of steps has been taken, the original objections to the process, or to this degree of it, now seem misplaced. The cumulative process has itself altered perceptions of that process. It is a mechanism very like that in terms of which Nelson Goodman explained the fact that increasingly incompetent forgeries by van Meegeren were accepted as genuine Vermeers. Each new one was compared to a reference class that contained the earlier ones, and it was only when all the forgeries were bracketed, and the latest ones compared to a class of Vermeers free from van Mergeerens, that it become obvious how awful that were. It is often this kind of process that critics have in mind when they claim the allowing some process will lead to a slippery slope. It is a process that they see in terms of corruption or habituation, just as reformers may see it as a process of enlightenment or of inhibitions being lost.

In my view, this is precisely the role of logic and argumentation theory can play in analysing arguments as Slippery Slope: to point out the obvious *forgeries* (that one grain of sand is not a heap, John Doe, with only 1 $, is not rich and so on) and in this way to show the lack of justification to accept universally *PoT*.

Logic alone is not able to detect the truth or falsity of the premises, except in cases where premises are tautologies or logical truths. In the Slippery Slope Arguments none of the premises are logical truths. However, we have also theories of argumentation. In terms of the well-known theory of Stephen Toulmin,[35] for *grounding PoT* it is necessary to endorse the idea that our vague concepts are insensitive to small changes, a *warrant*. But, when we intend to *back* this warrant we find some counterarguments, a *rebuttal*: for instance, locking my daughter for 5 years

---

[33] I am very thankful to Christian Dahlman who pointed me this relevant conclusion, which allows us to hedge the principle of treating like cases alike.

[34] Bernard Williams (1995, 218). The story about Vermeer's pictures comes from (see note 3 at 223 of Williams 1995) Goodman 1976, 110–111).

[35] See Toulmin (1958).

into her home is unacceptable, and we should either abandon our claim or use some *qualifiers* that hedge the scope of *PoT*.

If we are convinced of this enlightened force of argumentation, then we can oppose mechanisms of slippery slope presented in the public arena usually to persuade and seduce, or worse, to cheat us; but not to procure our rational acceptance only of those ideas, which are capable to overcome the filters of our more strict evaluation.

References

Ascher, Nicholas, Josh Dever, and Chris Pappas. 2009. Supervaluations Debugged. *Mind* 118: 901–933.

Bencivenga, Ermanno, Karel Lambert, and Bas C. van Fraassen. 1986. *Logic, bivalence and denotation*. Atascadero: Ridgeview.

Bentham, Jeremy. 1838–1843. *The works of Jeremy Bentham*. Published under the Superintendence of his Executor, John Bowring. Edinburgh: William Tait, 11 vols, Vol. 2. Accessed from http://oll.libertyfund.org/title/1921/114121 on 20 May 2013.

Boolos, George. 1991. Zooming down the slippery slope. *Noûs* 25: 695–706.

Burns, Linda. 1991. *Vagueness. An investigation into natural languages and the sorites paradox*. Dordrecht: Kluwer.

Cahill, Courtney Megan. 2005. Same-sex marriage, slippery slope rhetoric, and the politics of disgust: A critical perspective as contemporary family discourse and the incest taboo. *Northwestern University Law Review* 99: 1515–1610.

Cargile, James. 1969. The sorites paradox. *British Journal for the Philosophy of Science* 20: 193–202.

Cargile, James. 1993. Vagueness. An investigation into natural languages and the sorites paradox. *Philosophical Books* 34: 22–24.

Cicero. 1993. *On the Nature of the Gods (De natura deorum)/Academica*. Trans. H. Rackhman, Loeb Classical Library. Cambridge, MA: Harvard University Press.

Codd, Helen. 2007. The slippery slope to sperm smuggling: Prisoners, artificial insemination and human right. *Medical Law Review* 15: 220–235.

Corner, Adam, Ulrike Hahn, and Mike Oaksford. 2011. The psychological mechanism of the slippery slope argument. *Journal of Memory and Language* 64: 133–1523.

Corner, Adam, Ulrike Hahn, and Mike Oaksford. 2013. The slippery slope argument –Probability, utility and category reappraisal. In *Proceedings of the 28th annual meeting of the cognitive science society*, ed. R. Sun, 1145–1150. Mahwah: Erlbaum.

Dore, Clement. 1989. Abortion, some slippery slope arguments and identity over time. *Philosophical Studies* 55: 279–291.

Dummett, Michael. 1975. Wang's paradox. *Synthese* 30: 301–324.

Dummett, Michael. 1978. *Truth and other enigmas*. London: Duckworth.

Dworkin, Ronald, et al. 1997. (Thomas Nagel, Robert Nozick, John Rawls, Timothy Scanlon, Judith Jarvis Thomson). Assisted suicide: The philosopher's brief. *The New York Review of Books*, March 27.

Endicott, Timothy. 2000. *Vagueness in law*. Oxford: Oxford University Press.

Enoch, David. 2001. Once you start using slippery slope arguments, you're on a very slippery slope. *Oxford Journal of Legal Studies* 21: 628–647.

Fara, D.G. 2003. Gap principles, penumbral consequence, and infinite higher-order vagueness. In *Liars and heaps: New essays on the semantics of paradox*, ed. C. Bell, 195–234. Oxford: Oxford University Press.

Fine, Kit. 1975. Vagueness, truth and logic. *Synthese* 30: 265–300.
Gaifman, Haim. 2010. Vagueness, tolerance and contextual logic. *Synthese* 174: 5–46.
Goodman, Nelson. 1976. *Languages of art –An approach to a theory of symbols*. Indianapolis: Hackett Publishing.
Govier, Trudy. 1982. What's wrong with slippery slope arguments? *Canadian Journal of Philosophy* 7: 303–316.
Hartogh, Govert den. 2009. The slippery slope argument. In *A companion to bioethics*, 2 ed., eds. Helga Kuhse, Peter Singer, ch.28. Oxford: Wiley-Blackwell.
Horgan, Terence. 1994. Robust vagueness and the forced-march sorites paradox. *Philosophical Perspectives* 8: 159–188.
Hyde, Dominique. 2011. Sorites Paradox. In *The Stanford encyclopedia of philosophy* (Winter 2011 Edition), ed. Edward N. Zalta. URL = http://plato.stanford.edu/archives/win2011/entries/sorites-paradox/
Jacquette, Dale. 1989. The hidden logic of slippery slope arguments. *Philosophy and Rhetoric* 22: 59–70.
Kamp, Hans. 1975. Two theories about adjectives. In *Formal semantics and natural language*, ed. E. Keenan, 123–155. Cambridge: Cambridge University Press.
Kasiewicz, Jerzy. 1970. On three-valued logic [1920]. In *Selected works by J. Łukasiewicz*, ed. L. Borkowski. Amsterdam: North–Holland.
Keefe, Rosanna. 2000. *Theories of vagueness*. Cambridge: Cambridge University Press.
Keefe, Rosanna, and Peter Smith. 1996. Introduction: Theories of vagueness. In *Vagueness: A reader*, ed. R. Keefe and P. Smith, 1–57. Cambridge, MA: Harvard University Press.
Körner, Stephan. 1960. *The philosophy of mathematics*. London: Hutchinson.
LaFollette, Hugh. 2005. Living on a slippery slope. *The Journal of Ethics* 9: 475–499.
Lewis, David. 1983. General semantics. In *Philosophical papers*, vol. III, ed. D. Lewis, 189–232. Oxford: Oxford University Press.
Lode, Eric. 1999. Slippery slope argument and legal reasoning. *Harvard Law Review* 87: 1469–1543.
Machina, Kenton F. 1976. Truth, belief and vagueness. *Journal of Philosophical Logic* 5: 47–78.
McGee, Vann. 1985. A counterexample of modus ponens. *The Journal of Philosophy* 82: 462–471.
Mehlberg, Henry. 1958. *The reach of science*. Toronto: Toronto University Press.
Przelecki, Marian. 1979. The semantics of open concepts. In *Semantics in Poland*, ed. J. Pelc, 284–317. Dordrecht: Reidel.
Putnam, Hilary. 1983. Vagueness and alternative logic. *Erkenntnis* 19: 97–314.
Rizzo, Mario J., and Douglas Glen Whitman. 2003. The camel's nose is in the tent: Rules, theories, and slippery slopes. *UCLA Law Review* 51: 539–592.
Sainsbury, Mark. 1995. *Paradoxes*. Cambridge: Cambridge University Press.
Sainsbury, Mark. 2013. Lessons for vagueness from scrambled sorites. *Metaphysica* 14: 225–237.
Schauer, Frederick. 1985. Slippery slopes. *Harvard Law Review* 93: 363–383.
Schechter, Joshua, and David Enoch. 2006. Meaning and justification: The case of modus ponens. *Noûs* 40: 687–715.
Schwartz, Stephen P. 1987. Intuitionism and sorites. *Analysis* 47: 179–183.
Shapiro, Stewart. 2006. *Vagueness in context*. Oxford: Oxford University Press.
Sorensen, Roy. 1988. *Blindspots*. Oxford: Oxford University Press.
Sorensen, Roy. 1989. Slipping off the slippery slope: A reply to Professor Jacquette. *Philosophy and Rhetoric* 22: 195–202.
Sorensen, Roy. 2001. *Vagueness and contradiction*. Oxford: Oxford University Press.
Sorensen, Roy. 2012. The sorites and the generic overgeneralization effect. *Analysis* 77: 444–449.
Spielthenner, George. 2010. A logical analysis of slippery slope arguments. *Health Care Analysis* 18: 148–163.

Toulmin, Stephen. 1958. *The uses of argument*. Cambridge: Cambridge University Press.
Trianosky, Gerog W. 1978. Rule-utilitarianism and the slippery slope. *The Journal of Philosophy* 75: 414–424.
Unger, Peter. 1979. There are no ordinary things. *Synthese* 41: 117–154.
van de Burg, Wibren. 1991. Slippery slope argument. *Ethics* 102: 42–65.
van Fraassen, Bas C. 1966. Singular terms, truth-value gaps and free logic. *The Journal of Philosophy* 63: 136–152.
Varzi, Achille C. 2007. Supervaluationism and its logics. *Mind* 116: 633–675.
Volokh, Eugene. 2003. The mechanisms of slippery slope. *Harvard Law Review* 116: 1026–1037.
von Wright, Georg Henrik. 1983. Truth-logic. In *Truth, knowledge, and modality. Philosophical papers*, vol. III, ed. G.H. von Wright, 26–41. Oxford: Basil Blackwell.
von Wright, Georg Henrik. 1996. Truth-logics. In *Six essays in philosophical logic*, ed. G.H. von Wright, 71–91. Helsinki: Acta Philosophica Fennica.
Walton, Douglas. 1992. *Slippery slope arguments*. Oxford: Oxford University Pres.
Williams, Bernard. 1995. Which slopes are slippery? In *Making sense of humanity and other philosophical papers*, ed. B. Williams, 213–223. Cambridge: Cambridge University Press.
Williamson, Timothy. 1994. *Vagueness*. London: Routledge.
Woods, John. 2000. Slippery slope and collapsing taboos. *Argumentation* 14: 107–134.
Wright, Crispin. 1975. On the coherence of vague predicates. *Synthese* 30: 325–365.
Wright, Crispin. 1976. Language-mastery and the sorites paradox. In *Truth and meaning*, ed. G. Evans and J. McDowell, 223–247. Oxford: Oxford University Press.
Wright, Crispin. 1987. Further reflections on the sorites paradox. *Philosophical Topics* 15: 227–290.
Zadeh, Lotfi A. 1975. Fuzzy logic and approximate reasoning. *Synthese* 30: 407–428.

Chapter 5
Institutional Constraints of Topical Strategic Maneuvering in Legal Argumentation. The Case of 'Insulting'

Harm Kloosterhuis

Abstract Strategic maneuvering refers to the efforts parties make to reconcile rhetorical effectiveness with dialectical standards of reasonableness. It manifests itself in *topical selection, audience-directed framing* and *presentational devices.* In analyzing strategic maneuvering one category of parameters to be considered are the constraints of the institutional context. In this paper I explore the institutional constraints for topical selection for the legal argumentative activity type *insulting*. I will make a distinction between statutory constraints, constraints developed in case law and constraints regarding language use and the logic of conversational implicatures.

5.1 Introduction

Frans van Eemeren explains in *Strategic Maneuvering in Argumentative Discourse* (2010, p. 40) how the theoretical reconstruction of argumentation should incorporate *strategic maneuvering* of parties in a discussion. Strategic maneuvering refers to the efforts parties make to reconcile rhetorical effectiveness with dialectical standards of reasonableness. It manifests itself *topical selection,* the *audience-directed framing* of the argumentative moves, and in the purposive use of *presentational devices.* In analyzing strategic maneuvering the following parameters must be considered: (a) the results that can be achieved, (b) the routes that can be taken to achieve these results, (c) the constraints of the institutional context and (d) the mutual commitments defining the argumentative situation (Van Eemeren 2010, p. 163). In chapter 10 of his study – 'Setting up an agenda for further research' – Van Eemeren proposes further research to the theoretical exploration of these four parameters for specific argumentative activity types. In this paper I want to do this for a specific legal argumentative activity type: the discussions about the accusation

H. Kloosterhuis (✉)
Erasmus School of Law, Erasmus University College, Erasmus University Rotterdam, Rotterdam, The Netherlands
e-mail: Kloosterhuis@law.eur.nl

© Springer International Publishing Switzerland 2015

T. Bustamante, C. Dahlman (eds.), *Argument Types and Fallacies in Legal Argumentation*, Law and Philosophy Library 112,
DOI 10.1007/978-3-319-16148-8_5

of *insulting*. In these discussions there is often disagreement because language users can opt for *indirect insulting*. The problem of indirect insulting is that there is a difference between sentence- and speaker meaning. This difference results in problems regarding the interpretation and reconstruction of the argumentation for and against the accusation of insulting. This aspect of insulting has received little attention in legal research and it is my aim in this contribution to solve some of these problems by providing a theoretical framework for the analysis of strategic maneuvering in legal discussions about insulting, using the parameters distinguished by Van Eemeren. I will focus on topical selection and the parameter institutional constraints by giving a specification of the argumentative activity type *adjudication in cases about insulting* and an analysis of the constraints of this activity type. I will make a distinction between statutory constraints, constraints developed in case law and constraints regarding language use and the logic of conversational implicatures.

5.2 The Statutory Constraints of the Institutional Context

In order to shed some light on the constraints of the institutional context let us first take an example of an accusation of insulting, taken from Dutch case law. 10 March 2009 the Supreme Court of the Netherlands ruled in a case about the accusation of insulting. The case was about article 137c of the Criminal Code, which makes insulting statements about a group of people a crime. The Supreme Court acquitted a man who stuck a poster in his window with the text 'Stop the cancer called Islam' of insulting Muslims. According to the district court and the court of appeal, this statement was insulting for a group of people due to their religion, considering the strong connection between Islam and its believers. But the Supreme Court argued that criticizing a religion, is not automatically also insulting its followers. According to the Supreme Court the appeal court gave too wide an interpretation of the expression 'a group of people according to their religion' in Article 137c. People expressing themselves offensively about a religion are not automatically guilty of insulting its followers, even if the followers feel insulted. The Supreme Court ruled that 'the statement must unmistakably refer to a certain group of people who differentiate themselves from others by their religion'. While people may not insult believers, they can insult their religion. The sole circumstance of offensive statements about a religion also insulting its followers is not sufficient to speak of insulting a group of people due to their religion.

Discussions about the accusation of insulting can be analysed as species of the argumentative *activity type adjudication*. Van Eemeren argues that argumentative discourse in practice takes place in different kinds of activity types, which are to a greater or lesser degree institutionalized, so that certain practices have become conventionalized. Activity types and the speech events that are associated with them can be identified on the basis of careful empirical observation of argumentative practice.[1] One of the activity types Van Eemeren (2010, p. 147) distinguishes is *adjudication:*

> Adjudication aims for the termination of a dispute by a third party rather than the resolution of a difference of opinion by the parties themselves. It is commonly understood as taking a dispute to a public court, where a judge, after having heard both sides, will make a reasoned decision in favor of either one of the parties. The judge determines who is wrong and who is right according to a set of rules. Most of these rules are tantamount to specifications of rules for critical discussion aimed at promoting that the dispute be terminated in a reasonable way.

Now how is the practice of discussions about insulting conventionalized? Which institutional rules and constraints are relevant? In the following I will make a distinction between three types of rules: statutory rules, rules from case law and rules regarding language use.

In the first place there are *statutory* rules about this criminal act in the penal code. The relevant statutory rule in the example 'Stop the cancer called Islam' is Article 137c of the Dutch Penal Code:

> Article 137c
>
> He who publicly, verbally or in writing or image, deliberately expresses himself in a way insulting of a group of people because of their race, their religion or belief, or their hetero- or homosexual nature or their physical, mental, or intellectual disabilities, will be punished with a prison sentence of at the most one year or a fine of third category.

This rule contains the following partially complex necessary conditions for the application: (1) there is an act of insulting of (2) a group of people, (3) there is an intention to insult, (3) the insult is in public, (4) verbally or in writing or image, (5) because of race, religion or belief, or hetero- or homosexual nature or physical, mental, or intellectual disabilities. This structure implies that a successful defence of the standpoint that someone is guilty of the criminal act insulting contains a coordinative argumentation of five arguments based on the five necessary conditions in the norm. A successful attack of this standpoint results in single or multiple argumentation, based on a refutation of one or more of the five necessary conditions.

5.3 Constraints Developed in Case Law and Linguistic Constraints

In the second place there are rules developed in *case law*. These rules refine and specify the five necessary conditions, but the case law about 137c also resulted in a new condition for the application. According to the rules from case law about the application of article 137c three questions should be answered. The first question is whether or not an utterance is an insult and whether or not the other conditions of 137c are fulfilled. If the utterance is an insult and the other conditions are fulfilled,

[1] Unlike theoretical constructs such as a critical discussion and other ideal models based on *analytic* considerations regarding the most pertinent presentation of the constitutive parts of a problem-valid procedure for carrying out a particular kind of discursive task (Van Eemeren 2010, p. 145).

the next question is whether or not the utterance is part of a public debate. And if the insult is an utterance in a public debate the third question is whether or not the utterance is unnecessary offensive.

Let us now focus on the first question: is the utterance insulting? Here the relevant rules are not legal, but *linguistic* in nature. This third category of rules are conventionalized *semantic* and *pragmatic* rules. In answering the question about the insulting nature of the utterance a distinction has to be made between *direct* and *indirect* insulting. In order the qualify an utterance as a direct insult the words themselves and semantic rules may often suffice, but often one may require the *context* to understand the actual meaning of the words. It could be clear, for instance, that the tone of the entire text is ironic. Those few words which in isolation may be construed as insulting, would then in their totality, in conjunction, be ironic and hence have an entirely different meaning.

As I have shown in Kloosterhuis (2012) the cases of *indirect* insulting are often more complicated to analyse. In these cases semantic rules are not sufficient as basis for the qualifications that an utterance is an insult. Here we need *pragmatic* rules. Let us look at some examples. According to Dutch case law the following utterances count as insult Kloosterhuis (2012):

1. Calling a police-officer a 'homo'.
2. Greeting a police-officer with 'Heil Hitler'.
3. Saying 'I am gonna fuck you' to a police-officer.
4. Having a tattoo or a bomberjack with the text '1312' or 'ACAB' (All Cops Are Bastards).
5. Referring to a passage in the Bible where Pilatus washes his hands.
6. Saying or implicating that the Holocaust did not happen

These utterances are less clear than direct insults. This vagueness often results in discussions about meanings, between parties, between parties and judges and between judges. In example 1 for instance – Calling a police-officer a 'homo' – the judge of the district court ruled that the utterance 'homo' is not insulting, but a neutral term. In contrast with this decision the court of appeal decided that this utterance 'in context' had to be considered as an insult. Another form of defence to the accusation of insulting in these case is that there was no intention to insult. And sometimes the meaning – or to be more precise the propositional content – of a word is disputed. One of the counterarguments against the accusation of an insult in the ACAB-cases (example 4) was that ACAB does not mean 'All Cops Are Bastards' but 'Acht Cola Acht Bier' ('Eight Cola Eight Beer').

5.4 Constraints Related to the Logic of Conversational Implicatures

The interesting problem with the examples like 'I am gonna fuck you' is that there is a (possible) difference between the sentence meaning and the speaker meaning. According to Grices theory about conversational implicatures a speaker or writer can use utterances as 'I am gonna fuck you' and defend that there was no insult meant. To explain this logic of the conversational implicatures in cases of indirect insulting, we should first give a precise definition of the *speech act insulting*. In the analysis of speech act theory, language users performing speech acts have illocutionary and perlocutionary purposes. The successful and performance of an illocutionary act will always result in the effect that the hearer understands of the utterance produced by the speaker. But in addition to the illocutionary effect of understanding, utterances normally produce and are often intend to produce, further perlocutionary effects on the feelings, attitudes and subsequent behaviour of the hearers. An assertive speech act as asserting or argumentation may result in the perlocutionary effect of convincing or persuasion and a commisseve speech act as a promise may create expectations. Searle (1971) and Searle and Vanderveken (1985) claims that there are five and only five types of illocutionary acts:

1. *assertive* illocutionary acts that commit a speaker to the truth or acceptability of the expressed proposition, for example making a statement.
2. *directive* illocutionary acts that are to cause the hearer to take a particular action, for example requests, commands and advice.
3. *commissive* illocutionary acts that commit a speaker to some future action, for example promises and oaths.
4. *expressive* illocutionary acts that express the speaker's attitudes and emotions towards the proposition, for example congratulations, excuses and thanks.
5. *declarative* illocutionary acts that change the reality in accord with the proposition of the declaration, for example baptisms, pronouncing someone guilty or pronouncing someone husband and wife.

The successful performance of illocutionary acts is dependent on the fulfillment of different conditions (Searle 1971, p. 47; van Eemeren and Grootendorst 1984, p. 21). A successful performance of a speech act results in a perlocutionary effect, for example being convinced in case of the illocutionary act argumentation. Within the framework of speech act theory we are now able to give a more precise definition of the effect 'being insulted': *being insulted is a perlocutionary effect that is intended by the speaker or writer and that is based on rational considerations on the part of the addressee.*[2]

[2] In other to make clear what this perlocutionary effect involves Van Eemeren (2010, p. 37) makes the following distinctions. First, he distinguishes between effects of the speech act that are intended by the speaker or writer and consequences that are brought about accidentally. Van Eemeren reserves the term act, in contradistinction with 'mere behavior', for conscious, purposive activities based on rational considerations for which the actor can be held accountable. As a result, bringing about completely unintended consequences cannot be regarded as acting, so in such cases there can be no question of the performance of perlocutionary acts. According to Van Eemeren a rough and ready criterion for distinguishing between the performance of perlocutionary acts and the bringing about of unintended consequences is whether the speaker can reasonably be asked to provide his/her reasons for causing the consequences in question. Second, Van Eemeren distinguishes between consequences of speech acts whose occurrence may be regarded to be based on rational considerations on the part of the addressee and consequences that are divorced from reasonable decision-making, like being startled when someone shouts boo.

The next question now is how the perlocutionary effect of being insulted is related to the five types of illocutionary acts in cases of indirect insulting. How, in other words, is a language user capable of inferring an 'insult' from an assertion, a promise, a question, a compliment or a declaration? According to Van Eemeren and Grootendorst the associated perlocutions are connected to the essential condition or illocutionary point of the illocutionary act.[3] There are five and only five illocutionary points. (1) The assertive point is to say how things are. (2) The directive point is to try to get other people to do things. (3) The commissive point is to commit the speaker to doing something. (4) The declarative point is to change the world by saying so. (5) The expressive point is to express feelings and attitudes.

Now it is clear from these illocutionary points that none of the five illocutionary acts is related in a direct conventional way with the perlocution 'being insulted'. Calling a police officer a homo or comparing an employer with Pontius Pilatus are assertive illocutionary acts, in which a proposition is presented as representing a state of affairs, with an associated perlocution as accepting a description or being convinced, but not being insulted. Saying 'I am gonna fuck you' to a police-officer is a commissive illocutionary act – a promise or a threat – in which the speaker commits himself to carrying out an action. The associated perlocutionary effects of commissives are accepting the promise or being intimidated, but not being insulted. Greeting a police-officer with 'Heil Hitler' is an expressive illocutionary act with an associated perlocution as accepting the greeting but again – not being insulted.

So, the question now is: how is it possible to derive the perlocutionary effect 'being insulted' from illocutionary acts whose associated perlocutionary effects is primary a different one. The key to an answer to this question is treating the examples as forms *conversational implicatures* as analyzed by Grice. In order to analyze the difference between sentence meaning and speaker meaning, Grice (1975, pp 26–30) postulated a general Cooperative Principle and four maxims specifying how to be cooperative:

Cooperative Principle. Contribute what is required by the accepted purpose of the conversation.

Maxim of Quality. Make your contribution true; so do not convey what you believe false or unjustified.

Maxim of Quantity. Make your contribution as informative as is required for the current purposes of the exchange. Do not make your contribution more informative than is required.

Maxim of Relation. Be relevant.

Maxim of Manner. Be perspicuous; so avoid obscurity and ambiguity, and strive for brevity and order.

---

[3] Van Eemeren en Grootendorst (1984, p. 53) are of the opinion that there is a conventional relation between illocutionary acts and associated perlocutionary effects. They describe the associated perlocution as 'something like the rationale' for performing the illocution; it is, as it were, in the nature of the illocution to bring about the perlocution. Central in their analysis is the relation between the essential condition or illocutionary point of the illocutionary act and its rationale. They explain that the relation between the illocution argumentation and the perlocution convincing can be characterized as 'conventional' in Lewis (1977) sense of regularity, normativity and mutual expectations.

According to Grice it is common knowledge that people generally follow these rules for efficient communication and, so long as there are no indications to the contrary, assume that others also adhere to the maxims. Cases in which the speaker leaves certain elements implicit, yet the listener still understands what he means over and above what he 'literally' says, can then be explained by assuming that, in combination with the cooperative principle, these maxims enable the language users to convey conversational implicatures. So, if a speaker is able to adhere to the maxims, yet deliberately and openly violates one of the maxims, even though there is no reason to suppose that he has completely abandoned the cooperative principle, then it is possible to derive a conversational implicature.

In order to give a more precise description of inferring conversational implicatures Van Eemeren and Grootendorst (1984) propose to combine the maximes of Grice with Searles conditions for the performance of illocutionary acts. For the performance of an assertive the preparatory conditions are that the speaker has reasons for acceptance the truth of the propositional content and the sincerity condition is belief. For the performance of a commissive the propositional content condition is that the propositional content represents a future course of action of the speaker, the preparatory condition is that the speaker is able to perform this course of action and the sincerity condition is intention. For the performance of a directive the propositional content condition is that the propositional content represents a future course of action of the hearer, the preparatory condition is that the hearer is able to perform this course of action and the sincerity condition is desire. For the performance of a declarative there are no special propositional content conditions, the preparatory condition is that the speaker is capable of bringing about the state of affairs represented in the propositional content solely in virtue of the performance of the speech act and the sincerity conditions are belief and desire. For the performance of an expressive there are no general propositional content, preparatory and sincerity conditions. But most expressives have propositional content conditions (you cannot apologize for the law of *modus ponens*), the preparatory condition that the propositional content is true and the sincerity condition about a state of affairs that the speaker presupposes to obtain.

These conditions presuppose Grice's Cooperation Principle and can be viewed as specifications of the four maxims. Let us now try to explain how a hearer is able to derive an insult in our examples. The line of reasoning of the public prosecution defending the standpoint that an utterance counts as an insult would be s follows.

Someone who calls a police-officer a homo implicates an insult by openly violating one of the maxims. When the assertive is not true, the speaker violates the maxime of quality, or in terms of the conditions for performing an assertive, the speaker infringes the preparatory and sincerity conditions. When the assertive is true the speaker violates the maxime of relevance, or in terms of the conditions for performing an assertive, the speaker violates the essential rule, because there is no sense or point.

The fired employee who compares his employer with Pontius Pilatus does not say that his dismissal is like the condemnation of Jesus, but he is implicating it by openly violating the maxime of quality, or more precise the preparatory and sincerity conditions for an assertive illocutionary act.

Someone who greets a police-officer with 'Heil Hitler' implicates an insult by openly violating the maxime of relation, or more precise the sincerity conditions for performing an expressive illocutionary act. Someone who promises or threats a police-officer to fuck him implicates an insult by openly violating the maxime of quality of relation, or more precise the preparatory and sincerity conditions for performing a commissive illocutionary act.

Saying or implicating that the Holocaust did not happen counts as an insult because it is (or counts as) a violation of the maxime of quality. In terms of the conditions for performing the assertive illocutionary act this utterance can be analyzed as a violation of the preparatory and maybe also the sincerity conditions for performing an assertive illocutionary act.

5.5 Conclusion: The Constraints of Topical Strategic Maneuvering in Cases of Indirect Insulting

The analyses of insulting shows that there are three kinds of institutional constraints of strategic maneuvering: statutory constraints, constraints developed in case law and constraints regarding language. In cases of indirect insulting the rules of conversational implicatures are highly relevant constraints for the analysis of topical strategic maneuvering. In the cases discussed, I showed how indirect insults can be reconstructed as conversational implicatures. The violation of the gricean maxims results in a potential obstruction of the communication, for reasons that go beyond these maxims. But it is a *potential* obstruction, because of the uncertainty related to the implicature. The examples of indirect insulting illustrate two important characteristics of conversational implicatures. The first is that the presence of the implicature must be capable of being worked out for even if it can in fact be intuitively grasped, unless the intuition is replaceable by an argument, the implicature (if present at all) will not count as a conversational implicature. The second characteristic is that a conversational implicature is always *contextually cancellable* if one can find situations in which the utterance would simply not carry the implicature (Grice 1989, p. 44). In other words, in using an 'indirect insult' there is *plausible deniability*. These two characteristics are the explanation for the *topical space* in discussions about the accusation of an indirect insult. The party who claims that a certain illocutionary act carries the implicature 'insulting' and the perlocutionary effect 'being insulted' claims that there are good arguments for this standpoint, given the conventional meaning of the utterance and the conventional rules for conversations. Because of the plausible deniability the accused can argue that there was no insult at all. In the examples mentioned this was precise one of the types of argumentation to defend the standpoint that there was no insult.

Let us to illustrate this point take a closer look to the argumentation in the case 'Stop the Cancer called Islam' Is it possible to analyze this utterance as implicating an insult because the writer openly violates one of the maxims or conditions for performing a directive illocutionary act? The analysis of the utterance as an open violation of the maxime of quality and the sincerity conditions for the performance of an assertive – Islam is not a cancer – can easily be countered with the argument that it was meant metaphorically. The analysis of the utterance as a violation of the maxime of relation and the essential condition for an assertive, can be countered by arguing that this utterance was part of a public debate. This was in fact the point the defence made in this case.

References

Grice, H.P. 1975. Logic and conversation. In *Syntax and semantics 3: Speech acts*, ed. P. Cole and J. Morgan, 43–58. New York: Academic.

Grice, H.P. 1989. *Studies in the way of words*. Cambridge: Harvard University Press.

Kloosterhuis, H.T.M. 2012. The logic of indirect insulting in legal discussions. A speech act perspective. In *Explorations in language and law. An international, peer-reviewed publication series*, 69–82. Aprilia: NOVALOGOS/Ortica Editrice Soc. Coop.

Lewis, D.K. 1977. *Convention; a philosophical study*. Cambridge: Harvard University Press.

Searle, J.R. 1971. What is a speech act? In *The philosophy of language*, ed. J.R. Searle, 39–53. London: Oxford University Press.

Searle, J.R., and D. Vanderveken. 1985. *Foundations of illocutionary logic*. Cambridge: Cambridge University Press.

van Eemeren, F.H. 2010. *Strategic maneuvering in argumentative discourse. Extending the pragma-dialectical theory of argumentation*. Amsterdam/Philadelphia: John Benjamins Publishing Company.

van Eemeren, F.H., and R. Grootendorst. 1984. *Speech acts in argumentative discussions. A theoretical model for the analysis of discussions directed toward solving conflicts of opinion*. Dordrecht: Foris.

Chapter 6
One-Sided Argumentation in the Defense of Marriage Act

Janice Schuetz

Abstract The goal of this essay is to extend legal argumentation theory by identifying the traits of partisan and one-sided arguments found in legal appeals and reinforced by *amicus curiae* briefs supporting those appeals. Specifically, I describe the role of *amicus curiae* briefs commonly used in appellate argumentation in the United States. Then I identify six characteristics of these arguments: clarifying a legal principle, emphasizing amici interests, refuting oppositions' arguments, stipulating partisan definitions, using one-sided evidence, and citing precedents that reinforce my-side bias. I conclude by providing examples of these six characteristics from two *amicus* briefs in the U.S. Supreme Court decision entitled, *United States v. Windsor* (570 U.S. slip opinion. American Bar Association. http://www.supremecourtpreview.org. Accessed 1 Sept 2013, 2013), that overturned a section of the Defense of Marriage Act (DOMA) that declared marriage in the U.S. is only between a man and a woman.

6.1 Case Background

The argumentation for both sides in *United States v. Windsor* (2013, Case 12-307) centered on the legality of the Defense of Marriage Act (DOMA), a federal law defending the traditional definition of marriage passed by Congress and signed into law by President Clinton in 1996 (1 U.S.C. 7). Section 3 states that "the word 'marriage' means only a legal union between one man and one woman as husband and wife," and it does not consider a person in a same sex marriage as a legal spouse. Prior to the passage of the law, the U.S. House of Representatives conducted extensive hearings on this statute. In these hearings many members of Congress claimed that this legislation was part of their moral duty to protect traditional marriage.

J. Schuetz (✉)
University of New Mexico, Albuquerque, NM, USA
e-mail: jschuetz@unm.edu

© Springer International Publishing Switzerland 2015

T. Bustamante, C. Dahlman (eds.), *Argument Types and Fallacies in Legal Argumentation*, Law and Philosophy Library 112,
DOI 10.1007/978-3-319-16148-8_6

The case involved Edith "Edie" Windsor, the surviving spouse of Thea Spyer, a same sex couple who were legally married in Toronto in 2007 after nearly 40 years of living together as committed partners. After Spyer died in 2009, Windsor was required to pay $363,000 in federal estate taxes, money that she would not have needed to pay if she had been married to someone of the opposite sex. Although Windsor and Spyer's marriage was legal in their home state of New York, the federal law (DOMA) did not recognize the marriage for the purpose of federal benefits.

The key legal issues in the dispute were whether or not Section 3 of DOMA (1996) is constitutional and whether or not those in same sex marriages are entitled to federal benefits. Attorneys for Windsor and for the United States claim this statute violated the Equal Protection Clause of the Fifth Amendment of the U.S. Constitution, and attorneys for BLAG (Bipartisan Legal Advocacy Group) claimed that DOMA should be upheld as federal law because it follows the tradition of the U.S. Constitution and it is financially wise to grant federal health, military pension, and social security benefits only to those in opposite sex marriages. After the U.S. Court of Appeals for the Second Circuit (*Windsor v U.S.* 2012) agreed with Windsor and her legal advocates that Section 3 of DOMA was unconstitutional, BLAG decided to defend the legality of the statute and the case made its way to the Court. When the Court declared this section of DOMA unconstitutional in June 2013, thousands of couples around the United States applauded the decision, which initiated efforts in more than 30 states to legalize same marriages.

6.1.1 Required Briefs

One of the required briefs for the Supreme Court argued by U.S. Solicitor General Donald B. Verrilli, Jr. supported the position of the U.S. government that Section 3 of DOMA, which defines marriage as between a man and a woman, is unconstitutional. Paul D. Clement on behalf of BLAG claimed Section 3 is constitutional and necessary for preserving the federal government's financial resources and providing uniformity in federal law. The contested definition of marriage is significant because only those involved in opposite sex marriages are entitled to health, social security, or inheritance benefits whereas those in same sex marriages are not.

Summary of appellate arguments from required briefs

Verrilli's arguments (Verrilli et al. 2013)	Clement's arguments (Clement et al. 2013)
Section 3 violates equal protection for all citizens.	Section 3's definition of marriage should be retained because it is fiscally necessary.
Section 3 does not further federal interests of preserving federal resources.	Section 3 provides a uniform definition that helps the federal government administer programs efficiently.
Section 3 legitimizes discrimination.	Section 3 should be retained because it was passed by Congress, signed by President Clinton, and certified by the Justice Department.

(continued)

Verrilli's arguments (Verrilli et al. 2013)	Clement's arguments (Clement et al. 2013)
Section 3 excludes gays and lesbians from federal benefits solely because of their sexual orientation.	Homosexuals are not a powerless group deserving special legal consideration.
Court precedents show that the federal government cannot exclude a group from federal benefits based on conserving public resources.	Section 3 should continue because there is no compelling legal reason to change it.

The goal of this paper is extend legal argumentation theory by identifying the traits of partisan and one-sided arguments found in appeal and reinforced in *amicus curiae* briefs. The essay describes *amicus curiae* briefs and their role in appellate argument, explains one-sided legal arguments, and explicates the specific traits of this type of argument in two different *amicus curiae* briefs submitted in the DOMA case for consideration by the U.S. Supreme Court.

6.2 *Amicus Curiae* Briefs

The name, *amicus curiae,* means friends of the court. These briefs are partisan, biased, and one-sided arguments submitted by special interest individuals and groups to support a particular side of an appellate case. The *amicus* briefs express partisan interests and seek to persuade the judges on the Supreme Court that their position is the only correct one (Foggan and Dancey 2004). The *amicus* briefs also present specialized and unique information that legal advocates determine to be pertinent to the judges deciding a case. Specifically, these briefs are "no longer a mere friend of the court, the *amicus* has become a lobbyist, an advocate, and most recently the vindicator of the politically powerless" (Lowman 1992, 1245).

These briefs are a common type of legal advocacy that accompanies the required appellate briefs and addresses judges deciding a case. Since 1990, more than 90 % of all case appealed to the U.S. Supreme Court include a number of *amicus curiae* briefs (Kearney and Merrill 2000, 744), a fact demonstrating the prevalence of this type of legal argumentation in the U.S. In the DOMA case, 43 *amicus* briefs supported the U.S. government and the petition of Windsor, and 30 supported BLAG and the interests of conservative groups. My study selects one brief for each side as a representative example of the kinds of arguments and the credentials of the amici who constructed the briefs. Most of the *amicus* briefs supporting the government and Windsor's claim of discrimination came from congressional groups, government agencies, corporations, and academic groups; whereas most of the briefs supporting BLAG came from conservative political and religious groups and individuals.

6.2.1 Structure

Amicus briefs share a common structure, purpose, content, and social premises. Because of the prevalence of friends of the court briefs in the last three decades, the Supreme Court issued guidelines in 1997 about the form of these arguments that limited these briefs to 50 pages and forced the authors of these briefs to identify their commitments, biases, authority and sources of financial support for the production and submission of these briefs. All *amicus* briefs contain the following: table of authorities, interests of amici, and summary of arguments. These briefs present arguments in a detailed outline form that must be submitted to the Court no later than 7 days after the petitioners and respondents submit their required briefs (Foggan and Dancey 2004; Rule 29, *Federal Rules of Appellate Procedure*).

6.2.2 Purpose

The goal of this kind of appellate argument is to inform the court of the amici's (name for the people and groups that pay attorneys to create the briefs) "interests in the case," establish "the relevance" of amici's argument" to the case outcome, and justify "why the amici's interests" are not adequately addressed in the appeal briefs (Kearney and Merrill 2000, 38). For this reason, *amicus* briefs allow individuals, interest groups and activists to make additional arguments that they consider pertinent to one side of the appellate case (Flango et al. 2006; Collins 2004).

6.2.3 Content

The content of each *amicus* briefs is aligned with the partisan and one-sided arguments of required briefs. The *amicus* briefs do not take up all of the arguments that are presented in the required briefs, but instead focus on key evidence and reasons that they claim have significant bearing on the case. For example, in support of the brief presented by the U.S. Solicitor General Donald B. Verrilli, *amicus* attorney Miriam R. Nemetz et al. (2013) argued: (1) Gay men and lesbians do not have meaningful political power because they lack civil rights and sufficient political clout to prevent the passage of DOMA and other harmful legislation; (2) Section 3 of DOMA is unconstitutional because it is based on partisan lawmaking; and (3) DOMA does not preserve tradition, protect federal interests in procreation, or assure uniformity in federal law. On behalf of conservative groups who support DOMA and BLAG argued by Paul D. Clement, *amicus* attorney Herbert W. Titus et al. (2013) constructed the following lines of argument: (1) DOMA is constitutional based on several historical Court precedents; (2) DOMA is not prohibited by the Fifth Amendment and due process clause; (3) Homosexuals already have significant political power; and (5) DOMA aligns with Christian teachings about marriage as only between a man and woman.

6.2.4 *Premises*

The premises of amici briefs are intertwined with the social myths that adhere in the narratives of the briefs. Larson (2010) defines social myths as "real or imagined [features of] narratives that illustrate a society's values" (234). Social myths are connected to law because they come from social knowledge and beliefs (tradition and history) about legal issues as well as from the appellate advocate's values. One prominent and disputed myth in this case emphasizes socio-political beliefs about discrimination of gays and lesbians, and another stresses the importance of traditional religious definitions of marriage and the intentions of the framers of the U.S. Constitution. For example, Nemetz (2013) premises her arguments in a social narrative that centers on flawed U.S. laws that promote discrimination of gays and lesbians and situates DOMA directly within contemporary practices of oppression and discrimination in the U.S. On the other hand, Titus (2013) locates his arguments within a social narrative emphasizing the importance of precise legal language, the intentions of the framers of the U.S. Constitution, and Christian religious ideals that he says demonstrate the moral importance of the nuclear family and centrality of marriage as only between heterosexual couples. The disparate social myths appear both in the required and amici briefs in the form of premises that contain appellate arguers' commitments and social values in relation to the disputed legal issues of this case.

6.3 One-Sided Appellate and Amici Arguments

Both the required briefs and those of amici are examples of biased, partisan, and one-sided argument. The *amicus* briefs locate their one-sided arguments both in the facts as advocates understand them, the values of the interest groups they represent, and the social myths that provide the premises of their arguments. Although a common view is that partisan, biased and one-sided arguments oppose the standards of logical rigor and therefore create fallacies, partisan bias is both a necessary and positive trait of appellate argument. Walton (1999) emphasizes that bias in argumentation is not necessarily "incorrect or logically defective"; it is normative for various kinds of one-sided advocacy and therefore deserves critical attention (xviii). Appellate arguers often create partisan, biased and one-sided arguments in order reflect the standpoints of those they represent with persuasive arguments.

A more nuanced meaning of the term "bias" is needed here. One sense of bias is closed-mindedness where the commitments of the advocates are so strong that they refuse to consider the arguments of opponents. Legal advocates typically do not hold this kind of bias because the rules of the legal procedure force them to acknowledge some of opponents' arguments in order to bolster their own standpoints. Another type of bias is what Walton (1999) calls "my-side" bias in which arguers promote group interests from a particular point of view. Expressing "my-side" bias is the norm for appellate arguers because the rules of the court require these advocates to defend one side of a legal dispute, create reasons and evidence that support the people and interests they represent, and make sure the judges deciding the case will understand the reasoning for their partisan positions and interests. In other words, partisan and my-side bias is an integral part of legal advocacy because it is "a function of the avowed or supported purpose of the discourse" (62). Even though the legal system expects appellate judges to be unbiased, impartial and without pre-existing commitments, these traits do not apply to appellate advocacy. Specifically, my-side bias allows amici, always outsiders to a particular dispute, to present arguments they believe should be considered by appellate judges as part of the overall reasoning for each side of the case.

A partisan point of view adheres in one-sided argumentation since appellate arguers must present a compelling case for those they represent and reject arguments from the legal adversaries. In contrast to Walton's claim that one-sided arguments are not balanced, appellate arguers construct reasoned arguments based on evidence that support their side of the case. Admittedly, some of the arguments are stronger than others, but they nonetheless provide reasons and evidence defending distinctive standpoints. Both the required appellate and the *amicus* briefs contain compelling partisan and one-sided arguments that contain my-side bias in order to present and defend their positions and allow the adversarial argument process to take place in the appeal process. Since Walton's descriptors of one-sided arguments are not designed to explicate the content of required or the amici appellate arguments, I explain six common traits in order to clarify this prominent type of legal argument.

6.4 Traits of One-Sided Arguments in Amici Briefs

Several traits commonly found in the arguments of amici briefs include: clarifying a legal principle, emphasizing amici's interests, refuting oppositions' interests, stipulating partisan definitions, using one-sided evidence, and citing precedents that reinforce my-side bias. The following section explains these traits and then provides examples from two sample *amicus curiae* briefs in the DOMA. Nemetz, cited here using the name of the counsel of record, supports the arguments of the U.S. and of lower court rulings in Windsor by denying the constitutionality of Section 3 of DOMA. Titus, cited here using the name of the counsel of record, promotes the arguments for several conservative groups supporting BLAG. Nemetz argues that same sex couples should not be denied federal benefits solely because they are gay, DOMA denies these benefits, and therefore Section 3 must be revoked. She submits this brief on behalf of 172 members of the U.S. House of Representatives and 40 U.S. Senators. Titus's brief represents the interests of a coalition of many conservative groups, including Citizens United National Committee for Family Faith and Prayer, Guns Owners Foundation, Lincoln Institute, and the Conservative Legal Defense and Education Fund. He argues that Section 3 is constitutional and that those in homosexual marriage can legally be denied federal benefits.

6.4.1 Clarifying a Legal Principle

The primary goal of the *amicus* briefs is to support one side of an appellate case by clarifying a legal principle, that is, developing arguments that amici believe are missing or underdeveloped in the required appellate briefs. For Nemetz et al. (2013), one underdeveloped argument is the lack of federal purpose of the DOMA statute. In fact she claims DOMA has no federal purpose whatsoever; instead its purpose is to legitimize discrimination against gays and lesbians.

1. Nemetz (2013) asserts: "We all agree that Section 3 of DOMA—which divides married couples into two classes and denies all federal responsibilities and rights to one of them—lacks a rational connection to any legitimate federal purpose and therefore is unconstitutional" (1). Emphasizing the lack of federal purpose is essential to her argument since every law must have a legitimate purpose otherwise no reason for the law exists. Nemetz further claims that DOMA's definition of marriage as only between a man and woman was not designed to clarify constitutional guarantees, but instead it was created "to express moral disapproval of a disfavored minority group" (22).
2. From the standpoint of those represented by Titus, the undeveloped argument in Clement's brief is his claim that defining marriage is not a State responsibility. He emphasizes instead that for nearly 200 years it has been a legitimate congressional responsibility to develop definitions in federal law. Specifically he asserts: "The courts below mistakenly assume that DOMA Section 3 invades the exclusive authority of States to regulate family relations, including marriage. Instead, DOMA's definition of marriage is a rule of construction defining the meaning of marriage and spouse as those words are used in the United States Code.... DOMA is an exercise of power vested in Congress and governed by *McCulloch v. Maryland* 1819" (Titus 2013, 2). Moreover, this federal power to define terms, Titus claims, is needed "to maintain consistency and uniformity in distributing benefits" (11).

6.4.2 Emphasizing Amici Interests

The reason that amici clarify legal principles is to emphasize interests of those they represent, supplement required appellate briefs, and expand the scope of reasoning and the type of evidence.

1. Nemetz et al. (2013) represents 172 members of the House of Representatives and 40 members of the Senate whose names appear on the amici brief. This brief is significant because many of those she represents voted to pass DOMA 17 years earlier, but in 2013 many changed their minds about that vote. In fact her arguments fault the actions of many of those she represents in her brief for failing to study of the implications of DOMA before they voted for it. She asserts, "DOMA affects thousands of federal statutes … covering virtually every subject within the federal sphere, including Social Security, housing, nutrition, veterans and military benefits, employment, immigration, and many other areas. Yet Congress [in 1996] did not study a single affected law or program" (13). By faulting the amici that she represents, Nemetz implies that congressional members are confessing about once voting for DOMA, and inferring that now they want to right the wrongs that took place when they passed this law in 1996. This kind of confessional argument has two legal purposes. First, it shows that law is temporal and must change to adapt to evolving social practices; the other is that it allows Congress to take responsibility for their actions. This is a direct response to BLAG and some of the congressional members they represent, who insist that the federal statute's definition of marriage as only between a man and woman is legally and morally correct.
2. Titus et al. (2013) represents a number of conservative political and religious groups who use this amici brief to assert the legal and moral concerns they have about the legitimacy of same sex marriages. Although many of the interests of the amici are clearly moral, Titus frames the arguments in legal terminology by insisting that the U.S. Congress has the constitutional responsibility to define terms in a consistent way in order for the federal government to function efficiently. To make this argument, Titus stresses that "DOMA Section 3 is designed by Congress to define words that appear throughout the federal code … as a means of administering a wide variety of federal statutes and programs" (16). To support this claim, Titus quotes the words of Chief Justice John J. Marshall in the 1819 McCulloch decision that "words do not have a fixed character" so it is necessary for Congress to define words like marriage so that the term has the same meaning for every federal law (18). The premise of his argument is that the Constitution does not change and what the founders of the nation wrote at the time is as valid in 2013 as it was nearly 200 years ago. Titus's strategy for including the interests of the several amici's religious and moral views is to claim that the American Constitution should recognize "Christianity as its foundation" (31). He presents this deductive argument in a reverse order stating the premise after his conclusions. His chain of reasoning is as follows: Principles of the U.S. Constitution are rooted in Christianity. One of these principles is that the Constitution should be interpreted in the same way the framers did when they wrote the Fifth Amendment. The framers likely viewed marriage as only between a man and woman. Therefore, his inference is that DOMA is constitutional because it defines marriage in ways that the framers intended and as aligned with Christian beliefs.

6.4.3 Refuting Oppositions' Arguments

In order to bolster their arguments, both of these amici engaged in refutation of key arguments of the opposition related to the presence or absence of discrimination, as presented in the required briefs and as stated in the Defense of Marriage Act Hearings (1996) that supported the passage of DOMA as a federal statute.

1. Nemetz claims that homosexuals do suffer political and social discrimination. She offers two reasons—it creates a federal disability; and it assumes that gay and lesbian couples are unfit parents. First, Nemetz concludes that "DOMA imposes a sweeping and unjustifiable federal disability on married of same sex couples. It is a class of legislation that lacks any rational connection to a legitimate federal interest, thus violating the Fifth Amendment's equal protection guarantee" (38). Her point is that DOMA singles out gays and lesbians for discrimination. She directly refutes evidence presented in the 1996 hearings prior to the passage of DOMA that gays and lesbians are unfit parents, a claim supported by a report in a conservative magazine (Defense of Marriage Act Hearings 1996). She also blames the 1996 Congress for failing to "consult any family or children welfare experts on whether denying federal recognition to gay and lesbian couples would serve children's welfare and promote stability of American families." Instead she says scientific research shows that gay and lesbian parents are as fit and capable as heterosexual parents" (15). Nemetz also refutes the premise of the opposition that same sex marriages threaten traditional marriage and create dysfunctional families. This kind of reasoning likely appeals to the more liberal judges on the Supreme Court since it is repeated in the decision of Supreme Court Justice Anthony Kennedy.
2. Similarly Titus refutes the arguments of the lower courts as well as those presented by Verrilli asserting that homosexuals suffer no discrimination. One reason that no discrimination exists, Titus claims, is that "as a class, homosexuals and their supporters are hardly disenfranchised. As citizens of the United States, they [gays and lesbians] are well represented in Congress, the legislative body that enacted DOMA" (26). This refutation is weak since he offers no evidence about why this proves lack of discrimination. Additionally, he fails to indicate if any gay and lesbian congressional representatives supported the passage of DOMA in 1996. He also asserts that "Since the 1960s and 1970s, the political power of homosexuals and their libertarian and [right to] privacy has grown, not shrunk" (28). He provided no evidence for this argument probably because the special interests that he represented likely would assume his claim to be true based on their belief in the social myth that homosexuals experience no discrimination. However, this refutation is so weak; it likely will not be persuasive to the judges deciding the case. This kind of evidence did not appear in the opinion of judges writing the dissent in this case. Additionally, Titus affirms the social myth and an underlying premise of his argument as a whole that homosexual marriages threaten the traditional family, the foundation of American society. This kind of reasoning appeals to the interests of the conservative groups that Titus represents.

6.4.4 Stipulating Partisan Definitions

Appellate arguers use partisan and one-sided definitions to reinforce definitions pertinent to one side of the case with additional reasoning and to challenge opponents' definitions. Specifically, the required appeal briefs frame legal issues by stipulating different kinds of definitions at the same time they cast doubt on the definitions used by their legal adversaries (646). Stipulative definitions are pervasive in statutes as well as in appellate arguments about those statutes because definitions of this type stipulate meanings as if they were indisputable facts (McGee 1999; Schiappa 2003; Zarefsky 1998, 5). In the arguments about the constitutionality of Section 3 of DOMA, stipulative definitions are central since this statute defines marriage (1 U.S.C. 7). It is not surprising then stipulated definitions often are the contested legal issue in a case and the basis for the partisan, biased, and one-sided appellate arguments about that issue.

The arguments in the required briefs as well as in amici briefs center on stipulative legal definitions as well as myths embedded in current social narratives. Nemetz promotes views of the Constitution and social knowledge that align with the partisan interests of the Democrat legislators and government agencies that she represents, and Titus relies upon standpoints and social myths that align with the partisan interests of BLAG and the conservative religious organizations he represents.

1. Nemetz (2013) agrees with the stipulated definitions presented by Verrilli about opposite sex marriage, federalism, state sovereignty, discriminatory law, and heightened equal protection scrutiny. Nemetz also adds definitions from the records of the two previous courts that decided the DOMA case and from the precedent of *Cleburne v. Cleburne Living Center* (1985). She emphasizes that sexual orientation is not a characteristic that affects a person's ability to perform tasks or contribute to society (4); and she asserts that "gay men and women continue to be powerless" (9).
2. Titus (2013) agrees to the many of the stipulated definitions provided by Clement, including separation of state and federal power, rational review, equal protection, and uniformity of federal benefits. Additionally, Titus emphasizes the importance of Section 3 of DOMA by asserting that only heterosexual marriage results in procreation (10); heterosexual marriage promotes the raising of children by biological parents (12); and the definition of marriage between a man and women is the norm in U.S. history and tradition (17). Titus concludes that the definition in Section 3 is necessary to provide uniformity, administrative efficiency, and keep the federal budget in check. In the concluding part of his brief (41–51), he reiterates the benefits of heterosexual marriage echoing arguments in Clement's brief, and then adds that this traditional definition of marriage promotes responsible child bearing, forces parents to provide social and financial support to their children, fosters the success of children, and provides children with role models from both a mother and father. He offers these benefits as support for a definition of marriage as only between a man and woman.

6.4.5 Using One-Sided Evidence

Partisan and one-sided evidence is common in appellate argument. In ways similar to other kinds of legal evidence, one-sided evidence consists of facts, precedents, and predictions. Appellate advocates select one-sided evidence to reinforce my-side bias, accommodate their amici's interests and values, and show how this evidence supports premises derived from legal and social myths. Although one-sided evidence is necessary for the adversarial system, the issues of a legal dispute also predict some of the evidence and claims that appellate advocates will use. The arguments in the required briefs are constrained by legal rules in ways that those of the amici are not. For example in this case, the amici did not address every disputed legal issue, but instead selected what issues to emphasize based on their vested interests.

1. Nemetz (2013) reinforces and extends the evidence provided by Verrilli about the legal process called "heightened scrutiny," a Supreme Court practice that allows review of cases that appear to violate equal protection rights of certain minority groups, such as gays and lesbians. She concludes that gay men and women are powerless to secure basic rights within the normal political processes for a range of reasons, including "vulnerability to harmful ballot initiatives, underrepresentation in office, geographic dispersion, and entrenched opposition to their political advancement" (9). To develop her arguments, she cites legislation prohibiting discrimination of gays in the workplace that failed to pass Congress and contrasted this lack of congressional action with statistics from a Gallup poll that 89 % of Americans support this legislation (10). Additionally she refers to previous discriminatory policies in the U.S. Military and concludes that sexual orientation has no connection to work productivity or social contributions (12). In this way, Nemetz argues inductively adding examples of legislation that bolster her main claim that DOMA discriminates against same sex couples.
2. Amici supporting BLAG reinforced the correctness of the stipulative definitions of marriage in DOMA by adding new evidence and new lines of reasoning. For example, Titus (2013) presents a variety of evidence to support DOMA and embraces the traditional social narrative that makes heterosexual marriage the only acceptable definition of marriage. Titus develops this deductive sequence of reasons: The Court of Appeals erroneously concluded that homosexuals as a class are suspect because they have been singled out for discriminatory treatment. Thus, the Court of Appeals' decision is incorrect because it improperly contravenes federal law (4). Then Titus introduces a series of constitutional arguments not developed by Clement. He emphasizes that DOMA is clearly constitutional because the Constitution gives power to the Congress to "regulate marriage for federal taxing and spending purposes" (5) citing statements from the Constitution on federal and state powers as evidence. Then Titus concludes that the U.S. Congress has power to define marriage because it has the power to provide for the general welfare (6) and to tax citizens to provide federal benefits (10). His evidence for these claims comes from the dissenting opinion of Judge

Straub in the Second Circuit decision (*Windsor v. U.S.* 2012). Titus further asserts that DOMA Section 3 was "designed to limit the national impact of state-level policy" (10) allowing gay marriage. Supreme Court Justice Antonin Scalia emphasized this point in his dissenting opinion (*U.S. v. Windsor* 2013, slip opinion).

6.4.6 Citing Precedents That Reinforce My-Side Bias

Just as the required appellate briefs differ in their choice and use of evidence in support of their arguments, so do the amici that support them. In the required briefs, precedents are numerous because appellate attorneys believe that these are the most compelling evidence for judges to consider. Amici briefs can restate precedents cited in the required briefs in order to convince the Supreme Court judges about the legal grounds of key arguments, but amici usually supplement these precedents with other kinds of evidence that support amici's interests. Nemetz et al. (2013) cites, but does not explicate, 38 different precedents (previous appellate court rulings) related to the Tenth Amendment. The bulk of her argument emphasizes nine prior and related statutes; she also quotes legislators who supported and opposed DOMA in 1996, citing the Congressional Record (1996), and presents expert opinion from social scientists about gay men and women and harms they had suffered and abilities they had. This evidence refutes some of the claims made in Clement's brief.

1. One key precedent for Nemetz comes from *Lawrence v. Texas* (2003), which reinforces her conclusion that laws need to change to reflect changing times. She argues that laws have shifted since 1996. "DOMA is one of those laws that was enacted which … blinded us to certain truth; but that 'later generations can see … in fact serve only to oppress'." This precedent supports Nemetz's reasoning that DOMA, a statute passed by Congress in 1996, needs to be revoked so that marriage laws reflect changing social knowledge and practices. She repeats some precedents used in Verrilli's brief, including those that stress the need for people of all groups to have the equal protection of the Constitution regardless of their political standing in society.
2. In contrast, Titus (2013) refers to 26 precedents; most do not appear in the arguments of Clement. Instead the precedents he cites are related to the First Amendment and religious rights decided prior to 1950. In addition to these precedents, he quotes from Genesis in the *Old Testament* and from one legal journal essay explicating flaws of appellate judges' use of the equal protection clause of the Constitution. Titus relies on the *McCulloch v. Maryland* (1819) decision, which states that "all means which are not prohibited directly" by the Constitution and "are within its letter and spirit are constitutional" (11). He also quotes from *Marbury v. Madison* (1819), which reiterates the importance of what the framers of the Constitution intended when they wrote the Fifth Amendment. Titus then develops a unique argument in which he refutes appeal court decisions that

concluded that the Fifth Amendment contains an equal protection provision. His final argument is repeated by the dissenting opinion of Justice John Roberts in the final decision (*U.S. v. Windsor* 2013, slip opinion).

6.5 Conclusion

Clarifying a legal principle, emphasizing amici interests, refuting oppositions' arguments, stipulating partisan definitions, using one-sided evidence and citing precedents that reinforce my-side bias are six traits of one-sided appellate arguments that commonly appear in *amicus curiae* briefs submitted as supplements to the required briefs in cases heard by the U.S. Supreme Court.

At first glance, readers may find glaring weaknesses with the amici briefs. For example, the arguments of both sample briefs seem to be infused with ideological bias. Nemetz presents a liberal argument based on the social myth that discrimination against gays and lesbians is rampant, emphasizes that the U.S. Constitution must always change to meet the needs of minority groups in society, and demonstrates that the harm from DOMA to homosexuals is both extensive and reprehensible. To develop her inductive argument, she selects only that evidence that supports one side of the case. However, if readers understand that the goal of *amicus curiae* briefs is to provide partisan arguments based on my-side bias, then Nemetz's ideological position, emphasis of legal principles, refutation, use of definitions and evidence seems reasonable and necessary for this legal adversarial process.

Similarly, Titus presents a conservative ideological argument by premising his claims on the social myth that gays and lesbians have political power and do not experience discrimination, by clarifying the legal principle of equal protection, by stipulating traditional definitions of marriage as the correct ones, by emphasizing that Constitution is immutable and its original intent should be applied to present legal situations, and by relying on precedents from nearly 200 years earlier. Just as the arguments presented by Nemetz, the arguments of Titus about the Constitution can be interpreted as reasonable and worthy of the consideration by conservative justices on the Supreme Court.

These divergent ideological standpoints and the claims and evidence that support them are the norm for amicus briefs because as Lowman explains (1992) these type of briefs function as "lobbyist, advocate, and vindicator of the politically powerless" (1245). The legislators that Nemetz represented are a minority in Congress, and the religiously conservative groups that Titus represents constitute a minority voice in contemporary public debates about the morality and legality of gay marriage.

A reader can move beyond the different standpoints of these amici and make judgments about which of these amici make the strongest arguments based on standards from other contexts. By utilizing standards outside of the legal field that require validity and logical rigor, the arguments of both Nemetz and Titus could be faulted for making false generalization based on limited evidence or for using biased and out dated sources, but these same criticisms likely would apply to all *amicus curiae* briefs. This type of legal argument is essential to the adversarial process in appellate law just as partisan and biased one-sided arguments that promote the ideological standpoints and one-sided interests are. Although certainly, a critic could find a number of problems with the arguments of *amicus* briefs based on logical requirements, I chose a different route and concentrated on what the rhetorical features of these biased and partisan legal arguments in hopes of stimulating discussion about the importance of this understudied genre of legal argument.

References

Cleburne v. Cleburne Living Ctr. (1985). 473 US 432.

Clement, Paul, et al. 2013. Brief for respondents in *U.S. v. Windsor* (Case no. 12-307). Lyle Denniston Archive, Same Sex DOMA. http://www.scotusblog.com/2013/02/same-sex-marriage-doma-briefs). Accessed 1 Sept 2013.

Collins, Paul M. 2004. Friends of the court: Examining the influence of *Amicus Curiae* participation in Supreme Court litigation. *Law and Society Review* 38: 807–828.

Debate on DOMA. 1996, July 12. 142 Cong. Rec. H. 7501.

Defense of Marriage Act. 1996. 1 USC 7, para. # 3.

Defense of Marriage Act: Hearings before the Subcom. on the Constitution of H. Com. on the Judiciary. 1996. 104th Congress.

Flango, Victor E., Donald C. Bross, and Sarah Corbally. 2006. *Amicus Curiae* briefs: The court's perspective. *Justice System Journal* 27: 180–190.

Foggan, Laura, A., and D. Dancey Zedford. 2004, April. *Amicus Curiae:* Writing persuasive briefs and recruiting Amicus support. *Appellate Advocacy Committee,* 35–38. http://www.pkuy.k12.mo.us.nmckeever/file/How_to_write_an_Amicus_Brief. Accessed 1 Sept 2013.

Kearney, Joseph D., and Thomas W. Merrill. 2000. The influence of *Amicus Curiae* briefs on the Supreme Court. *University of Pennsylvania Law Review* 148: 743–855.

Larson, Charles U. 2010. *Persuasion: Reception and responsibility*, 12th ed. Boston: Cengage Learning.

Lawrence v. Texas. 2003. 539 US 558.

Lowman, Michael K. 1992. The litigating *Amicus Curiae*: When does the party begin after the friends leave? *American University Law Review* 42: 1243–1269.

Marbury v. Madison. 1819. 5 US (1 Cranch) 137.

McCulloch v. Maryland. 1819. 17 US (4 Wheat) 316.

McGee, Brian R. 1999. The argument from definition revisited: Race and definition in the progressive era. *Argumentation and Advocacy* 35: 141–158.

Nemetz, Miriam R., et al. 2013. Brief of 172 members of the U.S. House of Representatives and 40 U.S. Senators in Support of Respondent Edith Schlain Windsor, urging affirmance on the merits. American Bar Association. http://www.Supremecourt-preview.org. Accessed 1 Sept 2013.

Schiappa, Edward. 2003. *Defining reality: Definitions and the politics of meaning*. Carbondale: Southern Illinois University Press.

Titus, Herbert W., et al. 2013. Brief *Amicus Curiae* on the Merits of Citizen's United National Committee on Family, Faith and Prayer, Citizens' United Foundation, U.S. Justice Foundation, Gun Owners Foundation, the Lincoln Institute, Public Advocate of the US Declaration Alliance, Western Center for Journalism, Institute on the Constitution, Abraham Lincoln Foundation, Conservative Legal Defense Education Fund, English First, Protect Marriage Maryland PAC, Delegate Bob Marshal and Senator Dick Black [Virginia Legislature] in Support of Resp.

Bipartisan Legal Advisory Group. American Bar Association. http://www.supremecourtpreview.org. Accessed 1 Sept 2013.
U.S. v. Windsor. 2013. 570 U.S. slip opinion. American Bar Association. http://www.supremecourtpreview.org. Accessed 1 Sept 2013.
Verrilli, Donald B., et al. 2013. Brief for petitioners in *US v. Edith Windsor* (Case no. 12-307). Lyle Denniston archive, Same-Sex Marriage DOMA. http://www.scotusblog.com/2013/02/same-sex-marriage-doma-briefs. Accessed 22 Feb 2013.
Walton, Douglas. 1999. *One-sided arguments: A dialectical analysis of bias*. Albany: State University of New York.
Windsor v. U.S. 2012. 699 F.3d (2d.Cir.).
What is Needed to Defend the Bipartisan Defense of Marriage Act of 1996. 2003. Hearing Rights and Property Rights of the S. Com. on the Judiciary. 108th Congress.
Zarefsky, David. 1998. Definitions. In *Argument in a time of change: Definitions, frameworks, and critiques*, ed. J.F. Klumpp, 1–11. Annandale: NCA Publications.

Part II
Argument Types and Legal Interpretation

Chapter 7
Anti-Theoretical Claims About Legal Interpretation: The Argument Behind the Fallacy

Thomas Bustamante

Abstract Legal theorists disagree not only about the interpretation of a particular legal provision, but also about the procedure or the interpretive attitude that lawyers should adopt while interpreting statutes and other legal materials. Some of these theorists hold that theory and philosophy have nothing to offer jurists and play a very limited role in the justification of a legal decision. I call this thesis the "Anti-Theoretical Claim". This claim appears in two variants: a strong form states that no moral theory can ever provide a solid basis for a moral or a legal judgment, whereas a weaker form recognizes that no moral or legal claim can be grounded without a theoretical stance, but holds that participants in legal discourse may bracket their theoretical disagreements when they agree about the solution to a given case. I argue, here, that both versions of the claim are fallacious. While the strong version contains a performative contradiction, for it contains an implicit theoretical position about legal interpretation, the weak variant cannot be grounded without a moral argument to defend the value of incompletely theorized agreements, which is missing in the reasoning of its supporters. Nonetheless, there seems to be an argument behind this fallacy, which has to do with the need to take seriously the empirical circumstances which influence any theoretical account of law and legal reasoning.

Part of the contents of this chapter, at Sect. 7.3 and the first half of Sect. 7.4, has appeared previously in Bustamante (2013). I would like to thank Christian Dahlman and Bernardo Fernandes for helpful comments on a previous draft of this paper.

T. Bustamante (✉)
Law Faculty, Federal University of Minas Gerais (Universidade Federal de Minas Gerais), Avenida João Pinheiro 100, Belo Horizonte 30130-180, MG, Brazil
e-mail: tbustamante@ufmg.br; bustamantethomas@gmail.com

© Springer International Publishing Switzerland 2015

T. Bustamante, C. Dahlman (eds.), *Argument Types and Fallacies in Legal Argumentation*, Law and Philosophy Library 112,
DOI 10.1007/978-3-319-16148-8_7

7.1 Introduction

One of the most prominent theses which appear in recent writings on legal interpretation is the so-called anti-theoretical claim. This claim usually appears in two variants: a stronger and a weaker version. The strong form is advocated by Richard Posner, who holds that legal judgments must be grounded on a consequentialist reasoning that requires no value theory whatsoever. Legal decisions must be assessed on the basis of the political consequences that they ensue, rather than on any abstract theory about the legitimacy, morality or authority of the law (Posner 1990, 1998, 2003). The weak version, in turn, is held by Cass Sunstein and Adrian Vermeule. These authors believe that Posner is wrong to suppose that judges may reach any decision without a theoretical stance. If one is to evaluate a legal argument on the basis of its consequences, it is undeniable that one needs a value theory to determine which consequences are just, good or desirable, for this is the only way to ground any sort of consequentialist judgment. Sunstein and Vermeule uphold, however, that people with different background value theories may reach the same conclusions on the basis of an "incompletely theorized agreement" (Sunstein 2001). When this is the case, then any theoretical disagreement that participants may have should be bracketed and considered irrelevant for reaching the decision at hand (Vermeule 2006; Sunstein and Vermeule 2003). Although normative theories are necessary to support a legal judgment, they do not by themselves allow one to choose among different interpretations, and jurists should not spend much time and energy with them.

In this chapter, I argue that both versions of the anti-theoretical claim are based on a *fallacy*. To counter the strong version, I accept Dworkin's view that no practical decision about the interpretation of the law can be justified without a normative theory that leads to the conclusion adopted by the decision-maker. Even Posner's global scepticism about moral theory is based on a nihilistic moral argument which is as theoretical as any other form of moral philosophy.

By the same token, I argue that Sunstein and Vermeule's advocacy of incompletely theorized agreements is in no better position than Posner's decisionism. From the practical point of view, there is little difference between adopting Posner's strong version of the antitheoretical claim or bracketing all theoretical disagreements on the basis of an incompletely theorized agreement. Yet, though both versions of the anti-theoretical claim are untenable, there is a powerful argument underlying Vermeule's assumptions about the significance of empirical considerations in debates concerning the choice of an interpretive methodology. Though I am persuaded by Dworkin's objections to the Anti-Theoretical Claim, I believe that the advocates of its weaker version have successfully shown that no sensible theory of legal interpretation can be supported without a foundation provided by empirical evidence. To come to this conclusion, I proceed as follows. In Sect. 7.2, I introduce Posner's "everyday" pragmatism, which is grounded on the strong version of the anti-theoretical claim. In Sect. 7.3, I expound Sunstein and Vermeule's criticisms on Posner and their attempt to overcome the difficulties of the strong anti-theoretical claim by raising a "weaker" version of the same claim. Section 7.4, in turn, intends to dismantle the fallacy which underlies the anti-theoretical claim, while Sect. 7.5 acknowledges the strength of Vermeule's normative argument about the role of empirical research in legal argumentation.

7.2 Posner's Abstract Anti-Theoretical Pragmatism

In his Holmes Lectures delivered at Harvard Law School on October 14 and 15, 1997, Richard Posner shocked the world of legal philosophy with two theses concerning the role of moral theory in legal argumentation.

The first thesis is an abstract sceptical claim that concerns moral philosophy in general, and holds that *no moral theory can ever provide a solid basis for moral judgments* (Posner 1998, p. 1639).

This ambitious theoretical claim is based on the following assumptions. First, morality is always and necessarily local, for "there are no *interesting* moral universals" and the few principles of social cooperation that might be valid across different cultures are "too abstract to serve as standards for moral judgment" (Posner 1998, pp. 1640–1641). Second, "many of the so-called moral phenomena can be explained without reference to moral categories," as "most moral principles that claim universality are better understood as mere workaday social norms in fancy dress" (Posner 1998, p. 1641). The domain of moral theory is not composed of self-evident principles or moral truths, but conventional norms whose efficacy must be measured according to their ability to work as "means to a society's ends" (Posner 1998, p. 1652).[1] Third, moral theory or, as Posner prefers to say, academic moralism, is incapable of improving moral behaviour, since "knowing the moral thing to do does not furnish a motivation for doing it," as moral norms are "too feeble to override either narrow self-interest or moral intuitions." The vivid disagreement amongst academic moralists makes it possible for the reader to find a rationalization for any course of conduct, regardless of its moral merits (Posner 1998, p. 1641). Fourth, "exposure to moral philosophy may actually lead people to behave less morally by making them more adept at rationalization." And fifth, there is no uniform morality and it would be "a disaster" if academic moralists were successful in imposing their own moral view upon the majority (Posner 1998, p. 1642).

The second thesis, in turn, is specific about legal reasoning, and holds that *even if moral theory could provide a solid ground for some moral judgments, it should not be used as a basis for **legal** judgments* (Posner 1998, p. 1639).

The target here is limited to legal discourse. Yet in a certain sense the second claim is even more ambitious because it not only holds that moral philosophy is a mere tool for rationalizing one's idiosyncratic moral views, but also argues that the

[1] According to Posner's *instrumental* account of morality, this form of social inefficacy is the only defensible way of criticizing a moral code (Posner 1992, pp. 220ff).

separation between law and morality entails a sort of *firewall* that prevents moral considerations from influencing any relevant legal decision.

> Here I am arguing that moral theory has nothing for law, but I am not limiting myself to academic moralism. The idea that racial discrimination is immoral owes very little to academic moralists; it owes a lot to non-academic moral entrepreneurs such as Abraham Lincoln and Martin Luther King, Jr. Yet we shall see in considering *Brown v. Board of Education* that the courts do not rely on these moralists, either, to support decisions in racial cases, and we shall see that there are good prudential reasons for this forbearance. I do not mean that moral entrepreneurs are never cited in judicial decisions, but they are cited as representatives of *uncontested* moral positions, rather than as authorities for taking one side or another of a moral issue (Posner 1998, p. 1698).

Judges and lawyers, therefore, should narrow down their ambitions and give up making abstract moral judgments to justify their legal decisions. Rather than philosophizing and rationalizing moral principles, judges should adopt a pragmatic approach to adjudication that evaluates a legal decision on the basis of its social consequences, and not of its moral worth.

To distinguish this "practical" approach to adjudication from the philosophical theories of pragmatism, Posner advocates a normative theory of adjudication called "everyday" pragmatism, which could be described thus:

> Everyday pragmatism is the mindset denoted by the popular usage of the word 'pragmatic,' meaning practical and business-like, 'no-nonsense,' disdainful of abstract theory and intellectual pretension, contemptuous of moralizers and utopian dreamers. It long has been and remains the untheorized cultural outlook of most Americans, one rooted in the usages and attitudes of a brash, fast-moving, competitive, forward-looking, commercial, materalistic, philistine society, with its emphasis on working hard and getting ahead (Posner 2003, p. 50).

While adopting this "everyday" pragmatism, one bases one's judgments "on *consequences*, rather than on deduction from premises in the manner of a syllogism," without a commitment to any philosophical tradition on the basis of which these consequences will be evaluated (Posner 2008, p. 40).[2]

7.3 Vermeule's Weaker Version of the Anti-Theoretical Claim

In his institutional theory of legal interpretation, Vermeule claims that no interpretive theory can be defended without careful empirical research about the interpretive capacities of legal institutions and the systemic effects of the allocation of decision-making power between or among institutions. This is what he calls his "minimal point" about interpretive theories (Vermeule 2006, p. 81).

[2] A more developed account of the principles of pragmatic adjudication can be found in Posner (2003, pp. 59–85).

Nevertheless, his institutional theory of interpretation is based on a second and more ambitious claim that in some cases "a second-best assessment of institutional issues might not only be necessary but indeed sufficient to resolve conflicts over interpretive theories," inasmuch as people with different theoretical premises might agree on a particular interpretive strategy at the operational level (Vermeule 2006, p. 82).[3]

This argument is premised on the possibility of an "incompletely theorized agreement" in the sense defended by Cass Sunstein. Under this view, people who disagree about abstract moral principles might attempt a "conceptual descent," i.e., a "descent to a lower level of abstraction" with a view to achieving a consensus about "concrete outcomes" (Sunstein 2001, p. 50–51). According to Sunstein,

> The agreement on these points, more particular than their supporting grounds, is incompletely theorized in the sense that the relevant participants are clear on the practice or the result without agreeing on the most general theory that accounts for it. Often people can agree on a rationale offering low-level or midlevel principles. They may agree that a rule – protecting political dissenters, allowing workers to practice their religion – makes sense without entirely agreeing on the foundations for their belief (Sunstein 2001, p. 51).

The possibility of incompletely theorized agreements over the right interpretive theory for a given institution, therefore, allows meta-interpreters to put aside the theories on which they base their interpretive decisions at the operational level.

By relying on incompletely theorized agreements, judges should embrace what Sunstein has described as "decisional minimalism," which advises judges to say "no more than necessary to justify an outcome," and leave "as much as possible undecided" (Sunstein 1999, pp. 3–4). Decisional minimalism would have at least two important advantages which reduce the costs of judicial decision-making and contribute to the democratic justification of a legal ruling: first, it "reduces the burdens of judicial decision" and, more fundamentally, "is likely to make judicial errors less frequent and (above all) less damaging" (Sunstein 1999, p. 4).

This implies, according to Vermeule, that "institutional analysis might even enable interpreters to choose particular doctrines before, or in place of, choosing a value theory that specifies what counts as a good or bad consequence of interpretive practices" (Vermeule 2006, pp. 82–83). To give an example, Vermeule thinks that, "if, on certain empirical findings, it turned out that legislative history should be excluded on any high-level theory specifying what counts as a good or bad interpretation, then as far as the interpretive question goes, there would be no need to choose a fundamental theory" (Vermeule 2006, p. 83).

Vermeule's account is, thus, admittedly anti-theoretical as he believes that most of the theoretical disagreements in meta-interpretive debates may be "bracketed as

---

[3] Underlying this assertion lies the distinction between *first-best accounts* which specify "a value-theory that makes some interpretive regimes good, some bad" (Vermeule 2006, p. 80), and *second-best accounts*, which attempt to achieve an optimal point under the assumption that it is impossible to achieve the *first-best account* for a given case: "In economics, the idea of a second-best demonstrates that if perfect efficiency cannot be obtained, efficiency is not necessarily maximized by approximating the first-best efficiency conditions as closely as possible" (Vermeule 2006, p. 81).

irrelevant to the operational problems and thus dispensed with altogether" (Vermeule 2006, p. 63).[4]

According to Vermeule, meta-interpreters should bracket theoretical disagreements and concentrate on empirical *institutional analysis*, choosing an interpretive theory on the basis of a consequentialist assessment of the institutional capacities of the interpreters and the systemic effects of the interpretive methods in dispute.

An adequate empirical analysis of the performance of a formalist (or any other) interpretive method for our institutions should, as Vermeule argued in an earlier essay co-authored by Sunstein, provide a reliable answer to at least the following three questions, which deal mostly with empirical issues: (1) The first question, as Sunstein and Vermeule argue, is "whether and when formalist decisions that produce clear mistakes will be corrected by the legislature and whether making the corrections will have low or high costs" (Sunstein and Vermeule 2003, p. 917). (2) The second question, in turn, is "whether a nonformalist judiciary will greatly increase the costs of decision for courts, litigants, and those seeking legal advice. A large issue here involves planning; if nonformalist approaches make planning difficult or impossible, there is a real problem" (Sunstein and Vermeule 2003, p. 918). (3) Finally, the third question is "whether a formalist or a nonformalist judiciary, in one or another domain, will produce mistakes and injustices" (Sunstein and Vermeule 2003, pp. 918–9).

These questions, for Vermeule, refer mostly to the "institutional capacities" and "systemic effects" of interpretive theories, which according to his account are the most important variables that should be balanced in order to support a theory of constitutional interpretation.

If this meta-interpretive strategy is consistently employed, then Vermeule thinks that interpreters will not struggle to conclude that judges should adopt a *formalist* strategy of legal interpretation, following the "clear and specific meaning of legal texts, where those texts have clear and specific meanings," and deferring "to the interpretations offered by legislatures and agencies, where legal texts lack clear and specific meanings" (Vermeule 2006, p. 1). When interpreting the constitution, judges should "avoid high-level claims about constitutionalism, democracy, or the nature of law" and "enforce clear and specific constitutional texts according to the surface meaning," because this procedure "will produce the best ground-level consequences for legal institutions" (Vermeule 2006, p. 33).

Although Vermeule offers other institutional considerations in support of this formalist method of constitutional interpretation, my impression is that the main argument for this view is the (empirically verifiable) "epistemic superiority" of legislatures over courts (Vermeule 2009, p. 90), which should lead judges to construct a "codified constitution" (Vermeule 2009, p. 187) and to interpret constitutional

[4]This point is, again, very similar to what Sunstein has to say about his judicial minimalism. According to this author, "minimalists do not like to work deductively; they do not see outcomes as reflecting rules or theories laid down in advance. They pay close attention to the particulars of individual cases. They also tend to think analogically and by close reference to actual and hypothetical problems" (Sunstein 1999, p. 9).

provisions at the lowest possible level of abstraction, rather than following Dworkin's advice to read moral principles at the "most general possible level" (Dworkin 1996, p. 7).

Under Vermeule's understanding of institutions, the "major determinants of epistemic performance, for groups, are numerosity, diversity and average competence" (Vermeule 2009, p. 90). All of these variables, according to Vermeule, point towards the epistemic superiority of legislators over judges. Firstly, "there are many more legislators in a typical national legislature than there are judges on a typical high constitutional court," and this numerosity is "an important epistemic resource" (Vermeule 2009, p. 11).

Secondly, legislatures are "more representative than courts, and representation produces knowledge" (Vermeule 2009, p. 11). Vermeule follows Bentham on the assumption that representation "gives legislators information about local conditions and social judgments and preferences that judges cannot hope to match" (Vermeule 2009, pp. 10–11). While legislators benefit from a more accurate understanding of the social judgments and preferences on particular political issues, judges are normally fallible and uninformed public servants that suffer from a larger risk of error when they face the challenge of assessing high-level judgments of values and policies. The advice to seek a provision's "legislative history," for example, is subject to a high risk of judicial error because judges "lack the full capacity to remedy informational defects caused by the sheer volume of legislative history" (Vermeule 2006, p. 111).

Finally, and as Vermeule says, "crucially," legislatures have an epistemic superiority because of their greater diversity compared to a typical modern judiciary. The legislature's "professional diversity reduces group-thinking – the positive correlation of biases within decision-making groups – and is thus an important source of epistemic strength" (Vermeule 2009, p. 11). In sum, legislators are "far more diverse," what gives them "clear epistemic advantages under the Condorcetian model" (Vermeule 2009, p. 90).

A "more diverse and more numerous institution," therefore, can "easily outperform a smaller and less diverse group of ultra-competent experts, such as the judicial system capped by a multimember appellate court" (Vermeule 2009, p. 12).

This calls for a defence of judicial formalism, even if this formalism is coupled with a more policy-permissive method of legal interpretation for legislatures and administrative agencies (Sunstein and Vermeule 2003, p. 925–932).

7.4 The Anti-Theoretical Claim as a Fallacy

Thus far we have seen two different anti-theoretical claims that may be regarded as fallacies in meta-interpretive disagreements within legal discourse.

Let us examine, first, the more ambitious version supported by Posner, who claims that (a) *no moral theory can provide a solid basis for any given moral judgment*, and (b) *no moral judgment, whether or not supported by a philosophical moral argument, can provide a solid basis for choosing between or among alternative legal interpretations.*

One of the merits of Vermeule's institutional theory of legal argumentation is that it rightly acknowledges that Posner's "everyday pragmatism" is an untenable position because it fails to provide a value theory – of any imaginable sort – to evaluate the "consequences" or "policies" which determine how legal judgments are to be passed (Vermeule 2006, pp. 52–59; 71–72; 83–85). According to Vermeule, "Posner wants to say that a pragmatic interpretation is one that produces better consequences, but Posner resolutely refuses to say what, in his view, counts as a good consequence" (Vermeule 2006, pp. 6–7).

The root of Posner's strong anti-theoretical claim lies, as we have seen, in his "everyday pragmatism," the most fundamental aim of which is to free legal reasoning from *any* philosophical or conceptual claim about how policy decisions should be made by practicing lawyers.

Pragmatism in this non-philosophical or anti-theoretical sense advises us to put away abstract theories of government, rights, legitimacy, democracy, or law and replace them with common sense and a "practical" sense of what is "workable" or "reasonable." As Dworkin observes, Posner does not want "to rest his own recommendations on any philosophical thesis: he regards his views of adjudication as free-standing" (Dworkin 2006, p. 60), but ends up defending "one of the most ambitious and technocratic absolutisms philosophers have ever devised" (Dworkin 2006, p. 73), since it is exposed to the following objection:

> Pragmatists argue that any moral principle must be assessed only against a practical standard: does adopting that principle help to make things better? But if they stipulate any particular social goal – any conception of when things are better – they undermine their claim, because that social goal could not itself be justified instrumentally without arguing in a circle … So moral pragmatism has seemed to many critics an empty theory: it encourages forward-looking efforts in search of a future it declines to describe (Dworkin 2006, p. 91).

With regards to this version of "pragmatism," Vermeule recognizes that Dworkin's objection is sound and that Posner's advocacy of a decision-making process that lacks any "general account of what makes some judicial decisions good and some bad" suffers from an "incorrigible vice" (Vermeule 2006, p. 72).

Furthermore, Posner's anti-theoretical attitude gets even more implausible because it is also, as Dworkin points out, "a *moral judgment* of a theoretical and global kind" (Dworkin 1998, p. 1725), that is, a strand of moral nihilism that is as theoretical as the substantive moral theories that Posner disqualifies. Instead of a thesis *about* morality, as it purports to be, Posner's strong anti-theoretical claim is a thesis *of* morality, for "if they [Posner's theses] were only 'about' morality, they would in no way contradict the opinions of his academic targets, whose work, so far as he objects to it, is entirely of the 'of' variety" (Dworkin 1998, p. 1720).

Posner's insistence that judges should avoid all philosophical issues in adjudication, by relying on his "everyday" or "non-philosophical" pragmatism and evaluating the consequences of the purported decision, boils down into what Dworkin has described as a "patent fallacy" (Dworkin 2000, p. 10), since "lawyers and judges must appeal to (or in any case make assumptions about) moral or political principles in order to decide whether the projected consequences of one decision are better than those of another" (Dworkin 2000, p. 10). Let us call this fallacy the Anti-Theoretical Fallacy.

The Anti-Theoretical Fallacy, in its *strong* form, can be classified as a performative contradiction, for Posner stakes a moral claim to prove that moral arguments in general are flawed, relying his own judgment on an implicit adherence to a moral argument.

As Alexy explains,

> A performative contradiction is contradiction in the classical sense. The performative character results from the fact that only one part of the contradiction stems from what is explicitly stated by performing the legal act, whereas the other part is implicit in the claim necessarily connected with the performance of this act. (...) It [a performative contradiction] is based on the classical concept of contradiction, which can be applied to law-making acts because those acts express and imply assertorial or propositional contents (Alexy 2000, p. 141).

The anti-theoretical claim, therefore, is a fallacy because "its conditions of success cannot possibly obtain" (Searle and Vanderveken 1985, p. 151), being an example of a performative contradiction or a "self-defeating illocutionary act."[5]

The *weak* version of the anti-theoretical claim is an attempt to circumvent this fallacy. When Vermeule constructs his empirical model for assessing interpretive capacities of institutions, he is forced to distinguish his consequentialism from Posner's model of pragmatic adjudication. The former "requires some value theory," even though this theory can remain implicit, while the latter "quite self-consciously lacks any value theory of the sort consequentialism must provide" (Vermeule 2006, p. 71).

Here I argue, however, that Vermeule's belief that meta-interpreters can bracket their theoretical positions, replacing them with some incompletely theorized agreement, does not avoid the Anti-Theoretical Fallacy.

In effect, Vermeule himself is ready to recognize that his appeal to incompletely theorized agreements is not entirely different from Posner's radically anti-theoretical jurisprudence, as we can see in the following attempt to reconstruct Posner's "everyday pragmatism":

> In a charitable spirit we might also construe Posner's everyday pragmatism as a form of consequentialism that rests upon a suppressed, implicit, but indispensable appeal to convergence on particulars across a range of value theories. If this is what Posner means, then everyday pragmatism is a perfectly valid version of consequentialism; indeed, it is the version I am suggesting here (Vermeule 2006, p. 85).

We can see, therefore, that Vermeule's agnostic position on the strength of moral theories in constitutional reasoning is nearly the same as Posner's.

---

[5] For Searle and Vanderveken, speech acts such as Posner's reliance on moral claims to hold that moral assumptions are ungrounded are logically inconsistent: "since a set of illocutionary acts is consistent if it is performable, no self-defeating illocutionary act is consistent" (Searle and Vanderveken 1985, p. 151).

In particular, I think that Vermeule is wrong to assume, without stating the reasons for this assumption, that it is acceptable to ground an account of constitutional interpretation on an incompletely theorized agreement of the participants of meta-interpretive debates. When he asserts that meta-interpretive disagreements can be resolved on the basis of an implicit or unstated value theory, he fails to acknowledge that this sceptical position on the role of theoretical accounts of legal argumentation is also a theoretical position that needs to be based on a normative argument, rather than on empirical findings alone.

Implicit in the view that one may resort to incompletely theorized agreements to vindicate a method of interpretation lies a *normative (and not purely empirical) assumption* which holds that an incompletely theorized agreement over the choice of an interpretive approach is *better* than any type of disagreement on these matters.

This implicit supposition is not unanimously accepted. One can argue, for instance, that an incompletely theorized decision is in general poorly justified, and that this is too high a price to pay in order to get an agreement.

To defend his position Vermeule needs a *moral* or *political* argument to establish the value of incompletely theorized agreements. Without this moral or political argument, he is not able to explain why it is more appropriate to reach a consensus about concrete outcomes than to benefit from the justificatory force of deliberation and principled argumentation.

In effect, Vermeule would violate Hume's Law, which forbids one from deriving an "ought" from an "is". He would be guilty of the Naturalistic Fallacy if he intended to derive the value of incompletely theorized agreement (a *norm*) merely from the *fact* that people can agree on the level of operating principles. In other words, Vermeule needs a normative foundation for his own advocacy of incompletely theorized agreements, and this normative foundation cannot be provided by his empiricist approach to legal argumentation.

Vermeule must justify, as well, the importance of achieving a general agreement about a method of legal or constitutional interpretation, since his own theoretical approach to legal reasoning advocates that numerosity and diversity are some of the major determinants of the epistemic performance of institutions (Vermeule 2009, p. 11). It might be argued, therefore, that a multi-member court will be better-off if its members approach a case with different interpretive strategies, rather than struggling to find a shallow agreement which hides the foundations of their decisions. Once again, he needs a moral or political basis to respond to this objection.

The view that empirical considerations can be *sufficient* to decide which interpretive approaches should be adopted will be arguing in circle if it fails to explain *why* incompletely theorized agreements are desirable. In effect, one cannot bracket the arguments necessary to support a thesis according to which theoretical arguments can be bracketed, for this thesis, as any other claim, is not able to validate itself.

Perhaps an example will help me to illustrate this point. Let us consider, for instance, Neil MacCormick's theory of legal reasoning, which asserts that the law is "an argumentative discipline," in the sense that "one's opinion about the strength of a case depends on an evaluation of the rival strength of competing sets of arguments" (MacCormick 2005, p. 15). This arguable character of law, for MacCormick, contributes to the development of the law and is "admirable in an open society" (MacCormick 2005, p. 16). Instead of being a "pathological excrescence," the disagreements over the "proper interpretation of legal materials" are regarded as an "integral element of the ideal of the rule of law" (MacCormick 2005, p. 27).

An advocate of MacCormick's theory of legal reasoning, thus, will not be troubled by the fact that there is disagreement over interpretive methods. She will regard this disagreement as good for the practice of legal reasoning and as an important source of rationality and legitimacy for the theories of legal interpretation, for she believes that the discourse in which people attempt to resolve it can help developing the law even when the disagreement remains. She will need a very powerful moral argument to give up her convictions and trade off the benefits of deliberation for the benefits generated by an incompletely theorized agreement.

As we can see, the value of incompletely theorized agreements is far from obvious. Thought Vermeule's advocacy of incompletely theorized agreements has an intuitive appeal, the value of this way of resolving disagreements is not object of a consensus. Dworkin, for instance, agrees with MacCormick and objects that bracketing the theories that one needs for grounding a legal argument implies the "the paralysis of a process essential to democracy" (Dworkin 2006, p. 73).

How could Vermeule respond to Dworkin or to the supporter of MacCormick's theory, if not with a moral or political argument?

To provide a solid basis for his view on meta-interpretive debates, Vermeule cannot avoid a high-level theory about rights, government, constitutionalism, democracy, the value of legality, the rule of law, or the nature of law and legal reasoning. His own interpretive theory must be grounded on a normative theory of the same kind as those that he thinks should be bracketed because they are allegedly inapt for choosing an interpretive strategy.

To claim that this moral theory can also remain implicit or bracketed will not do, for one can neither accept nor criticize Vermeule's account of legal interpretation without considering the moral argument that is missing. One cannot know whether incompletely theorized agreements are acceptable without considering the moral reasons for bracketing people's theoretical disagreements.

Hence, Vermeule's weak version of the anti-theoretical claim is an arbitrary position in its current form, which is exposed to the same sort of objection that dismantles Posner's pragmatic model of adjudication. It is self-defeating, and another victim of the Anti-Theoretical Fallacy.

7.5 The Argument Behind the Fallacy

One of the main features of Posner's everyday pragmatism is that his prejudice against jurisprudence and moral philosophy is compensated by a clear understanding of the importance of an *empiricist* approach to adjudication (Posner 2003, pp. 75–76).

By the same token, Vermeule's stance on meta-interpretive debates is based on the advocacy of empirical analysis to discover the interpretive capacities of legal institutions and the systemic effects of adopting an interpretive theory. Nevertheless, Vermeule's account is more specific than Posner's and states very clearly the premises of its anti-theoretical attitude.

Vermeule's anti-theoretical claim is based on the *rejection* of the views that (1) "a value theory is, all by itself, enough to yield operational conclusions about what judges ought to do," and that (2) "a commitment to any particular value theory is required in order to do institutional analysis at the operational level" (Vermeule 2006, p. 84). While the first thesis is dismissed because of the incompleteness of a purely conceptual analysis, the second is denied because incompletely theorized agreements over interpretive practices can lead the meta-interpreter to remain agnostic about the first-best accounts of interpretation that led the parties to sustain a particular interpretive approach.

One of the problems in Vermeule's reasoning is that by denying these two claims he presupposes an implausible separation between "pure" abstract value theories and "pure" empirical institutional analysis at the operational level. Though it is possible to imagine a purely abstract philosophical reasoning concerning the right and the good, no real-world theory about what judges and other officials ought to do is feasible without certain empirical assumptions about the capacities and the functions of real-world judges.

To stay with Vermeule's favourite target, we can think of Ronald Dworkin's justification of a moral reading of the constitution, which is accused of being blind to institutional considerations. The core of Dworkin's case for the moral reading of the constitution within judicial review lies on the distinction between "arguments of policy," which "justify a particular decision by showing that the decision advances or protects some collective goal of the community as a whole," and "arguments of principle," which "justify a political decision by showing that the decision respects or secures some individual or group right" which is based on a *moral* value that precedes and overrides any political compromise of the majority (Dworkin 1978, p. 82).

The key theoretical claims that Dworkin attempts to defend with the moral reading of the constitution are the submissions that:

> [1] Courts should make decisions of principle rather than policy – decisions about what rights people have under our constitutional system rather than decisions about how general welfare is best promoted – and that [2] it should make these decisions by elaborating and applying the substantive theory of representation taken from the root principle that government must treat people as equals (Dworkin 1985, p. 69).

These submissions, in turn, are based on the following empirical claims: (1) The majoritarian process – the political process that leads to a legislative decision – "encourages compromises that may subordinate important issues of principle" (Dworkin 1996, p. 30). (2) Judicial review is a "pervasive feature" or our political life, "because it forces political debate to include argument over principle, not only when a case comes to the Court but long before and long after" (Dworkin 1985,

p. 70). (3) "Individual citizens can in fact exercise moral responsibilities of citizenship better when final decisions involving constitutional values are removed from ordinary politics and assigned to courts, whose decisions are meant to turn on principle, not on the weight of numbers or the balance of political influence" (Dworkin 1996, p. 344).

These are all empirical claims about the "institutional capacities" and "systemic effects" in Vermeule's sense. They refer to consequences deeply related, but not limited, to the "cost of the decision-making" or the probability of (technical) errors, or the number of people who will actually make the decision. When Dworkin argues that judicial review forces the political debate to respect and discuss the moral rights of citizens in a more open and public way, or that individual citizens are forced to exercise their moral responsibilities better, he is giving us a decisive argument for authorizing judges to adopt a moral reading of the constitution, which is still an empirical argument, but one that is perfectly accommodated into the abstract theory of constitutional adjudication that Dworkin is offering for our consideration.

As one can see, even Dworkin's advocacy of a moral reading of the constitution by the Supreme Court is based on an intertwining of empirical and normative claims about the performance and the role of legal institutions and about how the law is to be constructed. If Vermeule is right when he concludes that this account fails in providing a good interpretive theory of law, it must be because its empirical assumptions are undemonstrated or poorly vindicated in factual evidence, rather than because it lacks empirical considerations or its operational conclusions are based on a purely idealistic value theory.

Although Vermeule is right to dismiss the assumption that an abstract value theory can, all by itself, yield operational conclusions about what judges ought to do, I think that he is wrong to argue that one can do relevant institutional analysis (at the operational level) without making theoretical judgments about how these institutions ought to behave.

The claim that empirical analysis might suffice for choosing an interpretive theory is flawed because any interpretive theory is, by definition, *normative*, and therefore requires a normative assumption as its starting point. It seems to me implausible to hold, therefore, that a purely empirical assessment of institutional issues suffices to resolve conflicts over interpretive approaches.

Yet, behind this anti-theoretical fallacy lies an important argument for better institutional analysis of the empirical kind, which is necessary to test the empirical assumptions of any given theory of legal interpretation.

To come back to our example, Dworkin's assumption that courts are a forum of principle may be challenged on the basis of Segal and Spaeth's "attitudinal theory of adjudication," which depicts judges as policy-makers rather than guardians of principle (Segal and Spaeth 2002, pp. 6–27).

According to the attitudinal theory, North American judges behave differently according to their political commitments and personal preferences:

> Justices and judges appointed by Democratic Presidents are predicted to vote disproportionately for 'liberal' outcomes, such as outcomes favouring employees, consumers, small businessmen, criminal defendants (other than white-collar defendants), labour unions, and

> civil liberties plaintiffs. Judges and Justices appointed by Republican Presidents are predicted to vote disproportionately for the opposite outcomes (Posner 2008, 20).

As it is visible, this is an empirical hypothesis that must be verified by the sort of institutional analysis that Vermeule is arguing for.

The real argument behind the anti-theoretical claim has nothing to do with its despise for philosophical or moral considerations in legal reasoning or in meta-interpretive theoretical disagreements. Underlying this fallacy there is an important warning for jurisprudents and practicing lawyers: *ceteris paribus*, the more an interpretive theory incorporates empirical research and is sensitive to factual findings, the more reliable such theory is.

The performance of a court depends on several empirical findings, including reliable statistical data about the sort of cases on which it adjudicates. If we distinguish between "autarkic cases," in which the law is "self-sufficient and inward-looking," and "nonautarkic cases," in which the law is "outward-looking" and "the legal right answer itself incorporates by reference nonlegal domains of knowledge" (Vermeule 2007, p. 1582), then it becomes extremely relevant, for instance, to gather information about several factors, such as (*i*) the frequency with which a constitutional court is faced with each class of cases, (*ii*) the systemic effects of the interpretive attitudes of the court, including the effects of formalism or anti-formalism in the performance of other institutions, (*iii*) the psychological factors and biases that may affect the court's decisions, and (*iv*) the error-costs of granting trained lawyers the power to decide on the basis of extra-legal considerations.

It may well be the case, for instance, that in hard cases where moral judgments are required "professional legal training confers no special advantage to lawyers" in finding the right answer, even though this answer is, "by incorporation into law, the right *legal* answer" (Vermeule 2007, p. 1585).

It might even be the case, as Vermeule argues, that constitutional courts could benefit from the presence of lay Justices who would be free from some of the professional biases of lawyers, which make them more vulnerable to adjudicate on highly controversial moral issues (Vermeule 2007, p. 1569).[6]

---

[6]On the basis of the works of Daicoff (2004), Hedegard (1979), Plumlee (1981) and others, Vermeule (2007, p. 1569) asserts that "it is clear from this literature that lawyers are, compared to people generally, more rational as opposed to emotional, more judgmental, more competitive, aggressive and materialistic" (Vermeule 2007, p. 1569). There are even empirical studies that conclude that legal training gives lawyers "a strong status quo orientation and a bias to conventional morality, as compared to similar educated adults" (Landwehr 1982, quoted by Vermeule 2007, p. 1569) and that legal training "reduces law student's general concern for social justice" (Kay 1978, quoted by Vermeule 2007, p. 1569). These studies move towards the same conclusions as Jeremy Waldron, who thinks that legislators are in a better position than judges to reason about moral issues that concern the whole society, since their reasoning is not constrained by existing texts, doctrines and precedents, and "members of the legislature talk directly to the issues involved, in a way that is mostly undistracted by legal doctrine or precedents" (Waldron 2009, p. 60). Controversial as these empirical claims might be, it is obviously correct that no reasonable theory of constitutional interpretation can either ignore them or neglect to respond to them with similar empirical claims that must be equally grounded on factual investigations.

The choice of a theory of legal or constitutional interpretation will depend as much on empirical evidence as it does on value judgments justified by philosophical considerations. Authors like Posner, Vermeule and Sunstein have successfully shown that no interpretive theory can turn its back on these empirical concerns. Nowadays, no-one can take legal interpretation seriously without paying attention to the kind of empirical institutional analysis that Vermeule is arguing for, and this "institutional turn" is an extraordinary achievement for jurisprudence.

7.6 Conclusion

To conclude, both versions of the anti-theoretical claim are fallacious. On the one hand, the strong version claims that no moral theory can provide a solid basis for a legal judgment, but relies on an implicit moral theory to vindicate this claim. On the other hand, the weak version acknowledges that any form of consequentialism requires some value theory, but holds that in controversial cases these theories may be bracketed on the basis of an incompletely theorized agreement. But the very assumption that one does not need a commitment to any particular theory to do institutional analysis is flawed because it entails both a moral position in favour of relying on incompletely theorized agreements and a sceptical position on the role played by value theories in choosing between or among theories of constitutional reasoning, which are also *theoretical* positions that need to be justified, at least in part, on the basis of a normative argument, rather than empirical findings alone.

In both of its versions the anti-theoretical claim is self-defeating. Yet, the advocates of the anti-theoretical claim have a strong argument for grounding the choice of an interpretive approach also on empirical evidence, rather than relying exclusively on abstract philosophical theories. What they have, at the end of the day, is an argument about how normative legal theories should be, rather than an argument against normative legal theory.

References

Alexy, Robert. 2000. On the thesis of a necessary connection between law and morality: Bulygin's critique. *Ratio Juris* 13: 138–147.

Bustamante, Thomas. 2013. Comment on Gyorfi – Dworkin, Vermeule and Gyorfi on constitutional interpretation: Remarks on a meta-interpretive disagreement. *German Law Journal* 14: 1109–1146. Available at http://www.germanlawjournal.com. Accessed 5 Dec 2013.

Daicoff, Susan Swaim. 2004. *Lawyer, know thyself – A psychological analysis of personality strengths and weaknesses*. Washington, DC: American Psychological Association.

Dworkin, Ronald. 1978. *Taking rights seriously*, 2nd ed. Cambridge, MA: Harvard University Press.

Dworkin, Ronald. 1985. *A matter of principle*. Cambridge, MA: Harvard University Press.

Dworkin, Ronald. 1996. *Freedom's law – The moral reading of the American constitution*. Cambridge, MA: Harvard University Press.

Dworkin, Ronald. 1998. Darwin's new bulldog. *Harvard Law Review* 111: 1718–1738.
Dworkin, Ronald. 2000. Philosophy and Monica Lewinsky (review of An Affair of State: The Investigation, Impeachment and Trial of President Clinton, by Richard Posner, and The Problematics of Moral and Legal Theory, by Richard Posner). *The New York Review of Books*, March 9, 2000.
Dworkin, Ronald. 2006. *Justice in robes*. Cambridge, MA: Belknap.
Hedegard, James M. 1979. The impact of legal education: An in-depth examination of career-relevant interests, attitudes and personality traits among first-year law students. *Law and Society Inquiry* 4: 791–868.
Kay, Susan Ann. 1978. Socializing the future elite: The nonimpact of law school. *Social Science Quarterly* 59: 347–354.
Landwehr, Lawrence J. 1982. Lawyers as social progressives or reactionaries: The law and order cognitive orientation of lawyers. *Law and Psychology Review* 7: 39.
MacCormick, Neil. 2005. *Rhetoric and the rule of law*. Oxford: Oxford University Press.
Plumlee, John P. 1981. Lawyers as Bureaucrats: The impact of legal training in higher civil service. *Public Administration Review* 41: 220–228.
Posner, Richard. 1990. *The problems of jurisprudence*. Cambridge, MA: Harvard University Press.
Posner, Richard. 1992. *Sex and reason*. Cambridge, MA: Harvard University Press.
Posner, Richard. 1998. The problematics of moral and legal theory. *Harvard Law Review* 111: 1637–1717.
Posner, Richard. 2003. *Law, pragmatism and democracy*. Cambridge, MA: Harvard University Press.
Posner, Richard. 2008. *How judges think*. Cambridge, MA: Harvard University Press.
Searle, John R., and Daniel Vanderveken. 1985. *Foundations of illocutionary logic*. Cambridge: Cambridge University Press.
Segal, Jeffrey A., and Harold J. Spaeth. 2002. *The Supreme Court and the attitudinal model revisited*. Cambridge: Cambridge University Press.
Sunstein, Cass. 1999. *One case at a time – Judicial minimalism on the Supreme Court*. Cambridge, MA: Harvard University Press.
Sunstein, Cass. 2001. *Designing democracy – What constitutions do*. Oxford: Oxford University Press.
Sunstein, Cass, and Adrian Vermeule. 2003. Interpretation and institutions. *Michigan Law Review* 101: 885–951.
Vermeule, Adrian. 2006. *Judging under uncertainty – An institutional theory of legal interpretation*. Cambridge, MA: Harvard University Press.
Vermeule, Adrian. 2007. Should we have lay justices? *Stanford Law Review* 59: 1569–1611.
Vermeule, Adrian. 2009. *Law and the limits of reason*. Oxford: Oxford University Press.
Waldron, Jeremy. 2009. Do judges reason morally? In *Expounding the constitution – Essays in constitutional theory*, ed. Grant Huscroft, 38–64. Cambridge: Cambridge University Press.

Chapter 8
Frames of Interpretations and the Container-Retrieval View: Reflections on a Theoretical Contest

Pierluigi Chiassoni

Abstract Interpretive argumentation is saddled with uncertainty. The predicament is brought about by the presence of competing theories concerning the very notions of legal interpretation and general written-law norms. The paper describes and compares two theories: the frames of interpretations theory and the container-retrieval theory (in its conventional linguistic meaning variety). By means of a critical survey, the frames of interpretations theory will be defended as being both immune from a pretended capital flaw (the impossibility of tracing a clear-cut distinction between explicit and implicit norms), and preferable as a theory of written norms, interpretation, and argumentation, on the three counts of conformity to juristic commonsense, ideological neutrality, and conceptual adequacy.

8.1 A Puzzle for the Theory of Interpretive Argumentation

It is commonplace sorting out two main kinds of argumentation in law: evidentiary argumentation and interpretive argumentation. The former concerns statements about the relevant facts to a lawsuit (like, e.g., "John Smith stabbed Henry Doe to death"), and is typically deployed for claiming such statements to be "true", "false", "established beyond any reasonable doubt", "utterly (un)sound", etc. The latter concerns interpretive sentences (like, e.g., "Section Y of the Traffic code expresses the norm N_i", "The term 'T' in section Z of the Civil code refers to $C_1 \ldots C_n$"), and is typically deployed for claiming such sentences to be "correct", "right", "wrong", "true", "false", etc.

As soon as we move from the needs of ordinary law-jobs to the more demanding requirements of legal theory, however, the very notion and scope of interpretive argumentation appear saddled with uncertainty: What exactly does a piece of

P. Chiassoni (✉)
Istituto Tarello per la Filosofia del Diritto, Università di Genova,
Via Balbi 30, 16126 Genova, GE, Italy
e-mail: pierluigi.chiassoni@unige.it

© Springer International Publishing Switzerland 2015
T. Bustamante, C. Dahlman (eds.), *Argument Types and Fallacies in Legal Argumentation*, Law and Philosophy Library 112,
DOI 10.1007/978-3-319-16148-8_8

interpretive argumentation amount to? How can we tell genuine interpretive argumentation tokens from spurious ones? When is a purported instance of interpretive argumentation really "interpretive"?

Clearly, all such questions point to a boundary problem involving momentous jurisprudential issues like the proper concept and theory of legal interpretation, and the proper theory of legal norms, in so far as it intertwines with the former.

My purpose in this paper is describing and comparing two theories, both within the province of analytical jurisprudence (they have in fact very easily recognizable "godfathers" in such a line of inquiry), that provide alternative views about legal interpretation, written-law norms and interpretive argumentation. They are the frames of interpretations theory, on the one hand, and the container-retrieval theory (in its conventional linguistic meaning variety), on the other.[1]

Supporters of the container-retrieval theory suggest their view cannot be reasonably resisted by supporters of the frames of interpretations theory.[2] By a critical survey of both theories, I will bring to the fore a few arguments for considering the resistance to the container-retrieval theory as being by all means reasonable: indeed, a theoretical "must".

8.2 The Frames of Interpretations Theory

The frames of interpretations theory (hereafter, for brevity sake: "frames theory") is an interpretive (or "interpretivist") legal theory within analytical Kelsenian realism. It considers interpretation to be a key activity that intervenes at all crucial points in the working of "our" legal systems. It claims, accordingly, that the terminology and conceptual apparatus of a useful legal theory should accommodate to the pivotal role interpretation plays in legal experiences; it suggests that theoretical concepts, to be adequate, must be either *interpretation-dependent* (they must so far as possible bear a conceptual connection to interpretation), or *salva interpretatione* (they must openly rule out such a connection to some valuable theoretical purpose at hand).

The following components have to be considered in order to provide an account of the frames theory suitable to a comparison with the container-retrieval view: (1) the distinction between authoritative legal sentences, explicit norms, and implicit norms; (2) the distinction between interpretation and integration ("juristic

[1] The idea of staging a contest between the "frames of interpretations" theory and the "container-retrieval" theory came to me from a discussion on a book by R. Guastini (Guastini 2011), recently edited by V. Velluzzi (Velluzzi 2013b, 73–136), with essays by V. Velluzzi (Velluzzi 2013a, 73–76), G. Pino (Pino 2013, 77–101); E. Diciotti (Diciotti 2013, 103–123) and a reply by R. Guastini (Guastini 2013, 125–136). There, the usual terminology is employed and old characters are around. I thought worthwhile the experiment of upsetting terminology and disguising old characters; furthermore, the frames of interpretations theory does not correspond philologically to the theory of any individual author in that debate. It is, if you like, my own rendering and reconstruction of a set of ideas I deem worthwhile considering.

[2] Diciotti (2013, 118–122).

construction", "juristic law-finding", "juristic law-making"); (3) the argumentative conception of legal interpretation and integration; (4) the conception of interpretive and integrative argumentation as institutional games; (5) the distinction between practical and cognitive interpretation; (6) the twin claims of universal methodological ambiguity and potential axiological ambiguity; (7) the idea of general norms of written-law as frames of interpretations, with the related minimalist conception of "written law".

(1) The theories of law set forth by naïf normativism describe positive legal orders as normative orders: as discrete sets of interrelated *norms*. From their standpoint, the elementary, atomic component making up the law is the norm. As soon as we shift to the interpretive perspective advocated by the frames theory, however, the elementary, atomic notion of norm is to be replaced by three related notions: the notion of authoritative legal sentence, the notion of explicit norm, and the notion of implicit norm. *Authoritative legal sentences* (normative sentences, norm-formulations, or, for brevity sake, "legal clauses") are sentences enacted by law-making authorities; they make up the elementary components of such documents as written constitutions, charters, international treaties and covenants, civil and criminal codes, statutes, executive regulations, etc. *Explicit norms* are normative sentences (in the broadest sense of the phrase) that represent the meaning of a legal clause. *Implicit norms* are normative sentences which, by definition, are not the meaning of any legal clause, but can nonetheless be considered as components of a legal order by means of some "approved" method of identification (to this point I will come back in a moment).
(2) The notions of legal clause, explicit norm and implicit norm are interpretation-dependent. They all bear a conceptual connection to interpretation. Legal clauses are authoritatively enacted sentences that represent the matter of interpretation. Explicit norms are the meanings of legal clauses; they are identified by interpreting legal clauses: they are dependent variables of interpretation or interpretation-outputs. Implicit norms are normative sentences that cannot be identified by means of interpretation, but only by resorting to other approved methods.

The activity of interpretation – the matter of which are legal clauses and the outputs of which are explicit norms – as it is usually performed by judges, other legal officials, jurists and lawyers at large is *interpretation proper to practical purpose* (*practical interpretation proper*): it determines the "correct" ("proper", "true", "right") meaning of a legal clause; it translates a legal clause into the "correct" ("proper", "true", "right") explicit norm, either in view of deciding a lawsuit (judicial interpretation), or in view of affecting such a decision (forensic interpretation), or else in view of providing the "right" solution to an abstract *quaestio juris* (juristic interpretation). It is, in any case, a will-geared, decision-making activity: it decides for a meaning as "the correct" meaning of a legal clause, at the same time tacitly or expressly ruling out alternative possible meanings as "uncorrect".

By contrast whenever, for instance, a judge identifies an implicit norm in view of deciding a lawsuit, by definition such an activity of hers is not (practical) interpretation (proper): it is rather a piece of *law integration*; indeed, she determines the "proper" ("correct", "true") implicit norm to be applied to a case at hand, presupposing explicit norms have run out.

(3) Practical interpretation proper and integration, in their external, public, dimensions, are both – actually or at least potentially – *argumentative activities*.

Indeed, practical interpretation proper, according to the definition I have just offered, does not consist in translating a legal clause into an explicit norm whatsoever. It consists, rather, in providing "the correct" ("proper", "true", "right") translation of a legal clause: it consists, more precisely, in translating a legal clause into an explicit norm and presenting such a norm as "the correct" meaning of the clause to some practical purpose, on the ground of a (purportedly) adequate set of contextually formulated arguments. The arguments which may be used to justify such operations are *interpretive* arguments (like, e.g., the literal meaning, legislative intent, and teleological arguments). The argumentative apparatus may be dispensed with any time the explicit norm at hand is such a matter of course in the legal culture of the time that no argument is needed. This does not mean, however, that arguments cannot be provided, if necessary: for instance, to show a young lawyer which arguments a judge could deploy in favour of a usually never-argued-for explicit norm they commonly apply in their decisions.
Like remarks apply to integration, the results of which are (liable to be) supported by some set of *integration* arguments (like, e.g., integrative uses of analogical, *a contrario*, *a fortiori* or general principle reasoning).

(4) The activities of practical interpretation proper and integration, as they are actually performed by judges, lawyers and jurists, are tantamount to playing legally specific *argumentative games*. They are played by licensed players (judges, attorney at law, legal scholars). They are played by selecting discrete sets of tools out of a tool-box that is usually provided by the methodological tradition and is expressly or tacitly "approved" by the law.

Interpretive arguments are built upon interpretive directives: for instance, any literal argument concerning a piece of legislation has its ground and starting point in a directive like "Statutory clauses should be interpreted according to their literal meaning".[3] The discrete set of interpretive directives licensed players select and employ to present a norm as "the correct" meaning of a legal clause is an interpretive code.
The basic rule of the interpretive argumentation game runs, roughly, as follows: "Employ the interpretive code that enables you to deploy the best set of arguments in view of presenting the interpretive output you set forth as the only correct one for the case at hand".

[3] The first legal theorist who set the focus on "interpretive directives" is J. Wróblewski. See, e.g., Wróblewski (1992), chap. VII.

An interpretive code, as a tool for justifying interpretive outcomes, is typically made of three sorts of interpretive directives: primary translation directives, secondary procedural directives, and secondary preferential directives.[4]

Primary translation directives are instructions pointing to resources (empirical data, actual or imaginary pieces of information, actual or conjectural ingredients of the legal order and legal experience) by means of which a legal clause should be translated into some explicit norm. We may single out five different types of translation directives: (1) directives of linguistic interpretation (e.g., "Statutory clauses should be interpreted according to the ordinary linguistic meaning of their expressions at the time of their enactment"); (2) directives of intentional or genetic interpretation (e.g., "Statutory clauses should be interpreted according to the original semantic intention of the historical legislator"; "Statutory clauses should be interpreted according to the counter-factual semantic intention of the historical legislator"); (3) directives of teleological interpretation (e.g., "Statutory clauses should be given the meaning pointed out for them by the objective purpose they serve"); (4) directives of authoritative interpretation (e.g., "Statutory clauses should be given the meaning established for them by the Supreme Court"); (5) directives of substantive, normative-ethics, interpretation (e.g., "Statutory clauses should be given the meaning pointed out for them by the critical morality they refer to").

Secondary procedural directives are instructions pointing to the order that should be followed while deploying arguments from primary translation directives (e.g., "Deploy first an argument from primary directive PD1, and then from primary directive PD2, and then ...").

Secondary preferential directives, finally, are instructions pointing to the criteria that should be adopted to justify: (a) the ruling out of a given interpretive outcome (proposed, for instance, by the counsel of the plaintiff), as being "incorrect" in itself or by comparison with a different, "more correct" outcome (proposed, say, by the counsel of the defendant or by the judge); (b) the acceptance of a given interpretive outcome as all-things considered "correct". Secondary preferential directive typically include so-called "systematic (interpretive) arguments" (like, e.g., the argument from coherence and the argument from completeness: "Statutory clauses should not be given any meaning logically incompatible with constitutional principles", "Statutory clauses should not be given any meaning teleologically incompatible with the fundamental principles of the legal system", "Statutory clauses should be given the meaning, among the several ones identified by means of primary directives PD_1 ... PD_n, that is most instrumentally in tune with the requirements of fundamental principles", "Statutory clauses should not be given any meaning showing the law to be incomplete as to the case at hand", etc.).

One last remark seems in order, before proceeding. The methodological tradition (and the legal clauses that sometimes purport somehow to "approve" it) usually provide lawyers with a disordered set of indeterminate interpretive directives. Accordingly, when lawyers use interpretive codes to justify some interpretive

[4] Interpretive codes may also be used as heuristic devices: as tools for *getting to* the correct meaning of legal clauses. In such case, they belong to the "internal" stage of legal interpretation.

outcome (i.e., some explicit norm), such codes are often made of directives they themselves have somehow shaped, sharpened, made more precise as to the interpretive resources to be used, and put in the "proper" order. Fatally, such a shaping, sharpening, resource-selecting and ordering is likely to mirror, and be affected by, each lawyer's own methodological attitude, ideological stance and material interests. This suggests the following conclusion: the selection and use of an interpretive code by a lawyer interpreting a legal clause, i.e., playing the interpretive argumentation game, is a discretionary, value-laden, activity. This is one of the reasons – perhaps, the main reason – why, as I said before, practical interpretation proper ("textual interpretation", "adjudicative interpretation") is, according to the frames theory, a will-geared, decision-making activity. The same remarks apply to the game of law integration.

(5) Generally speaking, interpretation proper may be defined as any activity consisting in translating legal clauses into explicit norms. Explicit norms are norms that, on the ground of some interpretive code, may be presented as the correct legal meanings of a legal clause.

So far, we have considered the practical variety of interpretation proper: i.e., interpretation to practical purpose. However there are at least two further varieties of interpretation proper, not to practical purpose (at least: not directly and immediately so), but *to theoretical or cognitive purpose* (*cognitive interpretation proper*). These are the varieties of conjectural interpretation and creative interpretation.

While dealing with conjectural interpretation it is worthwhile distinguishing, in turn, two (sub)varieties: methodological conjectural interpretation and axiological conjectural interpretation.[5]

Methodological conjectural interpretation consists in laying bare, as to a given moment *t*', the meanings that can be ascribed to a legal clause (say, LC_i), on the ground of the interpretive directives the legal culture considers as "required" or "approved" "by the law".[6] In so doing, the interpreter must avoid qualifying any of such meanings as "the only correct" ("true", "right", "just") meaning of the legal clause. Rather, she should limit herself to working out a dispassionate inventory of meanings. This can be a minimal or a maximal inventory: in the latter case, she will claim it to account for (almost) *all* the methodologically viable meanings of legal clause LC_i, to exhaust the hermeneutical potentialities of LC_i, having reached, so to speak, the ultimate frontier of its possible meanings. The process of methodological conjectural interpretation may be recounted, tentatively, as including four stages.

In the first stage, the interpreter must identify the *set of allowed interpretive directives* (techniques, methods, criterions, rules) that may be considered as required

[5] The original source of these remarks is obviously the Kelsenian notion of "scientific interpretation" (see Kelsen (1960, chap. VIII).

[6] There may be methodological disputes in a legal culture as to the methods to be considered as "approved" by the law. In such cases, conjectural interpreters must record and take into account them in their inquiries.

or allowed by the law and/or the legal culture, in view of interpreting LC_i [$SAID_{t'} = ID_1, ID_2 \ldots ID_n$].

In the second stage, the interpreter must identify the set of possible combinations of interpretive directives, i.e., the *set of allowed interpretive codes* [$SAIC_{t'} = IC_1, IC_2 \ldots IC_r$].

In the third stage, the interpreter must identify, for each of the several interpretive codes previously singled out [$SAIC_{t'} = IC_1, IC_2 \ldots IC_r$], the related set(s) of interpretive resources [$SR_1, SR_2 \ldots SR_p$].

In the fourth, and last, stage, the interpreter must conjecture (calculate) the *set of meanings* that can be ascribed to the legal clause LC_i, from the standpoint of the several combinations of allowed interpretive codes and related sets of interpretive resources [$SMLC_i = EN_1$ [$f(IC_1, SR_1)$], EN_2 [$f(IC_2, SR_{2'})$] … EN_r [$f(IC_r, SR_r)$]. The set of alternative meanings so identified for the same legal clause LC_i – or, in other words, the set of alternative explicit norms ($EN_1 \ldots EN_i$) into which LC_i can be translated – makes up the "frame" of possible interpretations of LC_i. Each of those meanings is a methodologically correct meaning: i.e., it is correct, by hypothesis, from a purely methodological point of view.

Axiological conjectural interpretation represents a variety of methodological conjectural interpretation. Here, the interpreter aims at identifying, not just the methodological interpretive frame of a legal clause (say, LC_i), but its axiological interpretive frame. Such a frame depends not only on the interpretive methods and resources available, but also on social axiology: more precisely, on the ethical views prevailing, or in any case recordable as being influential, in the society. These views may make a methodologically viable interpretive outcome unviable, for reasons having to do with the prevailing negative substantive social value of such an outcome.[7] Accordingly, the scope of the axiological frame is likely to be narrower than the scope of the methodological frame.[8]

Creative interpretation consists, finally, in the identification of one or more meanings for a given legal clause (say LC_i) that, by hypothesis, are outside of its current methodological frame. Creative interpretation is a conjecture about "new" meanings for existing legal clauses, which can be grounded on some "new" interpretive directive that, by hypothesis, is not so far part of the available stock. Also in this case, the interpreter does not claim the "new" meanings she conjectures to be the only correct ones. She just wishes to point out some way of moving forward the frontier of the hermeneutic possibilities of a legal clause.

Conjectural interpretation and creative interpretation are interpretation proper, according to the broad definition I provided a moment ago. This is so since interpreters purport to show how legal clauses can be interpreted, and do provide

---

[7] For instance, a methodologically viable interpretation of a marriage clause to the effect of covering same-sex marriage may be unviable – i.e., likely to be considered "wrong" and rejected – from the standpoint of prevailing social axiology.

[8] Of course, a legal culture may be axiologically diversified. This is a sociological datum to be recorded and taken into account. Competing social axiologies may not exhaust the set of methodologically viable interpretations of a given legal clause.

interpretations for them, if only by way of hypothesis and without any (immediate) practical commitment. They are however cognitive forms of interpretation proper: they only bring to the fore the hermeneutic possibilities of legal clauses, and, by doing so, they are by design unable to settle any interpretive issue whatsoever. That further task needs an act of will, selecting one of the meanings in the frame as "the only correct one"; this is what goes on when interpreters play the practical interpretation game.[9]

The distinction between cognitive and practical interpretation can be gathered from the logical forms of their discourses.

The logical form of the discourse of practical interpretation runs roughly as follows:

To the purpose of providing a legally right answer to *quaestio iuris* QJ_i, the legally correct meaning of legal clause LC_i is explicit norm EN_i, as it is proved by interpretive arguments $IA_1 \ldots IA_n$, which are grounded on the correct interpretive code IC_i and the correct set of interpretive resources SR_i.

Contrariwise, the logical form of the discourse of conjectural interpretation in its methodological variety runs roughly as follows:

By way of methodological conjecture, legal clause LC_i can be interpreted, here and now, as capable of being translated (at least) into the following explicit norms: EN_1 [f (IC_1, SR_1)], *or* EN_2 [f (IC_2, SR_2)], *or* EN_4 [f (IC_4, SR_4)], … *or* EN_m [f (IC_m, SR_m)].

(6) The distinction between methodological and axiological conjectural interpretation, and the related distinction between the methodological and the axiological conjectural frames of the meanings of any given legal clause, suggest two claims that are paramount to the frames theory: the *universal methodological ambiguity* claim and the *potential axiological ambiguity* claim. According to the former, ambiguity of legal clauses is universal from a purely methodological standpoint: from the standpoint of the tools available in our methodological tradition, *every* legal clause is fraught with ambiguity; every legal clause is capable of different, alternative, readings (between the extremes of the broadest and the narrowest interpretation, passing through shades of ordinary meaning and defeasibility). According to the latter, ambiguity of legal clauses is potential from the standpoint of social axiology: not all the methodologically viable readings of a legal clause are at the same time viable (acceptable, right, proper) from the standpoint of prevailing, influent, social values and normative attitudes. This explains why there are easy interpretive cases: why lawyers consider certain interpretations of certain legal clauses as "settled" or "a matter of course".[10]

[9] Of course, an interpreter may choose to settle for what she knows to be an axiologically unviable interpretive-output, if only to challenge social orthodoxy and further its demise.

[10] To the purpose of the present paper, methodological ambiguity is not tantamount to linguistic ambiguity or "ambiguity proper". Not every legal clause, being methodologically ambiguous, is linguistically ambiguous.

(7) We are used to think that legislatures "produce" norms. From the perspective of the frames theory, however, such a commonplace view can be accepted only upon condition of making a few refinements. Surely, what legislatures do produce are statutory and constitutional *texts*: they produce sets of legal clauses that are the matter of statutory and constitutional interpretation. Do legislatures also produce statutory and constitutional *norms*? According to the frames theory, such a question is not for a simple answer. Statutory and constitutional interpretation, as you may recall, is an argumentative game. Which norm(s), if any, a statutory or constitutional clause does express depends on how the interpretive argumentation game is being played in a legal order – and this mirrors in turn contingent normative and methodological attitudes in the legal profession and the society at large. So, from the perspective of the frames theory, the only proper answer to that question runs as follows: legislators surely produce authoritative texts (documents made of legal clauses); legal clauses, on the ground of the interpretive directives "approved" in a legal culture, are usually capable of expressing frames of interpretations, sets of alternative explicit norms for each legal clause. Accordingly, if we stay with the idea of legislatures that "produce norms", we need to make clear that the norms they produce are frame-norms: a text plus the set of its methodologically and/or axiologically viable interpretations, as performed by licensed interpreters. These remarks hold, of course, for any other variety of so-called written law. Supporters of the frames theory hold a minimalist, counter-intuitive, view of written law.

8.3 The Container-Retrieval Theory

I said at the outset that, though it may sound a paradox, the very notion of interpretive argumentation is saddled with uncertainty. This is so because of a boundary problem: legal theorists do not agree upon the "right" way to draw the conceptual line between legal interpretation "proper" ("properly so-called", "properly and exactly conceived", etc.), on the one hand, and what lays beyond and outside of legal interpretation "proper", being instead tantamount to "law integration", "law making proper", "juristic construction", "juristic law-making", etc., on the other hand.

We have just seen how the frames theory proposes to draw such a line. That is not the only way to do so, however. Another way consists in adopting what can be regarded as a *container-view* of authoritative legal sentences (like, e.g., constitutional and statutory clauses); this view goes along with, and is matched by, a *retrieval-view* of interpretation proper. The key tenets of the container-retrieval theory, as we may call it for brevity sake, may be recounted as follows:

1. each authoritative legal sentence, each legal clause, contains a set of legal norms;
2. legal interpretation in a proper sense is, accordingly, the activity that consists in retrieving the legal norms contained in a legal clause (usually, one norm);
3. the legal norms of the normative set contained in a legal clause are *explicit* legal norms: they are the norms actually *expressed* by that text;

4. a legal norm that is not contained in any legal clause cannot by definition be identified by interpretation proper; its identification must consequently be the output of an activity of a different kind: namely, of some instance of law integration, juristic law making, juristic construction, etc.;
5. any such legal norm is an *implicit* norm: it is a norm that is not expressed by any legal clause, but can be identified and supported only by means of some form of reasoning from previously identified norms.[11]

The container-retrieval theory of interpretation is grounded on commonsense. Furthermore, it seems to provide a simple and working solution to the boundary problem we are considering.

Unfortunately, the appearance of simplicity and working virtue is tricky. Authoritative legal sentences are *not* containers, after all: they are linguistic entities, i.e., grammatically patterned strings of written words. It must be observed, as a consequence, that the container-retrieval theory provides a metaphorical account of legal texts and their interpretation. Metaphors are potentially misleading contrivances. Is there any viable way of showing the container-retrieval metaphor to be good to theoretical purpose?

It is here, apparently, that comes the conventional linguistic meaning variety I mentioned at the outset. It makes two basic claims in support of the container-retrieval metaphor.[12]

First, legal clauses *are* like containers after all: they are sentences in a natural language; hence, they contain the conventional linguistic meanings pointed out by the grammatical and semantic rules of that language.

Second, the conventional linguistic meanings of legal clauses are *the only* meanings properly "contained in" legal texts: they are the exclusive sort of meanings being "in the legal texts", "going along" with them, being "carried" or "expressed" by them, comes what it may.

It is worthwhile considering a few of the other key tenets of the conventional meaning variety of the container-retrieval theory. This will make possible appreciating how much that theory differs from the frames theory.

1′. If – as it is worthwhile doing – we consider legal interpretation proper as consisting *mainly* (this qualification will be made clear in a moment) in the retrieval of the meanings contained in legal clauses, provided there is only one

---

[11] A container-retrieval view like the one I consider in the text is apparently endorsed, e.g., by Diciotti (2013, 103–124), at 105 ff. Here and in other parts of my paper I will use Diciotti's views, as I see them, as endowed with exemplary value to the purpose of my argument.

[12] The archetype of the container-retrieval view in contemporary jurisprudence is usually located in chap. VII of Hart (1961). For a similar view of more recent cast see Soames (2007). In Hart (1967, 105–108) and Hart (1983, 7–8), Hart avows his former view was an "oversimplification", and makes clear that the determinate meaning of legal rules may depend not only on linguistic conventions, but also on the "special conventions on the legal use of words" and on interpretive techniques (like, e.g., resort to "the obvious or agreed purpose of a rule"). Apparently, in his rejection of a purely "retrieval conception" of legal interpretation, Joseph Raz goes along the same line as the "second" Hart. See Raz (2009), part III.

kind of meanings properly contained by legal clauses (i.e., conventional linguistic meanings), legal interpretation proper is basically the retrieval of the conventional linguistic meanings of legal clauses.

2′. Conventional linguistic meanings of legal clauses represent the objective meanings of legal clauses: they are "in there". Accordingly, legal interpretation proper is basically a cognitive activity: it basically consists in coming to know the objective meanings contained in legal clauses by means of grammatical and semantic rules of the relevant natural language.

3′. Provided explicit norms are the meanings of legal clauses, and provided legal clauses properly contain only one kind of meanings, i.e., objective linguistic meanings, explicit norms, properly considered, are tantamount to the objective, linguistic meanings of legal clauses.

4′. Provided explicit norms are objective meanings contained in legal clauses, provided they go along with legal clauses, comes what it may, the commonsense view according to which "legislatures produce norms" is by no means the result of a collective hallucination or self-deception. Legislatures do produce norms: they produce, more precisely, the explicit norms contained in the legal clauses they enact.

5′. Explicit norms, being the linguistic meaning of sentences in a natural language, may be defective. First, they may be indeterminate (ambiguous, vague, open textured); second, they may be determinate, but practically inadequate (because of over-inclusion, under-inclusion, or even flat incompatibility with superior norms).

6′. Whenever an explicit norm is defective because of linguistic indeterminacy, its simple "fixing up" is still to be regarded as legal interpretation proper. In such a case, however, interpretation is not anymore just a matter of cognition; it is, rather, a matter of decision (stipulation). In order still to stay within the borders of interpretation proper, such decision must consist: *either* in opting for one of the explicit norms simultaneously expressed by an ambiguous legal clause; *or* in making a vague explicit norm (more) precise, by including or excluding from its scope some class of objects dwelling in the penumbra of its reference. This qualification explains why legal interpretation proper is to be conceived *mainly* as a retrieval, cognitive job (see point 1′ above).

7′. Whatever activity does differ, either from the simple retrieval, or from the fixing up, of the objective, linguistic meaning of legal clauses, is not, by definition, legal interpretation proper. It is rather law integration ("juristic construction"), even though it may present itself as an activity purporting to translate a legal clause into an explicit norm ("the true", "the correct" explicit norm expressed by the clause). For instance, any activity by means of which an interpreter corrects (amends) some explicit norm deemed to be "under-inclusive" or "over-inclusive" is not interpretation proper but, rather, law integration; its outcomes are not explicit norms proper, but implicit norms "read into" the legal clause.

8′. The scope of interpretive argumentation proper is to be conceived in narrow terms: actually, it basically amounts to the deployment of linguistic arguments. Accordingly, the bulk of what the frames of interpretations theory regards as "interpretive argumentation" is properly to be regarded as *integrative argumentation*, by which lawyers amend or put aside legislatures' explicit norms.

9′. Conjectural interpretation, in so far as it goes beyond identifying the conventional, linguistic meanings of a legal clause, really is *conjectural integration*: the laying down of the several possibilities of amending or putting aside explicit norms available, from either a methodological or an axiological standpoint.

8.4 Frames Theory v. Conventional Meaning Container-Retrieval View

To supporters of the frames theory, the conventional linguistic meaning variety of the container-retrieval view appears objectionable. In the following, I will consider a few reasons why it is so.

1. *Ab posse ad esse non valet consequentia.* The conventional meaning variety insists, as we have seen, that legal clauses really are like containers. They are so, because they are natural language sentences; as a consequence, they have an obvious, "natural", objective *legal* content, represented by their conventional linguistic meaning. Such a line of argument, however, is flawed. Surely, legal clauses are sentences formulated by legal authorities using words and grammatical patterns borrowed from a natural language. Surely, we can read legal clauses as if they were just ordinary sentences of a natural language. Surely, we can maintain that the legally proper meaning of legal clauses, being sentences in a natural language, is their conventional meaning. Surely, the conventional meaning of legal clauses can be their legally proper meaning, at least *prima facie*. However, *ab posse ad esse non valet consequentia*: from the fact that it *can* be so, it does not follow that it is, or must be, so. This further step – from the statement that legal clauses are made out of the materials of a natural language, to the conclusion that their proper *legal* meaning is their ordinary linguistic meaning – is *not* warranted unless we add some further premise: like, e.g., the premise that the proper legal meaning of legal clauses depends on (the nature of) the language that has been used to formulate them; that whoever uses a natural language wishes his sentences to be understood according to the grammar and lexicon of that language, and has a legitimate claim to that, commanding respect; that legal authorities must be presumed to want their clauses to be interpreted according to the grammar and lexicon of the language they have chosen to employ, etc. However, the need for such premise is something supporters of the conventional meaning container-retrieval view seem to overlook, being somehow bewitched by a sort of "linguistic naturalism". There is indeed a further point they seem to overlook when they present the conventional linguistic reading of legal clauses as the "proper", "obvious", "natural", "evident" legal way of reading them. They seem to overlook that such a claim – whenever is not simply reported as made by somebody else – actually belongs to the normative theory of interpretation and

normative philosophy of law: since it is in fact a claim about the *proper*, natural, way of interpreting legal clauses, and, consequently, a claim concerning the proper, natural, way of establishing *what the law – what the actual content of legal systems – really amounts to.* A moment's reflection suggests that conventional meaning theory serves, perhaps unconsciously, a practical master: the legal policy master preoccupied with such ethical goals as "making practical sense of legislation", "restoring the dignity of legislation as a veritable legal source", "establishing legal security so far as possible", "making the law, so far as possible, readable and knowable to any competent speaker of the relevant natural language", etc. Notice that all these ethical goals belong to the Enlightenment theory of legislation. They belong to a specific normative view of legislation and statutory construction. That we may find such a doctrine greatly appealing and commendable on practical grounds should not obscure this fact.[13]

2. *No overwhelming theoretical reasons for the container-retrieval view.* I have just argued that the conventional meaning theory is either logically flawed (*qua* theory), or no theory at all, being rather (for good or bad) Enlightenment propaganda in disguise. Its supporters, however, maintain the conventional meaning theory to be theoretically warranted: to be, in fact, the only viable way we have to lay on the solid ground of an objective meaning – of a meaning "out there" – the distinction, which otherwise would be baffling, between explicit norms and legal interpretation proper, on the one hand, and implicit norms and legal integration (juristic law making, juristic construction), on the other. This would be so, they claim, for the following reasons:

    (a) the legal theorists who insist on the theoretical relevance of distinguishing between explicit norms and implicit norms usually maintain that explicit norms are the norms that can be identified as meanings of a legal clause by means of the "interpretive methods" (arguments, techniques) in use within "our" legal culture and experience;
    (b) such a claim however is sound if, but only if, it is possible to draw a clear-cut distinction between the methods and arguments which are properly and strictly *interpretive*, being apt to identify and justify explicit norms, on the one side, and the methods and arguments which play instead an *integrative* function, being apt to identify and justify implicit norms, on the other side; this is so since, if such a clear-cut distinction within "interpretive methods" is not viable, "interpretive methods" cannot be used as a reliable vantage-point for sorting out explicit norms from implicit ones[14];
    (c) unfortunately, the required clear-cut distinction between strictly interpretive and integrative methods is not viable; as a matter of fact, the most important methods (arguments) in "our" legal culture (like, e.g., the argument *a simili*

[13] A further possibility of making sense of the conventional meaning theory would be reading it as an empirical claim about what is the "common way" of reading legal clauses and establishing the content of legal system. As to "our" legal systems, however, such claim would be clearly false.

[14] "Se questa distinzione non è possibile, neppure è possibile distinguere le norme espresse dalle norme inespresse guardando ai metodi tramite i quali sono individuate" (Diciotti 2013, 106).

and the so-called dissociation argument) may be used to identify and justify *both* explicit norms *and* implicit norms; they may function *both* as strictly interpretive arguments, *and* as integrative methods;

(d) interpretive methods as a whole are accordingly *not* a viable vantage-point for distinguishing between explicit and implicit norms;

(e) there is, to conclude, only one way to make such distinction viable. And this way consists in resorting to the criterion of conventional linguistic meaning. A norm is an explicit norm if, but only if, it can be identified as belonging to the set of conventional linguistic meanings of a legal clause.

The preceding line of argument is appealing. Unfortunately, from the standpoint of frames theory, it does not work. For at least two reasons.

(I) In their reasoning, conventional meaning variety supporters deal with "the argument *a simili*" as if it were exactly one and the same argument, from the standpoint of *function* and *structure*, both in strictly interpretive and in its integrative uses. Such a claim is questionable.

In fact, it seems viable distinguishing two varieties of the so-called argument *a simili*: a strictly interpretive variety and an integrative one; they share the same function (dealing with gaps), but have a different structure.

The analogical argument in its interpretive variety is a means for arguing for a certain ascription of meaning to words and phrases contained in a legal clause. It contributes to the process of translating a legal clause into (explicit) legal norms. It supports the performance of so-called extensive interpretation of legal texts, and serves to overcome ("pre-empt") the gaps "revealed" by a first, literal or usual (authoritative, traditional, historical), reading of legal clauses.

Contrariwise, the analogical argument in its integrative variety is employed whenever interpretation proper is (deemed to be) over, and there is a need to argue for the existence and applicability of a further, implicit, norm, taking as starting point some previously identified explicit norm and the principle of analogical integration. This variety of analogical reasoning supports the performance of overt gaps-filling operations.

However, if we follow the suggestion of supporters of the container-retrieval view, we must consider both sorts of analogical reasoning as concerning the identification of *implicit* norms; we must apply the same label to two very different kinds of "implicit" norms, losing the possibility of sorting them out by appealing to the structure of reasoning employed to justify them.

(II) The examples provided by conventional meaning variety supporters to show the "competitive advantage" of their own view upon the frames theory are not, after all, convincing. Here you are the examples.[15]

Suppose that, on the main entrance to a public park, there is a legal clause (LC_i) saying "No vehicles in the park". Suppose three problems arise: (a) whether

[15] Diciotti (2013, 107–108).

roller-skates are a "vehicle" and should accordingly not be allowed into the park; (b) whether the prohibition to enter the park does hold also for horses, assuming that horses are not "vehicles" according to the conventional linguistic meaning of "vehicle"; (c) whether the prohibition to enter the park does hold also for an ambulance coming into the park to rescue a seriously injured man, though an ambulance is clearly a "vehicle" according to the conventional linguistic meaning of "vehicle".

By means of an argument *a simili*, it is possible to solve the first problem in a way that consists in making the content of the norm expressed by LC_i more "precise". This may be done, for instance, by the following line of reasoning: (a) there is an explicit norm not allowing vehicles into the park; (b) the explicit norm clearly refers to trucks and automobiles, but it is dubious whether it also refers to roller-skates; (c) the purpose (the *ratio*) of the norm is protection of the physical integrity of the people in the park; (d) surely, trucks and automobiles are a threat to the physical integrity of the people in the park; (e) surely, roller-skates too are a threat to the physical integrity of the people in the park; (f) hence, provided trucks, automobiles, and roller-skates are similar things from the standpoint of the *ratio* of the norm, we must conclude that roller-skates too are "vehicles" to the purpose of the explicit norm "no vehicles allowed into the park", and should not enter the park. In this case, notice, the argument *a simili* functions as a way to identify and justify an *explicit norm*: the norm according to which "no vehicles (i.e, no trucks, no automobiles, ..., *and no roller-skates*) are allowed into the park".

Reasoning by analogy also allows to cope with the second problem. Here, however, the argument *a simili* would be clearly a means for identifying and justifying an *implicit norm*: namely, the implicit norm according to which "horses are not allowed into the park". The reasoning goes as follows: (a) there is an explicit norm not allowing vehicles (i.e, trucks, automobiles, roller-skates, etc.) into the park; (b) surely, horses are *not* vehicles (according to the ordinary meaning of "vehicle"); (c) the purpose of the explicit norm is protecting the physical integrity of the people in the park; (d) surely, horses represent a threat to the physical integrity of the people in the park; (e) hence, we must conclude that, along with the explicit norm "no vehicles into the park" it goes by analogy the further, implicit, norm "no horses into the park".

Finally, the dissociation argument is useful to cope with the third problem. Here again, however, the argument would be a means to identify and justify an *implicit exception* to the explicit norm "no vehicles (i.e, no trucks, no automobiles, no roller-skates, etc.) are allowed into the park". The reasoning goes as follows: (a) there is an explicit norm not allowing vehicles (i.e, trucks, automobiles, roller-skates, etc.) into the park; (b) surely, an ambulance is a vehicle and, from the standpoint of the explicit norm considered in itself, it ought not to be allowed into the park; (c) the purpose of the explicit norm is protecting the physical integrity of the people in the park; (d) the ambulance clearly fulfils such a purpose, since it comes to rescue a seriously injured man; (e) hence the general prohibition of the explicit norm must be relaxed to allow into the park those vehicles performing valuable services to the people inside the park; (f) hence we may properly amend the explicit norm as follows: “no vehicles (i.e, no trucks, no automobiles, no roller-skates, etc.) are allowed into the park, *unless they serve a socially valuable function*”.

Now, according to the supporters of the conventional meaning view, the three examples above would show that only if we adopt their view it is possible to draw a clear-cut distinction between interpretation and integration. Example *A* would be a case of interpretation, while examples *B* and *C* would be cases of integration. According to the frames theory, on the contrary, all the three examples would be instances of interpretation: in all cases, the outcome either of reasoning by analogy, or of resorting to the dissociation argument, would be explicit norms, i.e., norms capable of being presented as the (legally correct) meaning of the legal clause “No vehicles in the park”.

Is the container-retrieval theory preferable? Are there overwhelming reasons to endorse it? I do not think so. First, the conventional meaning notion of interpretation proper classifies as genuine interpretation also the “fixing up” of vagueness in cases like example *A*. However, vagueness is a situation where linguistic rules have run out. So, if we use linguistic meaning as the benchmark to tell explicit norms from implicit ones, also such a fixing up should be regarded as a piece of integration, as concerning the identification of an implicit norm. Accordingly, from the very standpoint of a consistent and rigorous conventional meaning view, all the three examples above should be regarded, properly, as three instances of integration. Second, there seem to be at least three good reasons supporting the adoption of the frames theory: conformity to juristic commonsense, ideological neutrality, conceptual adequacy.

Juristic commonsense. The conventional meaning theory sets forth a highly counter-intuitive conceptual apparatus, far away from juristic commonsense. From its standpoint, the ongoing ways of thinking about legal interpretation and legal integration, explicit and implicit norms, should be radically amended. This is not the case with the frames theory. Provided that it is clear that both interpretation and integration are practical argumentative games, ongoing ways of thinking can be preserved. Why, if the reasonably arguable purpose of the legal clause “No dogs allowed into restaurants” is keeping dangerous dogs out of restaurants, should we present the teleological norm “No dangerous dogs allowed into restaurants” as an *implicit* norm?

Ideological neutrality. The conventional meaning theory may be charged, as we have seen, with (perhaps unaware) support to the Enlightenment case for the dignity and powers of legislators: with endorsing a substantive conception of what the law is, and must be, in any legal experience whatsoever. Contrariwise, no practical commitment whatsoever is to be found with the frames theory. The theory of interpretation (as an argumentative game) it sets forth is not committed to any determinate set of interpretive directives. On the contrary, it is compatible with whatever set of directives may prevail in any given legal culture. It does not rule out that the lawyers working in a given legal order may assume that the legislature, by enacting legal clauses, does produce the explicit norms corresponding to the conventional linguistic meanings of the clauses. Nor does it rule out that lawyers may adopt a different view about the proper way of conceiving legislation and interpretation (e.g., that the legislature intends to produce constitutionally legitimate norms, comes what it may of linguistic meaning). All these contingent ideological postures are as many data for the frames theory to record, and account for as possible features of ongoing legal systems.

Conceptual adequacy. The conventional meaning theory suggests that its own notions of legal interpretation proper and of explicit norm provide a better standpoint for establishing where lawyers simply "discover" the law (i.e., the objective meanings of legal clauses), on the one hand, and where, contrariwise, they "make" it, on the other. From the standpoint of the frames theory, however, such a claim is objectionable on two counts.

First, the proposal is misleading. Lawyers playing the interpretive or integrative argumentation games never do simply "discover" the law. They always establish what the law is by their own decisions. Obviously, their decisions may fall upon the objective linguistic meaning of a legal clause. But it is, in any a case, a decision for an interpretive sentence that is "correct" on the basis of an interpretive code that has been previously accepted as, in turn, "correct", which usually encompasses more directives than the single, literal, one (for instance, it usually includes secondary preferential directives of systematic kind).

Second, the conceptual framework of the frames theory is perfectly equipped to capture and bring to the fore the difference between *literal* explicit norms (that are justifiable on the ground of literal or conventional meaning argument), on the one hand, and, say, *teleological* explicit norms (that are justifiable on the ground of teleological argument from an assumed *ratio legis*), on the other.

True: the frames theory's notion of interpretation may seem tautological. As you may recall, interpretation proper is (intra-linguistic) translation of authoritative legal texts into explicit norms, according to allowed interpretive arguments. For the reasons I have tried to set forth, however, this is a virtuous tautology: respectful of theoretical neutrality and serving explanatory comprehensiveness.

References

Diciotti, Enrico. 2013. Norme espresse e norme inespresse. Sulla teoria dell'interpretazione di Riccardo Guastini. In *Interpretazione e costruzione del diritto. Riflessioni su Interpretare e argomentare di Riccardo Guastini*, ed. Vito Velluzzi, 103–123. Bologna: Il Mulino.

Guastini, Riccardo. 2011. *Interpretare e argomentare*. Milano: Giuffrè.

Guastini, Riccardo. 2013. Replica. In *Interpretazione e costruzione del diritto. Riflessioni su Interpretare e argomentare di Riccardo Guastini*, ed. Vito Velluzzi, 125–136. Bologna: Il Mulino.

Hart, H.L.A. 1961. *The concept of law*. Oxford: Clarendon.

Hart, H.L.A. 1967. Problems of the philosophy of law. In Id. *Essays in jurisprudence and philosophy*. Oxford: Clarendon Press.

Hart, H.L.A. 1983. *Essays in jurisprudence and philosophy*. Oxford: Clarendon Press.

Kelsen, Hans. 1960. *Reine Rechtslehre*. Wien: Deuticke, Zweite Auflage.

Pino, Giorgio. 2013. Interpretazione cognitiva, interpretazione decisoria, interpretazione creativa. In *Interpretazione e costruzione del diritto. Riflessioni su Interpretare e argomentare di Riccardo Guastini*, ed. Vito Velluzzi, 77–101. Bologna: Il Mulino.

Raz, Joseph. 2009. *Between authority and interpretation. On the theory of law and practical reason*. Oxford: Oxford University Press.

Soames, Scott. 2007, April 1–2. *Interpreting legal texts: What is, and what is not, special about the law*. Paper presented at "An International Conference on Law, Language, and Interpretation", University of Akureyri, Akureyri, Iceland.

Velluzzi, Vito. 2013a. Introduzione. In *Interpretazione e costruzione del diritto. Riflessioni su Interpretare e argomentare di Riccardo Guastini*, ed. Vito Velluzzi, 73–76.

Velluzzi, Vito., ed. 2013b. Interpretazione e costruzione del diritto. Riflessioni su Interpretare e argomentare di Riccardo Guastini. *Rivista di filosofia del diritto/Journal of Legal Philosophy* 1: 73–136.

Wróblewski, Jerzy. 1992. *The judicial application of law*. Edited by Z. Bankowski and N. MacCormick. Dordrecht: Kluwer.

Chapter 9
Argument Structures in Legal Interpretation: Balancing and Thresholds

Michał Araszkiewicz

Abstract This paper is a contribution to the development of a descriptive model of legal interpretation encompassing three areas: formulation of interpretive statements, generation of arguments that support or demote the interpretive statements, and comparison and balancing of arguments supporting incompatible interpretive statements. The focus of the paper is on the third layer. A case study is presented to demonstrate how a court uses a technique referred to as 'threshold conditions', instead of explicit balancing different values. The nature of this technique will be analysed in the framework of the developed model of legal interpretation. Although the purpose of the paper is theoretical, a practical objective of development of an AI-based legal interpretation support system creates an important background for the investigations.

9.1 Introduction

The nature of balancing of values and reasons in legal reasoning has been a subject of analysis in legal theory for at least three decades. However, the most important contexts for the discussion of this topic in the domain of legal argumentation theory are constitutional law and teleological reasoning, while general statutory interpretation has remained a relatively underrepresented field. The purpose of this paper is to make a contribution to this neglected area. Consequently, this paper focuses on the reconstruction of the mechanism of balancing in the context of interpretation of statutory expressions of civil law systems, and Polish tax law was chosen to serve as illustrative material. This reconstruction forms one part of the descriptive model of legal interpretation outlined in Araszkiewicz (2013b) and partially developed previously in Żurek and Araszkiewicz (2013). The model is designed to present the actual

M. Araszkiewicz (✉)
Department of Legal Theory, Faculty of Law and Administration,
Jagiellonian University in Kraków, Poland
e-mail: michal.araszkiewicz@uj.edu.pl

© Springer International Publishing Switzerland 2015

T. Bustamante, C. Dahlman (eds.), *Argument Types and Fallacies in Legal Argumentation*, Law and Philosophy Library 112,
DOI 10.1007/978-3-319-16148-8_9

structure of judicial interpretive argumentation in a precise manner and disregards the normative (postulative) questions of the theory of legal interpretation.

The emphasis on representing actual judicial argumentation instead of idealized reconstruction is motivated by a practical goal that prompted the development of the model, which is the creation of a workable AI-based legal knowledge representation system. The system should be able to analyse the argumentative structures of legal argumentation that are expressed in the actual wording of judicial decisions. The idea to develop an AI system that would include not only a simple representation of statutory rules but also the issues of legal interpretation has been recommended in the AI & Law literature for at least two decades (see Oskamp 1993); however, the construction of genuine legal expert systems appeared problematic for many reasons, including choosing a method for the representation of legal knowledge (Bench-Capon 2012). Extracting legal arguments from the actual wording of judicial decisions has been a frequent subject in contemporary research in Al and law (Ashley and Walker 2013). Focusing on actual rather than idealized judicial argumentation also possesses an important theoretical value in answering the question: what types of arguments are used in judicial reasoning as sufficient justifications of legal decisions? Hence, the purpose of this paper is to demonstrate how the comparison and balancing of different interpretive arguments are handled in actual legal cases in a civil law system. The illustrative material presented in the paper suggests that in legal practice balancing of values is replaced by use of certain types of default rules and that the use of these rules can be seen as sufficient for providing justification for legal decision-making. Apart from a theoretical insight concerning the discussion of argument schemes used in the mentioned context, the present study contributes to the development of AI-based model of legal interpretation. It shows how in certain cases the complicated procedures of balancing of values may be (and in actual practice are) substituted by far more simple, but non-trivial, reasoning patterns.

This study is divided into seven sections. In Sect. 9.2, we present a brief overview of the state of art concerning the discussion of balancing in legal theory. A general, multi-criteria decision-making framework for the analysis of the research problem is outlined in Sect. 9.3. In Sect. 9.4, the concept of statutory interpretation will be made illustrated in a model with an emphasis on the extensional aspect of this process, which is the legal interpretation as a determination for the extension of statutory expressions. Actual cases decided by the Polish Supreme Administrative Court will serve as illustrative material for extracting a mechanism of balancing in the context of competing interpretive arguments in Sect. 9.5. The illustrative material will show that the court applied what is referred to as the threshold technique to resolve the conflict between arguments supporting different interpretive conclusions and did not engage in an explicit balancing of values. Section 9.6 focuses on the discussion of the presented analysis with a particular emphasis on the use of the threshold technique of balancing. The final section includes conclusions and presents recommendations perspectives for further research.

9.2 Balancing in Legal Reasoning

Several accounts of legal balancing are presented in this section. The accounts discussed here are well-known proposals, and they provide an important contribution to legal theory by reconstructing the idealized models of weighing different values and reasons in the law. They generally abstract from actual wording of judicial argumentation by imposing elaborated theoretical structures on the represented phenomenon. This is not a disadvantage of these proposals from the point of view of aims adopted by the authors of these models; however, from the practical and theoretical point of view adopted in this paper, their usefulness is limited. The contributions discussed below suggest that balancing of values (and broader: teleological considerations) are crucial as regards resolution of questions of law that are not resolvable on some more basic level. We contend here that there is a large scope of different argumentative structures used for answering of such questions where purely linguistic techniques and full-blown balancing of values create the extreme points of the spectrum.

The author who introduced the topic of balancing to a very broad legal-theoretical audience is Robert Alexy, who presented a theory of constitutional principles as optimization requirements (Alexy 2002, 47). Alexy transformed the famous dworkinian distinction of legal norms into legal rules and legal principles. While legal rules may or may not be applied to a case in such a way that *tertium non datur*, legal principles may influence the outcome of a given case to a certain degree. Conflicts between legal rules are resolved in abstract by using the traditional criteria to resolve apparent antinomies in a legal system (such as *lex posterior* or *lex superior*), while collisions between legal principles have to be resolved by balancing (Alexy 2007). Legal principles should be understood as optimization requirements, ie, legal norms that require certain values to be realized to the greatest extent possible given factual and legal limitations. In his later work, Alexy called for the application of the Weight Formula as a scheme for the resolution of the collisions of legal principles (Alexy 2003, 2007). The principle of proportionality described by Alexy (and adopted in German constitutional jurisprudence, see Alexy 2002, 66), encompasses three important sub-principles: the principle of necessity (the adopted measure must be necessary for realization of the assumed aim), the principle of suitability (the adopted measure must be suitable for realization of the assumed aim), and the principle of proportionality in the strict sense. The latter, also referred to as the Law of Balancing, is the most relevant sub-principle to this study and was formulated in the following manner:

> [The Law of Balancing]: "[T]he greater the degree of non-satisfaction of, or detriment to, one principle, the greater the importance of satisfying the other," (Alexy 2002, 102).

Alexy adopts a triadic scale for measuring both the degree of non-satisfaction of the principles and the importance of their satisfaction, which encompasses the following levels: Light, Moderate, and Serious (Alexy 2003, 440). Each of these degrees of intervention or satisfaction may be further classified into three sub-steps.

Once numbers from this scale are assigned to deliberate legal decisions, it is quite simple to determine which of the competing principles (or groups of principles) should prevail in a certain situation. Of course, the assignment of numbers may be controversial and subject to debate.

In summary, Alexy has developed a theory in which balancing is a method for the resolution of collisions between legal principles understood as optimization requirements. The objects compared are degrees of the satisfaction of principles and degrees of importance of the realization of principles. These degrees are represented on a triadic scale and the collisions between or among legal principles are resolved by means of an arithmetical Weight Formula. Alexy's model is a reconstructive idealization because arithmetical formulas are not used in actual judicial argumentation. Interestingly, the choice of a triadic scale was motivated by Alexy's goal to remain faithful to the actualities of legal reasoning (Alexy 2007), but the idealization feature dominates his proposal.[1]

The concept of finding a proportional balance between colliding legal principles (or values; or, more generally speaking, reasons) has become appealing to many legal scholars, who are not only followers of Alexy but are also authors who have developed their own accounts of the role of balancing in legal reasoning.

A relatively recent and very well-developed theoretical model of legal balancing and maximization has been proposed by Giovanni Sartor (2010). Sartor provides a generalized and partially formalized framework for legal balancing and adopts Alexy's approach in choosing constitutional review as a prototypical context for the discussion of this topic (Sartor 2010, 176). He applies a modified terminology that divides legal norms into action-norms and goal-norms instead of rules and principles (due to the notorious lack of clarity in regards to the notion of legal principles). Action-norms assign to certain actions the status of obligatory ones or specify the conditions of validity of legal acts, while goal-norms involve certain objectives (Sartor 2010, 177). Sartor adopts a broad conception of values, which are defined as any valuable state of affairs. He presents counterparts of important decision-theory concepts in the field of legal balancing. For instance, he defines the notion of Pareto-superiority in terms of teleological reasoning. Informally speaking, a choice is Pareto-superior to another choice if the former choice is better than the latter one in regards to with regard to the realization of a certain value and if the former choice is not inferior to the latter with regard to any other value.[2] A given choice is Pareto-optimal if no other choice is Pareto-superior to it.

Sartor rightly acknowledges that in legal contexts, particularly in the context of legislative choice, these choices are often not Pareto-comparable; no choice is Pareto-superior with respect to another one. He proposes in his theory that trade-offs between conflicting values may be represented by means of indifference curves

[1] It is of course possible to also use other types of scales to compare the relative weight of principles or values. See Bench-Capon (2011, 14) for an outline of the problem and Araszkiewicz (2011) for a brief elaboration of this subject. A triadic scale seems to be a convenient choice because of the for semi-formal modeling of legal balancing. See the proposal of Grabmair and Ashley (2010).

[2] For a formal definition, see Sartor (2010, 185).

(Sartor 2010, 193). This idea was present in Alexy's account also (Alexy 2002, 103–104). Although Sartor adopts a quantitative scale for representing the degree of the realization of values, he also acknowledges that certain degrees of realization are qualitatively different. The degree of the realization of value referred to as the *core of value* should be satisfied in any legally acceptable decision. In other words, any legal decision leading to an infringement of the core of value should be assessed as legally wrong (Sartor 2010, 191). Moreover, Sartor presents a thorough, partially formalized analysis of each of the components of the principle of proportionality with particular emphasis on the third balancing component. Following Barak's general suggestion, Sartor develops and presents a scheme of value judgment concerning the balancing of colliding values that affect legislative choice using a marginal analysis (Sartor 2010, 200). He further discusses the different levels of intensity of a judicial review of legislative choices as well as several other topics involving balancing in the context of precedents (2010, 208–210).

Sartor's proposal is presumably one of the most developed accounts of legal balancing involving decision-theory based rationality. The concept of the optimization of the degree of realization of legally relevant values is particularly evident in his discussion of teleological Pareto-superiority. He combines quantitative and qualitative aspects of scales that measure the realization of values, preferring the use of natural numbers. Like Alexy, the illustrative material Sartor chose is the conflict of (mainly: constitutional) values in the context of legislative action. The model proposed by Sartor is highly idealized due to the application of the mathematical decision theory to legal balancing and differential analysis to create a fully-fledged formulation of legal value judgments.

Grabmair and Ashley (2010) are AI and law scholars who advocate a formal framework for reasoning with values in the context of legal case-based reasoning. They adopt certain ideas similar to Alexy's ideas by adopting a triadic scale concerning realization (promotion) or demotion of legally relevant values in particular (Grabmair and Ashley 2010, 69–70). Among the set of definitions formulated by the authors, there is also an account of value judgment, which is a scheme for the comparison of value effects sets (the effects concerning promotion and demotion of value tuples) in different factual situations (Grabmair and Ashley 2010, 70). The authors use the famous *California v. Carney*[3] case as illustrative material for their analysis (Grabmair and Ashley 2010, 73). They enter into a discussion with Bench-Capon and Prakken (2009, 2010) and criticize their approach for adopting an abstract (fact-independent) ordering of values and for using a static (instead of dynamic) account of the threshold degrees of the realization of a given value. According to Grabmair and Ashley, if there are at least two colliding values, their thresholds are relative to one another. In other words, for each threshold value of the realization of a given value (leading to a certain legal consequence), there is a threshold value of the realization of a conflicting value, which leads to avoiding the previously mentioned legal consequence (Grabmair and Ashley 2010, 75). Hence, the authors strongly emphasize the dependence of the outcome of legal balancing on

[3] 471 U.S. 386 (1985).

contextual information. The model proposed by Grabmair and Ashley is a moderate idealization because they attempt to join the rigor of a semi-formal framework with a heavy emphasis of its descriptive adequacy in regards to the actualities of judicial argumentation of American courts.

Jaap Hage advocates the theory of qualitative comparison of alternative decisions in the law (Qualitative Comparative Reasoning, Hage 2005, 102 ff.). Notably, Hage's account is broader than the teleological account because he uses the term "reasons" to refer to entities that may plead for or against a certain choice (Hage 2005, 103); however, he asserts that sets of goals are important types of reasons as well. To compare reason sets, Hage uses qualitative ordering operators, such as "stronger," "weaker," or "equal." He also acknowledges the possibility of using quantitative methods in the context of comparing the probabilities of consequences of certain actions, for instance. He formulates a set of conditions for establishing preference relations between sets of alternatives, and he is aware that a comparison of certain (more complicated) sets of alternatives involves additional evaluation and that the category of preference in qualitative comparison may not satisfy all axioms of the classical decision theory. For instance, the relation of preference in this context is only weakly, that is defeasibly, transitive (Hage 2005, 107). Hage devotes considerable attention to the role of the realization of goals in the comparison of different decisions. Eventually, he presents a formalized framework for comparison sets of reasons as an extension of his Reason Based Logic (Hage 2005, Chap. 3) that encompasses many interesting heuristic rules (Hage 2005, 122 ff.).

Hage's proposal is an example of a formalized and qualitative framework for the comparison of (sets of) alternatives. The framework is very general and thus applicable not only to any context of legal reasoning but also to other domains of deliberation. The illustrative materials chosen by the author are case-based reasoning and reasoning with legal proof. Although the author does not discuss the problem of optimization or maximization directly in this context, he does define solutions as right, wrong, or indifferent in terms of the preponderance of pro-reasons over con-reasons and the preponderance of con-reasons over pro-reasons and their equality, respectively. In summary, Hage's proposal is a very general framework for legal balancing that may be applicable to any context of legal argumentation. Due to its abstract character, it can be instantiated in different domains of legal discourse. Due to the moderate application of the scales of measurement, the framework is easily applicable to actual legal cases (an example of two analysed cases are discussed in Hage 2005, 114 ff.).

Legal balancing and teleological reasoning have also been topics of interest for argumentation researchers working with the theoretical framework of pragma-dialectical theory (Feteris 2008). The basic approach for the reconstruction of teleological argumentation in legal interpretation is as follows: application of a legal rule (interpreted in certain manner) to a given legal case, may lead to consequences that are desirable or undesirable in the perspective of the goal of a rule (Feteris 2008, 490 ff.). Feteris is aware that in actual judicial argumentation certain choices underlying the application of the presented scheme are often left implicit, and she advocates the method of "rational reconstruction" of legal balancing in teleological interpretation in order to indicate how the judge uses her or his discretionary powers in the interpretation and application of legal rules.

Feteris' analysis of legal balancing is less general and less formalized than the previously discussed analyses. Its value lies in focusing on the specific context, which is provided by the interpretation of statutory rules. The purpose of Feteris' study explicitly involves reconstruction and rationality. She intends to reveal hidden assumptions that are rarely made explicit in actual legal argumentation. On the other hand, she does not use any concrete measurement scale in her reconstruction; she uses binary concepts for an assessment of the consequences of interpretation (desirable / undesirable).

The amount of literature on the subject of legal balancing is enormous and includes not only thorough elaborations of the reasoning of constitutional principles (for instance: Borowski 2007) but also legal-theoretical accounts that are generally based on the concept of weighing and balancing (Peczenik 2008). The different terminology that is used by the different authors makes the comparison and the application of their concepts difficult; however, the main feature that makes the proposals discussed above less useful for the purposes of this paper is that they all impose a certain well-developed formal (mathematical) or semi-formal structure on the actual judicial argumentation. Moreover, the developed concepts of legal balancing do not deal directly with the problem of statutory interpretation.[4] In addition, the frameworks developed in the context of constitutional review might not be directly applicable to the domain of statutory interpretation. Therefore, for the purposes of this paper, it is worthwhile to look at the process of balancing in legal statutory interpretation from a more general perspective, which enables us to proceed with a descriptive analysis.

9.3 Balancing in Legal Interpretation: A General Framework

Legal balancing is naturally, although not necessarily exclusively, seen as an optimization problem. This stems from Alexy's account of legal principles as optimization requirements; however, the analysis of literature quoted in the preceding section suggests that legal balancing does not take place only in the context of application of legal principles. This seems to contradict contrast Alexy's position who argues that while balancing is a mode of the application of principles, legal rules are applied by means of subsumption. It is necessary to note here that according to Alexy's account, the balancing of legal principles leads to the formulation of legal rules (Alexy 2002, 54) and basically all rules (if rationally justifiable) are the results of the balancing of principles. Moreover, the interpretation of statutory expressions may be seen as the process of balancing of values (Alexy's letter published in

[4] With an exception of Sieckmann (2009, 151–168).

Bustamante 2005, 323).[5] Even if we agree that it is always possible to reconstruct certain values that have to be balanced in order to obtain the justification of a legal decision, this is not always apparent in actual legal argumentation. Even if legal arguments that are actually used are themselves interpretable as results of balancing certain values, this study focuses on the structure of these arguments as they are actually formulated in the language of judicial opinions. In order to analyse these structures without imposing any elaborate conceptual scheme, we will adopt a very general and neutral perspective here. The theory of multi-criteria decision-making (Ehrgott 2005) is a mathematical framework that is useful for providing a more general account of legal balancing. Each decision-making problem consists of a set of decisions (variables), a set of criteria that are applicable in assessing the decisions, and a notion of assessment (typically optimality) that is applied (Ehrgott 2005, 1). The purpose of this study it to reconstruct the counterparts of each of these three elements in the context of judicial interpretive argumentation.

Jerzy Wróblewski (1992) designed a model for the judicial application of law, which he referred to as a material decision model of the application of law. For Wróblewski, the judicial application of law can be viewed as a sequence of partial decisions that ultimately lead to the final decision of applying a law. These partial decisions are the decision of validity (deciding whether or not a legal norm in question is valid), the decision of proof (connected with establishing the facts of the case), the decision of interpretation (related to the determination of meaning of relevant legal rules), the decision of subsumption (qualification of a given state of affairs as belonging or not belonging to the scope of the application of a legal rule), and the decision regarding legal consequences (choice of legal consequences that stem from the application of a legal rule to a given state of affairs). Making a decision regarding partial problems leads the judge to the ultimate decision concerning the application of law.

Wróblewski's model of the judicial application of law is a good starting point for the analysis of legal balancing in judicial reasoning in continental law systems. It enables us to separate certain stages of judicial reasoning and to indicate what elements are relevant to the decision-making process in each of these stages. For instance, regarding the decision of the interpretation of legal rules, the decision space will be constituted by a set of interpretive alternatives, or different possible interpretations of statutory expressions. The set of criteria that are applied for an assessment of these interpretations is the set of different reasons that may justify the choice of different interpretations. If we follow the classical typology of the canons of legal interpretation, which are accepted by Wróblewski (1992), these reasons

[5] I am grateful to Thomas Bustamante for calling my attention to this problem. In this connection, let us also note that the process of balancing colliding values may be represented as a coherence problem in a constraint satisfaction framework (for an introduction to this theory see Thagard 2000; for the discussion of the limits of the theory cf. Hage 2013 and Araszkiewicz 2013a). Araszkiewicz (2010) asserts that the interpretation of a general legal rule may be understood as a process of balancing two competing legal principles in the context of the circumstances of a case; however, clearly, the constraint satisfaction framework is a conceptual scheme that is imposed on actual argumentative structures used by the court. As this papers adopts a descriptive perspective on the problem of legal interpretation, this type of analysis should be avoided.

may be divided into linguistic, systemic, and functional reasons. It is important to note that all of these canons of interpretation are related to different values and that the structure of these values and their mutual interrelations are often complicated. These values often affect the decisions of legal interpretation indirectly; the canons of interpretation are used without explicitly mentioning the value(s) that are realized by utilizing a given canon. There is no fixed theory regarding an optimality of judicial interpretation. Different philosophies of law contribute to this problem in different manners. For instance, according to the economic analysis of law, the chosen interpretation should lead to the maximization of welfare or wealth. In legal practice, a (relatively incomplete) theory of choice between competing criteria favouring different interpretive outcomes may be reconstructed from the so-called directives of preference, which are typically accounted for as collision rules governing the process of resolving conflicts between incompatible interpretive results.

The application of the basic framework of the multi-criteria decision-making theory to the problem of legal interpretation enables us to look at this problem from a very general perspective.

The structure of the interpretive alternatives is generally unclear. Although many scholars devoted much attention to clarifying the structure of interpretive propositions in law, their syntactic and semantic character of these alternatives is still debatable. In Sect. 9.4, a certain proposal of accounting for them will be presented.

Regarding the criteria that are applied for the assessment of different interpretive propositions, the problem of their representation is even more complicated for four reasons. First, as discussed previously, the reasons expressed in the canons of legal interpretation can be viewed as the criteria of assessment and justification of different interpretive alternatives; however, the use of these canons is justified by certain values. Consequently, there is a multi-layered set of criteria of a rather complicated structure. Second, the use of certain interpretive reasons is no longer theoretically neutral. For example, a legal formalist may acknowledge a narrower set of legally relevant reasons than an adherent of dworkinian jurisprudence. Third, the canons of legal interpretation are open to interpretation because there are no "authoritative" formulations of them. Fourth, it is not easy to answer questions concerning scales used for indicating the extent to which a given criterion is fulfilled by different solutions.[6]

As for an examplary notion of optimization, Alexy's concept of optimization expressed in his Law of Balancing has been presented previously; however, the question of whether or not the process of legal balancing is (descriptively) a process of optimization is raised. Do the judges actually strive for an *optimization* of realization of legally relevant values? Is the process of legal reasoning best explained in terms of finding a certain kind of maximal point or best answer? For obvious reasons, it is not possible here to discuss these important questions in detail; however, a case study presented in Sect. 9.5 will enable us to provide preliminary insight regarding the relation between legal balancing and the concept of optimization.

[6] In review, the problem with the scales of measurement of the realization of different values was discussed in Araszkiewicz (2011).

Table 9.1 Problems of legal interpretation in the framework of multi-criteria decision-making

Multi-criteria decision-making category	The set of decisions	The set of criteria	The applied notion of optimization
Instantiation of a category in the field of judicial interpretation	The set of interpretive alternatives	Compatibility of interpretative alternatives with canons of legal interpretation with the values that are protected by the canons of legal interpretation	The maximum value of function given by all relevant legal reasons
Problems	The syntactic and semantic characteristics of interpretive alternatives	1. The relation between canons and values justifying them	Is legal reasoning about maximization or optimization of any function at all?
		2. "Legal" character of certain arguments	
		3. Openness of the canons to interpretation	
		4. Measuring scales	

The analysis of the challenge of balancing in judicial interpretation of statutory law in terms of the general framework of multi-criteria decision-making is summarized in Table 9.1.

The model of statutory interpretation outlined in the next section addresses some of the problems presented in this Table in a satisfactory manner.

9.4 A Model of Statutory Interpretation Incorporating Teleological Argumentation

In this section, a model of statutory interpretation, which is outlined in Araszkiewicz (2013b), is presented. The model itself has mainly descriptive purposes. The purpose of the model is to represent actual judicial interpretive argumentation in the context of statutory legal systems. The model's objective is not to criticize the actual judicial reasoning, but to faithfully represent its actual structure and argumentation patterns for the possible implementation in a legal knowledge system in the future. The presentation of the model here is informal.[7]

The model outlined here is designed to represent the extensional aspect of legal interpretation which is determination of extension of statutory terms. This operation takes place in the context of an operative, judicial interpretation of law as well as the abstract, doctrinal interpretation of law. For example, if we deliberate if John should be classified as an object subsumed under the statutory expression "thief" we cannot

[7] For a formalized, set-theoretical account, cf. Araszkiewicz (2013b). For a logic-based model of teleological interpretation, cf. Żurek and Araszkiewicz (2013).

state, by simply assertion, that John is a thief to justify this conclusion; in fact we have to use another general linguistic expression such as 'a person who deliberately takes the property of other' and only after classifying John as an object of such intermediate legal concept (for instance, in the process of evidence inquiry) we are able to classify John as a thief. Once the evidentiary reasoning is concluded, the determination of the extension of statutory expressions consists in arguing about extensions of different general terms and expressions. We refer to the propositions concerning extensions of statutory expressions as extensional statements. Here are three examples of extensional statements:

1. According to this Act, a forest is also a land that is capable of forest production.
2. A legal claim is a subjective right that entitles a person to demand that another person behave in certain way.
3. According to the provision P, "5 years of driving experience" means "5 years of driving experience in the municipality where the applicant applied for the licence."

The first extensional statement is taken from the text of a statute, the second from a doctrinal textbook, and the third from case law. They are formulated in different contexts of legal argumentation, but they all have one thing in common: they establish set-theoretical relations between sets of objects belonging to the ranges of predicates used in linguistic expression. This relation may be a relation of inclusion, equality, or another type of extensional relation such as strict superiority, etc. Extensional statements that encompass at least one occurrence of a term that is not extracted from the wording of a normative act is referred to as an Interpretive Statement (IS). The extensional statement (1) presented above is not an IS, but the remaining two statements are.[8]

The formation of IS represents the first layer of the model of legal interpretation; however, an IS should be justified (supported by reasons). Therefore, the second layer of the model consists of the use of argumentation schemes to produce arguments (argument tokens) supporting or attacking a particular IS. Argumentation schemes are abstractions of patterns actually used in argumentation (Walton 2006; Walton 1996). Because the concept of argumentation schemes is well-known in the literature and in legal reasoning, a very brief description of this concept will suffice here. Argumentation schemes are based mainly on content and not on premises and conclusions. Consequently, the arguments are non-deductive and defeasible. By default, an argument based on an argument scheme provides for the justification of a given conclusion. Each argument scheme is accompanied with a set of critical

[8] In the following presentation, we will use a simplified notation to express both the content of legal rules and the structure of extensional relations in Interpretive Statements. We will make use of the general scheme [predicate] [object] and also use informal logical connectives such as AND, OR, and BUT NOT. For instance, the IS (3) discussed here would take the following form: [5 years' experience] [driver] = [5 years' experience] [driver] AND [experience in the same municipality] [driver].

questions that are used to scrutinize the actual strength of the argument based on the argument scheme.

Classical canons of legal interpretation can be reconstructed as argumentation schemes. Although this topic has not been fully developed yet, there are already interesting studies to show how the directives of legal interpretation can be understood as argumentation schemes (Macagno et al. 2012).

In order to explain how an argumentation scheme can be developed on the basis of a classical canon of legal interpretation, let us present a scheme for a teleological interpretation of statutory expression. This is an informal (and simplified) description of a formalized, logic-based framework that was presented in Żurek and Araszkiewicz (2013)[9]:

Normative Premise Statutory expression E should be interpreted in such a way that is satisfies the rule's goal to at least a minimally acceptable extent.

Factual Premise According to the objective of the satisfaction of the rule's goal, a statutory expression E should be interpreted in accordance with [an interpretive statement].

Conclusion A statutory expression E should be interpreted in accordance with [an interpretive statement].

According to the argument scheme presented above, accepted Interpretive Statements should satisfy the goal of a rule at least to some minimally acceptable extent (threshold). As Żurek and Araszkiewicz (2013, 164) argued, this type of threshold formation is actually used in the teleological interpretation of the Polish courts.

Consequently, the second layer of the model of legal interpretation involves reasons that support or demote the acceptance of certain Interpretive Statements. These reasons are included in arguments, or in instantiations of argumentation schemes.

As a result, the present model provides precise answers to the questions formulated in the preceding section in which the process of legal interpretation was discussed from the perspective of a general theory of multi-criteria decision-making. The set of decisions (alternatives) is given by competing Interpretive Statements; their structure is well-defined in the present model, and it does not seriously alter the syntactic and semantic structure of the actual interpretive statements as expressed in legal decisions. The set of criteria of assessment is formed by arguments that are instantiations of argumentation schemes built on the canons of legal interpretation. The third layer of the model, which concerns the optimization function (if any) used in legal interpretation needs further development. Because the model should perform mainly descriptive functions, a preliminary version of an account of legal balancing will be extracted from the actual legal cases discussed in the next section.

[9] In Żurek and Araszkiewicz (2013), the goals of the conditions of rules and of the rules themselves were discussed separately. Here, we only focus on the goals of rules for simplicity.

9.5 Case Study

The purpose of the case study presented is to show the usefulness of the model of interpretation discussed in the preceding section and to develop its third layer concerning the comparison and balancing of interpretive arguments.

The illustrative material is provided by a series of cases decided by Polish administrative courts (with particular emphasis on the case law of the Polish Supreme Administrative Court, hereafter referred to as the PSAC) concerning the application of a rule extracted from the Inheritance and Donation Tax Act of July 28, 1983, as amended[10] (hereafter referred to as the Act). Generally, according to the Act, the acquisition of material goods and monetary rights by means of inter alia, inheritance, or donation[11] is subject to taxation. As in most tax statutes, there are many exceptions to this general rule as well as tax reliefs and exemptions. One of these exemptions is the housing exemption. For the sake of simplicity and because it is sufficient for the purposes of this paper, let us state that the acquisition of a property (a flat or a residential building) is generally exempted from inheritance tax provided that the exempted taxpayer fulfils a set of conditions. It is not necessary to present an exhaustive set of these conditions, but an important condition is that the (exempted) taxpayer does not dispose of (sell or donate, etc.) the inherited property for a prescribed amount of time. The time period relevant to this study is 5 years from the date of acquisition of the property.

The rationale behind the "housing exemption" is quite obvious: the legislator is aware that property is often included in an inheritance to provide younger generations with housing. The acquired property must actually be used as a residence for at least 5 years. This period is prescribed to ensure that the acquired property is not sold or donated to third parties in a short time following the date of acquisition. As a result, if the acquired real property is transferred in a shorter period of time, the exemption is no longer valid, and the taxpayer is obligated to pay the tax.

The Act also provides certain exceptions to the conditions that are generally necessary to obtain the exemption. One of the exceptions to this condition that was enforced from the 22nd of June in 2004 to the 31st of December in 2006 caused a series of complicated cases and diverging opinions. This exception may be explained as follows:

[Exception] The disposal of acquired property does not lead to the termination of the exemption if it is justified by the necessity of a change in living conditions and if the acquisition of another building, the acquisition of permission for building, or the acquisition of a premises takes place no later than 6 months from the date of disposal.

The [Exception] rule obviously contains the implication the two conditions of which must be satisfied in conjunction. Following the simple formalism defined in the preceding section, this rule should be represented in the following way:

[10] Journal of Laws of 1983 no. 45, position 207 with amendments.

[11] For the sake of readability, only inheritance will be mentioned in further parts of the paper.

[Exception-formalized] IF [justified by the necessity of a change in living conditions] [disposal] AND [no later than 6 months after the date of disposal] [acquisition of new property] THEN [not terminated] [exemption].

Although one might have supposed that the first vague condition (necessity) caused more interpretive problems, it was in fact the second one that led to serious disagreement. More precisely, the expression "no later than" was assessed as ambiguous, which led to the formulation of two incompatible Interpretive Statements:

IS 1. [acquisition of new property no later than 6 months after the date of disposal] = [acquisition 6 months after the date of disposal] BUT NOT [earlier acquisition].

IS 2. [acquisition of new property no later than 6 months after the date of disposal] = [acquisition 6 months after the date of disposal] OR [earlier acquisition].

These two Interpretive Statements are contradictory regarding the acquisition of new property before the inherited property is transferred, which also includes the time before the inherited property is acquired. It is obvious that the (exempted) taxpayer is entitled to dispose of the inherited property and to acquire new property without losing his or her tax exemption in a period of 6 months. The interpretive question was whether he or she is entitled to acquire new property earlier and then to transfer the inherited property without causing the termination of the exemption.

As is common in such cases, the courts adopted different interpretive views. Some courts argued that "no later than x months from the point in time y" means "x months from the point in time y, but not earlier" (as in IS 1), and some courts argued that "x months from the point in time y or earlier" (as in IS 2) is the right interpretation. Even the different panels of the PSAC took opposing sides. Below, we reconstruct arguments favouring IS 1 and IS 2, respectively, on the basis of real cases decided by the PSAC.[12]

We begin with the reconstruction of the argument supporting IS 1 as it was argued in the judgment of the PSAC o13th of October in 2006, II FSK 1311/05 (hereafter: Judgment 1). The PSAC formulated only one argument in support of its thesis, which, in fact, had the form of argument from wrong consequences of adoption of IS 2. Because IS 1 and IS 2 are contradictory regarding the possibility of retaining the tax exemption in the case of the acquisition of new property before the inherited property is transferred, the rejection of IS 2 requires the acceptance of IS 1.

Argument 1 (Negative Consequences)

Premise 1 (normative). Statutory expressions should be interpreted in a way that avoids negative consequences.

Premise 2 (factual). Adoption of IS 2 leads to negative consequences.

[12] It is worth noting that the PSAC acts as the highest court in the hierarchy of administrative courts in Poland, although its judgments do not have formal precedential force in general.

Subpremise 2.1. The adoption of IS 2 ([earlier acquisition]) leads to the result that the acquisition of new property any time earlier than the transfer of inherited property does not terminate tax exemption concerning the acquisition of the latter.

Subpremise 2.1.1. The adoption of IS 2 leads to the result that the acquisition of new property even before the testator is deceased does not terminate the tax exemption concerning the acquisition of inherited property.

Subpremise 2.1.1.1. The acquisition of new property even before the testator is deceased should not have a legal effect on tax exemption concerning the acquisition of property by inheritance.[13]

Conclusion. IS 2 should be rejected.

Due to the fact that IS 1 and IS 2 are contradictory, the rejection of IS 2 leads to the immediate acceptance of IS 1.

As illustrated above, Argument 1 certainly has persuasive power, and the obvious intention of the legislator was to introduce the [Exception] rule to allow taxpayers to sell an inherited property in the event that the property would not provide a suitable living arrangement. In actual situations, due to many economic circumstances, the taxpayers acquired new property slightly before they eventually acquired the inherited one; however, according to IS 2, the purchase of new property before the inheritance takes place can also lead to tax exemption as regards acquisition of property by means of general succession. The PSAC ruled that this consequence is undesirable because these two legal events could be unrelated; it is natural to assume that a later disposal of inherited property has no economic connection with a (much) earlier acquisition of new property.

Let us note that the structure of the argument presented by the PSAC is enthymematic. The legislative goal of the regulation in question is not mentioned at all. Also, the possible reasons supporting the possible contrary decision are not discussed. The PSAC only claims that its argument against IS 2 is based on its alleged negative consequences and pleads for acceptance of IS 1.

The majority of the panels of the PSAC (and also lower administrative courts) adopted an opposing view and argued for IS 2. Let us reconstruct their argumentation on the basis of the judgment of the PSAC on the 7th of January in 2010, II FSK 1159/08 (hereafter: Judgment 2).

The PSAC initiated its argumentative process for favouring IS 2 on the basis of the canon of linguistic interpretation, which was ignored by the panel of PSAC in Judgment 1.

Argument 2 (Linguistic Interpretation)

Premise 1 (normative). Statutory expressions ought to be interpreted in accordance with the rules of (ordinary) language.

[13] The adding of subpremises to arguments based on argumentation schemes provide for justification of the premises.

Premise 2 (factual). The statutory expression "no later than x months from the time y" does not entail "no earlier than y" according to the rules of (ordinary) language.

Subpremise 2.1. IS 2 is in accordance with rules of (ordinary) language.

Conclusion. IS 2 should be adopted.

The conclusion stemming from argument 2 is strengthened by an additional argument based on the concept of legislative intent.

Argument 3 (Legislative Intent)

Premise 1 (normative). Statutory expressions ought to be interpreted in accordance with the legislative intent.

Premise 2 (factual). If the legislator intended to mean that the acquisition of new property should take place no earlier than the acquisition of inherited property, he would have omitted the expression "no later than."

Subpremise 2.1. The legislator used the expression "no later than," so he did not intend to mean "no earlier."

Conclusion. IS 2 should be adopted.

So far, three arguments were reconstructed. One argument pleads for IS 1, and the other arguments support IS 2. The question of how the relative strength of arguments should be compared is now raised. Fortunately, the PSAC made reference to Judgment 1 and criticized it in Judgment 2. Most of the criticism pointed out that in Judgment 1, the PSAC did not used the linguistic interpretation argument that should have been used by default and that conditions for acceptance of the results stemmed from other types of interpretive arguments, including the argument that negative consequences adopted in Judgment 1 were not fulfilled. A list of the conditions for disregarding the results of the linguistic interpretation in Judgment 2 is as follows:

- Contradiction with fundamental constitutional values,
- Flagrant injustice,
- Absurdity,
- Necessity to remedy a legislative error.

By providing this list of conditions, the PSAC attacked Premise 2 of Argument 1 by implying that the situation in question could not be classified as any of the conditions for the adoption of extra-linguistic types of interpretive arguments. Let us note that the use of this relatively simple argumentative move enabled the PSAC to not engage explicitly in the process of the balancing of values. Although a certain type of balancing has been performed by the court, it was presented in a form of rule-based reasoning and did not involve the application of any measurement scale or even a comparison between competing conclusions.

The competing arguments extracted from the cases discussed above are depicted in the following figure. Solid lines represent the informal relation of compatibility,

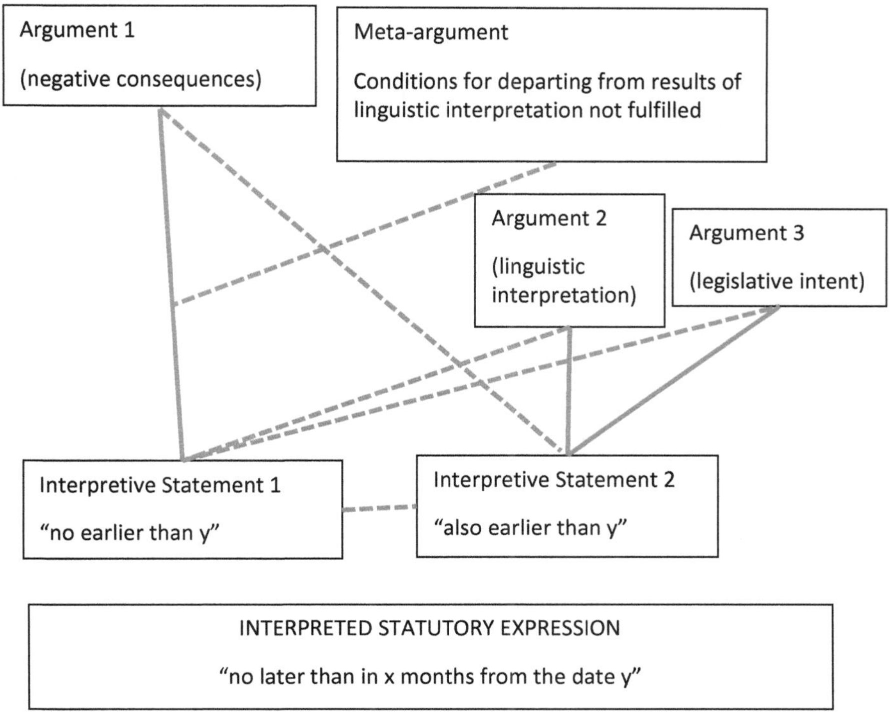

Fig. 9.1 Comparison of arguments in polish tax exemption cases

and dotted lines signify relations of incompatibility. Please note the relation of attack between the meta-argument employed in Judgment 2 and the applicability of the argument regarding negative consequences (Fig. 9.1).

9.6 Discussion

The case study discussed in the preceding section reveals the usefulness of the model outlined in Sect. 9.4 for the representation of the structure of interpretive arguments in the context of statutory law. The two layers of the model are the layer of Interpretive Statements and the layer of arguments based on argumentation schemes. The concept of Interpretive Statements as propositional representations of extensions of statutory expressions enables us to identify very clearly what legal issue is at stake in a given legal case. The layer of argumentation schemes illustrates that Interpretive Statements are supported by certain sets of premises.

As discussed previously, the third layer of the model, which concerns the comparison and balance between different arguments and is based on argument schemes, is yet to be developed. Because the model has a descriptive purpose, it should be designed using a bottom-up method with the use of legal cases as illustrative material. The case study presented in the preceding section provides useful information regarding the representation of the process of comparing competing arguments and assigning priorities to competing interpretive statements. The concepts of threshold and default priorities play central roles in this context. In the case analysed in this paper, a default priority has been assigned to the interpretive statement supported by linguistic interpretation. Moreover, certain threshold conditions were formulated for the assignment of priority to results generated by other types of elements. Because neither of these thresholds were met in Judgment 2, this case has been determined to favour the interpretive statement supported by linguistic interpretation.

The application of thresholds "activating" certain types of interpretation and the default priority assignment to the linguistic interpretation are arguably the result of balancing certain values; however, these considerations remain implicit. The PSAC stated instead in Judgment 2 that the argument based on negative consequences could not be applied because threshold conditions for its application have not been met. This technique enabled the court to not use any type of scales for the comparison of the strength and justification of competing arguments; even a simple ordinal scale was not applied (the PSAC in Judgment 2 implied that Argument 1 had in fact no foundation because threshold conditions have not been met). Notably, the avoidance to discuss any scale of comparison of the strength of the arguments was made possible due to the strict contradiction between the relevant parts of the competing interpretive statements. This reinforced the binary type of reasoning of the court: if one of the competing interpretive statements is to be accepted, the second one should be rejected, *tertium non datur*.

As a result, the present case study demonstrates that the balancing of values (which does not occur explicitly in the cases) has been represented by a rule-based argumentation framework encompassing default rules. The use of this framework enabled the PSAC to choose a justified interpretation of a statutory expression without addressing the complicated theoretical problems concerning the presence of values behind the statutory expression being analysed.

Żurek and Araszkiewicz (2013) argued that teleological arguments that are used in the statutory interpretation in *jus civile* legal systems often have threshold character: non-satisfaction of certain threshold of realization of a given value enables the reasoned to perform restrictive or extensive interpretation. The case analysed in the preceding section enables us to generalize this statement: the use of thresholds is also used on the meta-level and governs the choice between alternative interpretive statements generated by different types of arguments. Although the balancing of values is obviously present in the background of using thresholds, this does not have to be the case with maximization. The use of the threshold technique shifts the focus to *sufficient* conditions for adoption of a certain argumentative structure but not on maximization. It is contingent whether in certain jurisdiction or line of cases thresholds will be set in such way that they will actually lead to maximization of certain values. On the contrary, they (arguably) create a sufficient, reasonable level of realization of these values. Furthermore, the concept of proportionality is only implied here and reconstructed from the default preference orderings and the formulation of thresholds that "activate" certain types of arguments.

Interestingly enough, the argument schemes discussed above, and the meta-argument in particular, have the degree of justificatory force on their own. In this respect, they are to large extent detached from potentially explicable value-based framework that may be claimed to back them. Let us also note that it is possible to reconstruct different competitive sets of values that could justify the judicial decisions presented in this paper. The threshold-based descriptive model of decision on rival interpretation enables us to avoid overly complicated and potentially inconclusive investigations concerning those reconstructed sets of values and arguments based on them. At the same time it is worth noting that the use of threshold technique is not arbitrary. Let us recall that in Judgment 2 the PSAC disregarded the argumentation presented in Judgment 1 and justified its conclusions.

Regarding inaccuracies of the account presented above, it must be noted that a bias resulting from limited illustrative material may be present here. Another possibly problematic factor is that the transformation of argument schemes into argument tokens are very domain-dependent (see subpremises of Argument 1 and 2 above), so the model presented here should be seen as a tool for the description and reconstruction of actual judicial argumentation and not as a tool for a development of new legal argumentation. The completion of the latter purpose would involve gathering a huge database of common-sense reasoning patterns and combining them with complicated ontologies[14] designed for certain legal subdomains.

9.7 Conclusions and Further Research

In this paper, the topic of balancing in the context of statutory interpretation was discussed. Although the topics of balancing and proportionality have a vast amount of literature resources, especially in the context of constitutional review, it has not been discussed systematically in the context of comparing the strength of different types of interpretive arguments. The paper partially contributes to the topic and leads to the following conclusions.

First, the problem of legal interpretation may be generally described by the theory of multi-criteria decision-making. The general framework provided by this theory enables us to identify crucial features of any developed model of legal interpretation without commitments related to more concrete, or domain-dependent, models of legal balancing.

Second, the descriptive model of legal interpretation encompasses three layers: the formulation of Interpretive Statements, the use of argumentation schemes for the production of arguments and the resolution of conflicts between arguments.

Third, the analysis of the case study discussed in this paper using the three-layered model enabled us to present the structure of legal balancing in the context

[14] For the topic of legal ontologies in AI and Law, cf. Sartor et al. (eds.) (2011).

of statutory interpretation. Instead of an explicit balancing of legally relevant values and goals, the court used a technique of thresholds that should be met in order to use certain types of arguments (an argument regarding negative consequences in this context). If any of these thresholds are not met, interpretive decisions are resolved by using a default assignment of preference. It is plausible to claim that both argument schemes used in statutory interpretation (which form the second layer of the model) and the rules used for the resolution of conflicts between competing arguments (the third layer of the model developed in this paper) may be viewed as general and defeasible abstractions from the results of balancing background values. As such, they contribute to the economy of judicial reasoning and simplify the structures of knowledge representation used by courts. The use of such approximations is also present in common law judicial reasoning when the direct balancing of values is often substituted in actual judicial wording by collecting factors, or stereotypical fact patterns that tend to strengthen the position of the parties in the dispute.[15] On the other hand, the argument schemes and the threshold meta-arguments discussed are rather abstract rule constructs that tend not to focus on the circumstances of particular cases but on the determination of the meaning of general rules of law. Let us note in this connection that rules as generalizations may be over- or underinclusive with respect to their underlying justification (Schauer 1991, 31 ff.). We would like to point out that this feature applies not only to the rules of law and legal interpretation but also to threshold meta-arguments similar to the one discussed in this paper. Consequently, sometimes the result of the application of thresholds may be assessed as suboptimal from the point of view of the (underlying) balance of values. As a result, certain judicial decisions cannot be explained in terms of the balancing of values because the use of threshold arguments may lead to deviation from the result that would have been obtained were the court engaged in the explicit balancing of values. We contend that there is a huge gap between the application of rules by means of subsumption and the weighing of values that may contribute to the interpretation of rules and that there are layers of the application of arguments based on argument schemes and the application of thresholds, which are not reducible to the weighing of values.[16]

We argue that the model used in this paper may serve as a useful tool for further clarification and descriptive representation of the process of legal interpretation. The model should be tested on a larger corpus of legal cases in order to test the assertions of this paper. A different and potentially fruitful perspective for research is the comparison of the results obtained by the present model and other formalisms, such as the Carneades system developed by Gordon and Walton (2006).

[15] The topic of factors has ample literature resources in AI and Law research, cf. Ashley (1990) and Aleven (1997) for important expositions. The topic of substituting value-based arguments by factor-based arguments in Case-Based reasoning was discussed in Araszkiewicz (2011).

[16] Another important issue is the possible disagreement concerning the identification of values and the assignment of their relative weight that may accompany agreement concerning the application of certain argument schemes and threshold meta-arguments. This possible disagreement may explain the eagerness of the courts to refrain from the explicit balancing of values.

As for theoretical issues that are connected with the problems mentioned in this contribution, the concept of the burden of argumentation (Gizbert-Studnicki 1990) should be discussed in the context of analysing the threshold conditions for the application of different types of arguments. As noted in the case study, the fact that the threshold conditions were not satisfied was simply asserted and not justified. The concept of the burden of argumentation is useful in classifying statements in the process of legal interpretation into statements that may be simply asserted and statements that (according to the views accepted in judiciary practice) should be supported by argumentation.

Acknowledgements I am grateful to Thomas Bustamante for his valuable comments on an early draft of this paper and I thank Jaap Hage for excellent discussion concerning the late version. Also the comments of two anonymous reviewers contributed to making this paper better. All remaining mistakes are sole responsibility of the author.

References

Aleven, Vincent. 1997. Teaching case-based reasoning through model and examples. PhD thesis, Intelligent Systems Program, University of Pittsburgh.

Alexy, Robert. 2002. *A theory of constitutional rights.* Trans. J. Rivers. Oxford: Oxford University Press (1st German ed. 1985).

Alexy, Robert. 2003. On balancing and subsumption. A structural comparison. *Ratio Juris* 16: 433–449.

Alexy, Robert. 2007. The weight formula. In *Studies in the philosophy of law 3*, ed. Jerzy Stelmach, Bartosz Brożek, and Wojciech Załuski, 9–27. Kraków: Wydawnictwo Uniwersytetu Jagiellońskiego (Jagiellonian University Press).

Araszkiewicz, Michał. 2010. Balancing of legal principles and constraint satisfaction. In *Legal knowledge and information systems, JURIX 2010: The twenty-third annual conference*, ed. Rabboud Winkels, 7–16. Amsterdam: IOS Press.

Araszkiewicz, Michał. 2011. Values and factors in legal balancing. *Jusletter IT*, 29.

Araszkiewicz, Michał. 2013a. Limits of constraint satisfaction theory of coherence as a theory of (legal) justification. In *Coherence: Insights from philosophy, jurisprudence and artificial intelligence*, ed. Michał Araszkiewicz and Jaromír Šavelka, 217–242. Dordrecht: Springer.

Araszkiewicz, Michał. 2013b. Towards systematic research on statutory interpretation in AI and law. In *Legal knowledge and information systems, JURIX 2013: The twenty-sixth annual conference*, ed. Kevin Ashley, 15–24. Amsterdam: IOS Press.

Ashley, Kevin. 1990. *Modelling legal argument reasoning with cases and hypotheticals.* Cambridge, MA: MIT Press.

Ashley, Kevin, and Vern Walker. 2013. From information retrieval (IR) to argument retrieval (AR) for legal cases: Report on a baseline study. In *Legal knowledge and information systems, JURIX 2013: The twenty-sixth annual conference*, ed. Kevin Ashley, 29–38. Amsterdam: IOS Press.

Bench-Capon, Trevor. 2011. Relating values in a series of Supreme Court decisions. In *Legal knowledge and information systems, JURIX 2011: The twenty-fourth annual conference*, ed. Katie Atkinson, 13–22. Amsterdam: IOS Press.

Bench-Capon, Trevor. 2012. What makes a system a legal expert? In *Legal knowledge and information systems, JURIX 2012: The twenty-fifth annual conference*, ed. Burkhard Schäfer, 11–20. Amsterdam: IOS Press.

Bench-Capon, Trevor, and Henry Prakken. 2009. A case study of hypothetical and value-based reasoning in US Supreme-Court cases. In *Legal knowledge and information systems, JURIX 2009: The twenty-second annual conference*, ed. Guido Governatori, 11–20. Amsterdam: IOS Press.

Bench-Capon, Trevor, and Henry Prakken. 2010. Using argument schemes for hypothetical reasoning in law. *Artificial Intelligence and Law* 18: 153–174.

Borowski, Martin. 2007. *Grundrechte als Prizipien*, 2nd ed. Baden-Baden: Nomos.

Bustamante, Thomas. 2005. *Argumentação contra legem. A teoria do discurso e a justificação jurídica nos casos mais difíceis*. Rio de Janeiro: Renovar.

Ehrgott, Matthias. 2005. *Multicriteria optimization*, 2nd ed. Berlin/Heidelberg/New York: Springer.

Feteris, Eveline. 2008. The rational reconstruction of weighing and balancing on the basis of teleological-evaluative considerations in the justification of judicial decisions. *Ratio Juris* 21: 481–495.

Gizbert-Studnicki, Tomasz. 1990. The burden of argumentation in legal disputes. *Ratio Juris* 3: 118–129.

Gordon, Thomas, and Douglas Walton. 2006. The Carneades argumentation framework — Using presumptions and exceptions to model critical questions. In *Proceedings of the first international conference on Computational Models of Argument (COMMA 06)*, ed. Paul E. Dunne and Trevor Bench-Capon, 195–207. Amsterdam: IOS Press.

Grabmair, Matthias, and Kevin Ashley. 2010. Argumentation with value judgments. An example of hypothetical reasoning. In *Legal knowledge and information systems, JURIX 2010: The twenty-third annual conference*, ed. Radboud Winkels, 67–76. Amsterdam: IOS Press.

Hage, Jaap. 2005. *Studies in legal logic*. Berlin: Springer.

Hage, Jaap. 2013. Three kinds of coherentism. In *Coherence: Insights from philosophy, jurisprudence and artificial intelligence*, ed. Michał Araszkiewicz and Jaromír Šavelka, 1–32. Dordrecht: Springer.

Macagno, Fabrizio, Giovanni Sartor, and Douglas Walton. 2012. Argumentation schemes for statutory interpretation. In *ARGUMENTATION 2012: International conference on alternative methods of argumentation in law*, ed. Michał Araszkiewicz, Matej Myška, Terezie Smejkalová, Jaromír Šavelka, and Martin Škop, 31–44. Brno: Masaryk University.

Oskamp, Anja. 1993. Model for knowledge and legal expert systems. *Artificial Intelligence and Law* 1: 245–274.

Peczenik, Aleksander. 2008. *On law and reason*, 2nd ed. New York: Springer.

Sartor, Giovanni. 2010. Doing justice to rights and values: Teleological reasoning and proportionality. *Artificial Intelligence and Law* 18: 175–215.

Sartor, Giovanni, Pompeu Casanovas, Maria Angela Biasotti, and Meritxell Fernández-Barrera (eds.). 2011. *Approaches to legal ontologies*. Dordrecht/Heidelberg/London/New York: Springer.

Schauer, Frederick. 1991. *Playing by the rules. A philosophical examination of rule-based decision-making in law and in life*. Oxford: Clarendon.

Sieckmann, Jan. 2009. *Recht als normatives system*. Baden-Baden: Nomos.

Thagard, Paul. 2000. *Coherence in thought and action*. Cambridge, MA/London: MIT Press.

Walton, Douglas. 1996. *Argumentation schemes for presumptive reasoning*. Mahwah: Lawrence Erlbaum Associates.

Walton, Douglas. 2006. *Fundamentals of critical argumentation*. Cambridge: Cambridge University Press.

Wróblewski, Jerzy. 1992. *The judicial application of law*. In eds. Zenon Bankowski and Neil MacCormick. Dordrecht: Springer.

Żurek, Tomasz, and Michał Araszkiewicz. 2013. Modelling teleological interpretation. In *ICAIL 2013: Proceedings of the fourteenth conference on artificial intelligence and law*, ed. Bart Verheij, Enrico Francesconi, and Anne von der Leith Gardner, 160–168. New York: ACM.

Chapter 10
An Analysis of Some Juristic Techniques for Handling Systematic Defects in the Law

Giovanni Battista Ratti

Abstract The contribution carries out an analysis of some of the main techniques used by legal scholars in order to systematize the law, i.e. to provide it with a systematic character. In particular, the contribution first reconstructs some of the juristic operations consisting in deriving (deductively or not) implicit norms from expressed ones. It then goes on to analyze the operations consisting in reformulating a certain set of norms, singling out the "founding" elements of a normative system, highlighting the formal and axiological characteristics, and suggesting, if necessary, the expulsion, from the normative set, of the norms that do not allow this set to have a genuinely systematic nature. Then, the paper carefully examines, in the light of the conceptual dichotomy first/second interpretation, the systematizing tools employed by jurists in order to create, avoid, or ascertain systematic defects of the law, such as normative gaps and inconsistencies. The operations consisting in ordering legal materials in light of a set of underlying principles are finally examined.

10.1 Foreword

Both in common law and civil law systems alike, academic jurists are said to play a basic role in the description and cognition of law. According to a traditional thesis of legal positivism, jurists' main task is to provide a clear and systematic image of the law actually in force in a given (subset of a) legal system, at a certain time t_1.[1] Thus, the jurists' perspective is, at the same time, eminently static and partial.[2]

Jurists – unlike theorists and philosophers of law – do not seem to be interested in the legal system considered as a whole; they rather aim to analyze subsets of the legal system: private law, criminal law, business law, or even more restricted sets

[1] See Aarnio (2011, pp. 177–184) and Jori (1985, pp. 263 ff.).

[2] See Alchourrón and Bulygin (1971).

G.B. Ratti (✉)
Tarello Institute for Legal Philosophy, Department of Law, University of Genova,
Via Balbi, 30/18, 16126 Genoa, Italy
e-mail: gbratti@unige.it

© Springer International Publishing Switzerland 2015

T. Bustamante, C. Dahlman (eds.), *Argument Types and Fallacies in Legal Argumentation*, Law and Philosophy Library 112,
DOI 10.1007/978-3-319-16148-8_10

such as torts, homicide, the powers of the prime minister, the legislative procedure, and so on.

As Carlos Alchourrón and Eugenio Bulygin (1971, pp. 68–69) have pointed out, “it must be emphasized that the jurist is always concerned with a limited field of problems and although every legal problem is studied by some jurist, no jurist can take an interest in all the problems at the same time”.[3]

Moreover, even though jurists are often concerned with the evolution and the possible future developments of the topic they are focusing on, their principal purpose is to reconstruct the present state of a given subset: more precisely, the actual set of rules and their normative consequences with regard to a specified topic.

In order to do so, they usually carry out a plurality of activities that, although mixed in everyday practice, conceptual analysis must keep separate.[4] The epistemological *status* of such activities is rather controversial. In fact, the activities carried out by jurists are not, considered as a whole, a mere descriptive (i.e. cognitive) enterprise. In the perspective of the analytical legal theory, legal scholarship is commonly regarded as a set of “discursive” activities, composed of several operations.

In particular, at least 11 typical juristic operations can be singled out[5]:

1. Identification of a “relevant” normative problem[6];
2. Identification of the legal sentences forming a “sentential basis”;
3. Validation of the sentences which belong to the sentential basis;
4. Interpretation of each of the sentences belonging to the sentential basis (the product thereof being a normative basis)[7];
5. Argumentation of the interpretations that have been provided;
6. Development of the normative basis, by means of either logical rules of inference (*stricto sensu* logical development), or of different rules of inference commonly used by jurists (e.g.: argument *a simili*), in order to infer implicit norms that cannot be derived by the simple interpretation of the sentential basis[8];
7. Analysis of some possible defects of the normative basis: in particular, gaps and inconsistencies;
8. Conservative reformulation of the normative basis, by means of generalizing methods (so called “legal induction”), which allows one to eliminate the possible redundancies;
9. Removal of inconsistencies;
10. Filling of gaps;
11. Ordering the normative material according to a certain scheme.

[3] Alchourrón and Bulygin (1971, pp. 68–69).

[4] Bulygin (1986) and Guastini (2013 b).

[5] See Guastini (1986).

[6] Cf. Alchourrón and Bulygin (1971, ch. I). In a comparative perspective, see Sacco (1988: pp. 48 ff.).

[7] See Aarnio (1977, pp. 16 ff.); (1986, pp. 161–162); Alchourrón (1986, pp. 172–175).

[8] See Bobbio (1994, ch. XV).

In the following pages, I aim to analyze, in particular detail, the activities consisting in systematizing and ordering a normative basis (operations 7–11), being a normative basis a set of norms understood as the main product of previous identifying, interpretive, and developing operations (1–6). Accordingly, I shall briefly summarize such hermeneutic and inferential activities in the next two sections, while I shall devote the remaining sections to the thorough examination of the strictly systematizing tasks, such as the identification and filling of gaps and the identification and solution of inconsistencies. When examples are needed, I shall refer mainly to the Italian legal scholarship, the one I happen to know a little about, but I suspect that its *modus operandi* is not very far away from that of legal scholars in other Western legal systems.

10.2 The Identifying and Interpretive Activities of Legal Scholarship

What jurists are mainly interested in, when carrying out their "expository" task, is the determination of the normative qualification of a certain conduct, according to the law in force. In such case, it is the set of all the relevant actions that may be performed when some circumstances obtain that determines the identification of a certain normative problem. If, for instance, a certain jurist wants to determine the legal *regime* of the patrimonial assets of cohabiting couples in Italy, she has to single out all those normative provisions that, at least at first sight, seem to refer to the different actions which are related to. In other words, if a jurist wants to provide her normative problem with a solution, she has to single out all those provisions whose propositional contents describes the action or the actions, whose deontic *status* is determined by the normative qualification. In so doing, she can follow the order imposed on the topic by the lawgiver (if such order exists) or by the courts, or substitute this order with another one. Indeed, the jurist's first step is to identify an action: the action the normative qualification thereof she is interested in. The second step is to find the legal materials (statutory and constitutional, but also judicial and doctrinal) which are relevant for the solution of the problem, in the light of previous judicial and doctrinal interpretations.

The outcome of the operations analyzed so far is the identification of some legal sentences, belonging to the legal sources. Put in other words, what jurists do, after having approached a particular normative problem and after having identified a specific topic, is to cut out, inside of legislation (typically in civil-law legal systems) or case-law (typically in common-law legal systems), or both, "a finite set of relevant sentences".[9]

In civil-law countries, this operation can be reduced to singling out some statutory provisions assumed to be relevant with regard to the solution of the original

[9]Guastini (1986, p. 296).

normative question. This happens when, using the same conceptual categories used by the legislator in systematizing a certain topic, jurists identify the relevant provisions according to legislative design.[10]

When a legislative systematization is lacking, jurists may find themselves in front of a fragmentary normative discipline, dispersed in many legal documents,[11] or even in front of an inexistent one. The selection of every relevant sentence can be anything but easy with regard to some topic, alternatively either because of the modern legal systems enormous amount of legislation and the consequent difficulty of knowing all the relevant sentences, or because of the nearly total lack of legal provisions related to some specific topics. It must be added, however, that often jurists approach a topic in the light of previous identifications, carried out by other jurists, which make it easier for them to find the relevant legal sources, also in the extreme cases of super-abundance or complete lack of legal provisions.

The identification of the sentential basis logically involves (and temporally is accompanied by) other two important operations: (1) the *prima facie* (or first) interpretation of involved sentences; (2) their formal validation.

In the first interpretation phase, often in the light of previous doctrinal analysis, jurists identify a language segment as a sentence and ascribe a first tentative meaning to it.[12] This meaning, "fruit of a not pondered comprehension", seems not to be mechanically identified with the product of so-called "literal" interpretation (i.e.: with the "literal" meaning). It is rather its current legal meaning, diffused in the legal community, on the basis of consolidated scholarly and judicial views.[13]

---

[10]Alchourrón and Bulygin (1971, p. 76): "When the source is legislation, the problem has been usually solved in advance (at least in part) by the legislator himself who normally orders the statutes and their contents according to some criterion. This means that he also is engaged in the activity of systematization. This tendency to legislate in a systematic way has increased remarkably since the enactment of the Code Napoleon (the trend towards codification of the law). The characteristic feature of this procedure is that the statutes or the paragraphs of a code are grouped according to different topics [...] It should be noted that so far as theory is concerned, the legislator who draws up a statute is engaged in exactly the same activity as the dogmatic jurist: both are constructing a normative system, although the former is not bound by pre-existing (valid) sentences, but chooses them more or less freely".

[11]Cf. Van Hoecke (1986, p. 219): "D'un pont de vue historique la dogmatique juridique a longtemps eu comme objectif principal la systématisation d'un droit coutumier et d'une jurisprudence fragmentaire et hétérogène. Les grandes codifications [...] ont d'ailleurs été le travail d'éminants jurisconsultes".

[12]Chiassoni (1999a, p. 91): "At the first-interpretation stage, interpreters perform the following activities: (a) they identify an object as a sentence, or a string of sentences, in a (to them) familiar language; (b) they ascribe to the sentence(s) a first, tentative, meaning – or an array of tentative, possible, meanings".

[13]See Bowers (1989, pp. 49 ff.), who distinguishes "semantic meaning" and "situational meaning", observing about the latter. At p. 52, the author states: "Although the detailed exposition of situational meaning is complex, involving factors of social background, culture, participants' knowledge of the world, and the formal status of a text, the basic principles are simple; the effect of an utterance is strongly coloured by its "field", "tenor", and "mode". The field of a discourse is the social action of which it forms a part, including its subject-matter; its tenor is the set of relationships existing among the participants in the discourse – the social roles and status of speakers, hearers and overhearers; the mode of a discourse is its form of expression – spoken, written, formal, informal, private, public, and so on to the details of its actual physical qualities".

When jurists select a set of the sentences to form a sentential basis, from which they will start their exposing enterprise, they make sure that these sentences present determined requirements so that they can be considered formally valid or applicable.[14]

To do so, they use some criteria, which "establish what requirements legal sentences must satisfy in order to be valid".[15] The notion of formal validity is, accordingly, relative to a given set of criteria, which, following Alchourrón and Bulygin's terminology, we can call "criteria of identification". Criteria of identification consist, roughly, of two classes of rules: (1) rules of admission, which establish the conditions for a sentence to be valid; and (2) rules of rejection, which establish the conditions under which a sentence, previously valid, is no longer valid. A sentence, enacted in accordance with the rules of admission and not eliminated because of a rule of rejection, can be chosen as a basic sentence.

By "applicable" I mean a norm, the application thereof is prescribed by another valid norm.[16] In legal scholarship, it may be (and often is) the case that the normative systems built-up by jurists are made also (or even eminently) of applicable norms: think for example of foreign norms which are to be applied in a jurist's domestic legal system, or moral norms which are applied in decisions bearing on ethically sensible issues.

We have seen that the prima facie or first interpretation is the juristic operation that makes it possible to pass from a set of legal sources to the narrower set of prima facie relevant sources, by assigning a first, tentative, meaning to them and identifying their linguistic function.[17]

Second or all-things-considered interpretation (also dubbed "reinterpretation") is the operation that makes it possible to pass from the (relevant) legal sources to legal norms, or, from a slightly different perspective, from a sentential basis to a normative basis, which constitutes the foundation of all the following juristic operations.

The activity of reinterpretation consists in assigning to a certain text a particular meaning, which is the "final interpretative response" of the jurist and constitutes the final product of a complex exegetic process which is articulated in four phases: (a) the evaluation of the results of first interpretation; (b) the enumeration of some (or even all) the further interpretive options which may reasonably pursued by the interpreter; (c) the choice of one of such options or the creation of a new interpretive option; (d) making more precise the content of the chosen interpretation.[18]

---

[14] Alchourrón and Bulygin (1971, pp. 72–73); Guastini (1986); and Niiniluoto (1981).

[15] Alchourrón and Bulygin (1971, p. 72).

[16] Applicability, as a consequence, is a concept which is parasitic to that of validity. On applicability, see at least Bulygin (1982) and Rodríguez (2014, pp. 265–270).

[17] It cannot be excluded that only after having carried out one or more reinterpretations, the jurists regard as useless, due to an ascription of meaning different from the one carried out prima facie, some sentences that she had considered prima facie relevant for the solution of the normative problem at hand.

[18] Chiassoni (1999b).

On such an interpretive result (which is the product of reinterpretation), the jurist founds her main non-interpretive responses, such as the possible construction of a general doctrine (e.g. of sanctions, of contracts, of torts, etc.), the coherentization and integration of a normative set, and the subsequent elaboration of a dogmatic system. Each of such operations may involve the modification of the normative basis and, consequently, the changing (not only of first interpretation, but also) of the reinterpretation which is at the foundations of each of them.

10.3 The Derivation of Implicit Norms from a Normative Basis

The activities of jurists do not end with the construction of the normative basis. Quite the opposite: it is a widespread view that the *main activity* of legal scholars consists in logically developing and reformulating the normative bases of the different sectors in which the legal order is subdivided, according to criteria of concise exposition and systemic elegance.

The "empirical" observation of the activities of jurists shows that they complete the discourse of legal authorities deriving unexpressed norms, from the expressed norms which are assumed to be the meaning-contents of normative provisions.

More precisely, seven kinds of unexpressed norms can be singled out, depending on the reasoning and/or the premises from which they can be derived[19]:

(1) Norms derived from expressed norms by means of deductive reasoning;
(2) Norms derived from expressed norms by means of non-deductive reasoning, not expressly allowed/contemplated by positive law;
(3) Norms derived from expressed norms by means of particular rules of inference expressly allowed by positive law (e.g. analogy);
(4) Norms derived from expressed norms by means of particular rules of "legal logic" (such as the *a contrario* argument or the *a fortiori* argument);
(5) Norms derived from expressed norms by means of (sound or unsound) reasoning the premises thereof are made not only of expressed norms, but also of doctrinal theses;
(6) Norms derived from expressed norms by means of finite induction;
(7) Norms derived from unexpressed norms by means of non-finite induction.

For the sake of brevity, the analysis of each kind of derived norm cannot be completely carried out here. Here I shall only touch on them quickly.

[19] See Guastini (2013 b, pp. 155–157).

10.3.1 Deductively Derived Norms

The theory of normative systems claims that, a posteriori, many (if not all) juristic arguments can be reconstructed as deductive, often under the condition of making implicit premises explicit.[20] However, one can find some clear doctrinal examples of deductive reasoning, intended to produce implicit norms (understood as strict logical consequences of expressed norms).

An example of such kind of reasoning is apparent in the case of vicarious liability for culpable conduct of the employee within the Italian legal system; this, according to legal scholars, is not limited to the specified work duties of the employee, but reaches out to voluntary conducts of the employee exceeding his specific work incumbencies[21]:

> The liability for the negligence of the employee is not limited to the execution of the task specifically entrusted to him, but extends to deviations from the activities specifically ordered, and completion of related operations that the employee has voluntarily undertaken. Thus, if a skilled worker, sent by a company that supplies electricity to install a meter at a private place carries out, beyond the scope of his duties, the testing of the electrical power alimented by the meter he put in place, and, during this testing, negligently causes injury, his employer responds for damages.

Such kind of reasoning can be formalized as follows[22]:

[1] $\forall x(Dx \rightarrow ORx)$[23]
[2] Da

---

[3] ORa

Indeed, the conclusion (the employer's obligation to compensate the damages) necessarily follows from the premises (the norm [1] and the statement [2] which describes the employee's damage): this is so-called deontic modus ponens. Observe that, in the passage under scrutiny, so-called "logical enrichment" is also applied.[24] If there is a damage caused by the employee, there must be a compensation granted by the employer, both in the case that the damage is caused by the employee in carrying out her "ordinary" tasks (let's symbolize them by "I") and in the case it is caused by the employee in carrying out "extraordinary" tasks he has voluntarily undertaken (symbolized by "L").

---

[20] Alchourrón and Bulygin (1971), Navarro and Rodríguez (2014).

[21] Trimarchi (1961, p. 159). Translation from Italian, here and elsewhere, is mine.

[22] "D" is for "damages", "R" is for "responding for damages".

[23] Which reads: "If there is damage caused by the employee, then the employer is obliged to restore it".

[24] Logical enrichment is the rule according to which if a certain proposition *p* is a sufficient condition of another proposition *q*, no matter how many proposition we add to *p*, in case *p* is instantiated, *q* will continue on following from *p* anyway. In symbols: "$(p \rightarrow q) \rightarrow (p \,\&\, r \rightarrow q)$".

In symbols:

$$[1'] \ \forall x(Dx\&(Ix \vee Lx \vee \ldots Nx) \rightarrow ORx)$$
$$[2'] \ Da\&(Ia \vee La \vee \ldots Na)$$

---

[3] ORa

The identification of new *relevant* properties does not alter the nature of reasoning, provided that the normative basis is enlarged in order to contain further norms from which one can derive such properties: i.e. provided that implicit exceptions are made explicit. If relevance of properties is only recognized implicitly, then what we have is a case of enthymematic reasoning.

A relevant property, ruling out enrichment (or, from a slightly different perspective, calling for the revision of the premises) in the case at hand, is found in the following lines[25]:

> An employee may carry out, at times, without the employer knowing, a task that was up to another employee. If damages arise therefrom, in order to determine whether this is within the risk of the enterprise, one should consider the greater or lesser affinity between the duties of the employee and the specific activities carried out by him, and the extent to which the performance of the enterprise activities may be divided into branches, offices, and factories.

According to Trimarchi (who "introduces" this norm into the Italian legal system, inspired by the U.S. *Restatement of the Law of Agency*),[26] when an employee undertakes an activity which is up to another employee, without having the skills, exceeding his competences, and without the employer knowing (let's symbolize by "M" this set of circumstances), the employer does not respond for damages. In symbols:

$$[4] \ \forall x(Dx\&Mx) \rightarrow \sim ORx$$

In the passages we have quoted, Trimarchi enlarges the normative basis of vicarious liability of the employer, first reconstructing norm [1] regarding the liability for the employee's conduct, and then identifying the properties which rules out the application of such a norm, or more precisely rules out "logical enrichment" regarding [1] in a certain context – as it happens in [4]. However, it is manifest that if one wants to avoid inconsistencies within the system, the normative basis must be reconfigured as follows:

$$[1''] \ \forall x(Dx\& \sim Mx) \rightarrow ORx$$
$$[4] \ \forall x(Dx\&Mx) \rightarrow \sim ORx$$

[25] Trimarchi (1961, pp. 159–160).

[26] This norm is considered in force within the Italian legal order due to its implicit derivation from the principle of liability based on (direct or indirect) negligence of the employer: here we have a first example of non-deductive reasoning.

Indeed, deductively developed, such a normative basis constitutes a complete and consistent normative system.[27]

10.3.2 *Other Kinds of Derived Norms*

From the point of view of the "empirical" analysis of juristic reasoning, it can be observed that jurists carry out many kinds of reasoning which are not deductive in nature.

According to a widespread opinion among jurists, deductive reasoning is insufficient to reconstruct the conceptual content of a legal system. This is due, among other things, to the important fact that the law itself admits, in addition to deductive reasoning, also other types of reasoning.[28] As is known, it may be the case that a legal order admits (and in certain cases even requires) that legal officials, jurists and lawyers reason in a non-deductive way (e.g. analogically).

In addition to this, there is a widespread view among jurists, according to which legal scholars cannot confine themselves to deductively developing a set of norms (unless they want to build a merely "tautological" science) but should instead "systematize" legal materials, which, at first, often appear under the forms of an unordered set of normative provisions.[29] Therefore, it is common for jurists to derive norms from legal materials by means of logically unsound reasoning.

From the point of view of rational reconstruction, it is possible to distinguish the procedures used by jurists to develop legal requirements, at least between: (1) arguments expressly based on specific provisions of law; (2) arguments that have no explicit recognition in the law, but which are implicitly required by the law; and (3) arguments, not expressly provided or implicitly required by law, but developed by legal scholarship.

---

[27]Of course, the system at hand is made complete by what we can call "the norm of closure of liability" ([NCL] ~Dx → ~ORx), which is implicit in Trimarchi's discourse and is generally recognized by legal scholarship.

	[1″] Dx & ~Mx → ORx	[4] Dx & Mx → ~ORx	[NCR] ~Dx → ~ORx
Dx & Mx		~ORx	
Dx & ~Mx	ORx		
~Dx & Mx			~ORx
~Dx & ~Mx			~ORx

[28]Guastini (2013a): 134–135.

[29]Trimarchi (1961, p. 6): "With the only tool of formal logic one can infer from legal norms nothing more than what it is expressed by them, since formal deduction is tautological. To go further, to solve the problems that the legislature did not contemplate, or did not solve, often with the stated purpose of entrusting the solution to judges, it is necessary to study the functions that can be regarded as pertaining to the norms, by adequately coordinating and developing them".

Some qualifications are in order here.

(1) The first category contains those arguments, specifically productive or integrative of the law (such as analogy in the Italian legal order, or the variety of integrative arguments allowed by the first section of the Swiss Civil Code[30]), which have their foundations in legal provisions.

Although these arguments are generally deemed to be invalid from a logical point of view, there is no doubt that they are more than "sound" from a legal point of view, since they are allowed, if not imposed (at least in some cases), by law itself.

(2) The second category includes those kinds of reasoning that, though not being expressly recognized by the law, are implicitly required by the law in order to regard it as a complete and consistent whole. In particular, the judges, who are the addressees of a general prohibition of denial of justice and of the obligation of justifying their decisions on the basis of pre-existing legal norms, cannot but conceive the law as a complete and consistent normative set,[31] otherwise they could not judge or could not base their decisions on legally valid norms. Well, all the (logically unsound) procedures which, from time to time, the judges (and jurists) use to reach a solution for an unqualified case or a inconsistently qualified case, are admitted in so far as law requires the court to resolve any dispute whatsoever. In other words, there are situations where the only existing option for the judge of deciding a case on a legal basis consists in using arguments, not explicitly provided by the law, which allow one to fill in a normative gap or to solve an antinomy. These arguments usually make use of positive norms to create other norms. A paradigmatic example of such kind of arguments is the *a contrario* argument in its productive function (*Expressio unius est exclusio alterius*).

(3) Finally, there are procedures that are used to produce unexpressed norms, which are neither provided for, nor implicitly required by the law, but are grounded on extra-legal elements, and especially on the ideological theses defended (often surreptitiously) by legal scholars. For instance, jurists interpret constitutional provisions in a "dissociative" way, in order to distinguish cases that were not differentiated by the lawgiver.[32]

We have just seen that jurists often use different rules of inference to reach, on several occasions, diverging results. It is even more common, though, that they change the premises of their reasoning (rather than the rules of inference), by adding to positive norms non-positive premises derived by legal scholarship.

[30] Section 1 of the Swiss Civil Code provides: "1. The law applies according to its wording or interpretation to all legal questions for which it contains a provision. 2. In the absence of a provision, the court shall decide in accordance with customary law and, in the absence of customary law, in accordance with the rule that it would make as legislator. 3. In doing so, the court shall follow established doctrine and case law".

[31] Alchourrón (2012, pp. 40–44).

[32] Parodi (1996, pp. 102 ff.).

As a consequence, the development of the normative basis can be carried out, not only by changing the rules of inference (as we have explained so far), but also (and even more frequently) by *adding "non-positive" premises of different kinds.* Unluckily, this feature of the logical development of a normative basis has seldom been taken into account in relevant literature.[33]

In addition to specific dogmatic theses elaborated by jurists, the discourse of legal scholarship is full of conceptual theories, which are not only used to "integrate" the discourse of normative authorities, but are likely to affect the interpretation of the relevant statutory provisions and the normative consequences which can be derived from them.

Examples are legion. It suffices here to record just one of them, concerning the "legal nature" of pre-contractual responsibility in the Italian legal system, where section 1337 of the Italian Civil Code[34] has been interpreted, alternatively, as bearing upon an offense tort or as a responsibility of a contractual nature. The former thesis has been propounded on the basis of the theory according to which interest protected in terms of pre-contractual liability is that of freedom of contract. The latter thesis has been defended by arguing mainly that "the responsibility is of a contractual kind, on the assumption that torts would require violation of absolute rights, while those at play in negotiations are of a relative nature".[35]

Another major operation carried out by legal scholarship is so-called "legal induction", which consists roughly in deriving principles from specific rules. In other words, it consists in "summing up" a large number of rules, which have aspects in common, by means of one or more general principles. The logical nature of this process is controversial. Some authors hold that it has a deductive nature, whereas others believe it is a genuine inductive process.

For Alchourrón and Bulygin (1971, pp. 78–84), for instance, in reformulating several norms (which have at least one common element) into a more general norms containing such a common element and normatively equivalent to the original norms, the inferential nature of the procedure is ensured by the fact that the number of norms is finite (and that the conclusion necessarily follows from the premises). From the norms N_1 ($Dx \& Ix \rightarrow OR$); N_2: ($Dx \& Lx \rightarrow OR$); N_3: ($Dx \& Sx \rightarrow OR$) one can surely infer the norm ($Dx \rightarrow OR$). It is a strictly deductive inference, since the transition from more detailed norms to the more general rule is a strict inference, and not merely a "probable" one.

It should, however, be noted that, in addition to N1, N2, N3, one can derive from N4, by means of enrichment, many other norms, which were not previously belonging to the legal order. This evidently shows that the argument according to which legal induction is not a creative process can be maintained in so far as the context (i.e. the normative system in which the induction is carried out) does not change.

---

[33] But see Guastini (2011, pp. 155–163) and (2013 b).

[34] Section 1337 of the Italian Civil Code provides: "The parties, in negotiating and forming the contract, must act in good faith".

[35] Musy (1997, p. 400).

A view which runs counter to that of Alchourrón and Bulygin is defended by Jori, who holds that "any group of norms that have something in common can be used to 'induce' an infinite number of principles, that justify them (for example, by varying the level of generality at which 'induction' is stopped): from each of these different principles, then, it will also be possible to deduce the correct set of original norms".[36]

At any rate, one can find in legal scholarship examples of both deductive generalization (*à la* Alchourrón e Bulygin) as well as examples of strictly inductive generalization (*à la* Jori).

An example of the first kind of generalization is derivation of the so-called "principle of safety and health of the workers in working places", which is drawn from several provisions of the Italian legal system, such as sections 2, 32, 35, 41 of the Constitution, and section 2084 of the Italian Civil Code, as well as from many provisions of the legislative decree N. 626/1994. Generalization seems to be deductive in the case at hand, since given those premises (i.e. that specific meaning-attribution to that sentential basis) one cannot but derive such a principle (and there are no other norms of labor law which put such a principle into doubt).[37]

By contrast, an example of a principle extracted by means of a genuine inductive generalization is given by the principle of strict liability for enterprise risk.[38] Such a principle may be inferred, although not in an uncontroversial way, from some of the norms regarding torts. However, there are many other norms which justify the opposite principle, according to which the employer only responds in case of negligence. It is clear that also in this case the induction of the principle of strict liability is a "finite" one. But such finiteness is always capable of being jeopardized by adding new norms to the normative basis. As a consequence, its results are merely, as it were, "probabilistic".

10.4 Reformulation and Choices Among Alternative Normative Systems

Legal principles – often the product of the "inductive" activities we have just analyzed – play a twofold "systematic" role: (1) on the one hand, they constitute the ultimate "axiomatic basis" of a certain system of norms; (2) on the other hand, they justify the norms of the system, in that they are the axiological foundations of such norms. From combining such two functions, one can infer the distinction between "justifying" axiomatic bases and "non-justifying" axiomatic bases and observe that, generally, jurists prefer the former over the latter.

[36] Jori (1985, pp. 320–321).

[37] Cf. Minale Costa (2004, pp. 206 ff.).

[38] Cf. Trimarchi (1961, pp. 1–6).

According to this view, principles are the elements which are capable of making a certain normative set consistent, complete, and axiologically coherent.[39] This would be for the following reasons. First, a principle is often (if not always) "in collision" with (at least) another principle, so that by introducing a preferential ordering among principles one can order the whole normative set (in other words, by making consistent the set of the axioms one makes consistent the theorems too). Secondly, a principle allows one to infer other norms in addition to those from which it was derived (i.e. the completeness of the axioms warrants the completeness of the theorems). Finally, it is a widespread view that principles allow one to reduce a certain normative set to its ultimate values, highlighting its possible axiological defects and disharmonies. In the example above, the principle of strict liability, inferable from some of the norms on torts, was in conflict with other norms of the same field, from which it was possible to induce the principle of negligence or fault liability: in lieu of a unique system of liability for enterprise risk, legal scholarship has produced two, each of which may be traced back to a different principle.

The reformulation of the system makes it possible to single out the "founding" elements of a normative system, highlighting the formal and axiological characteristics, and suggesting, if necessary, the expulsion, from the normative set, of the norms that do not allow this set to have a genuinely systematic nature.

In particular, such a reformulation makes it possible to reconstruct a normative system as a deductive set, from which all the consequences can be derived by deduction. In other words, if it is true that before the reformulation, a normative set may have gaps and contradictions, as well as axiological disharmonies, it is also true that, after that the reformulation took place, it is easier to connect the normative set to the systematic characters of which the law is predicated.

This can be demonstrated, by formalizing the Italian regulations on strict liability for enterprise risk which were mentioned previously.

In "axiomatic" terms, the system of torts in Italian legal scholarship is formed by the two following principles, each of which is (supposedly) derivable from some provisions of the civil code:

$$[1]\ \forall x(Dx \rightarrow ORx)$$

Which means "For any *x*, if *x* is a damage, then it is obligatory to redress it"; and

$$[5]\ \forall x(Dx \& \sim Fx \rightarrow \sim ORx)$$

This means "For any *x*, if *x* is a faultless damage, then it is not obligatory to redress it". This is tantamount to the usual slogan in Italian legal scholarship "No liability without fault".

---

[39] See Ratti (2014).

Clearly, this set of norms is inconsistent, to the extent that [1] connects "Dx & ~Fx" to the contrary solution to the one connected by [5] to the same case.[40] If one rephrases [5] in the sense that it includes negligence or fault in its formulation, one can clearly grasp that, for the principle at hand, it is irrelevant whether there is fault or not:

[6] $\forall x(Dx \& (Fx \vee \sim Fx)) \rightarrow ORx$

In this sense, [6] is a happy formulation of the principle of strict liability, since one can derive from it – as well as [1] – both the norm "Dx & Fx → ORx" and the norm "Dx & ~Fx → ORx".

There is no way of making the system of torts consistent, if not by "repealing" one of these two general norms. In order to make such a system consistent, one must reject those norms from which the principle of fault liability can be derived or reinterpret the provisions from which such norms are derived. By contrast, if one wants to make consistent the system of fault liability, then one has to reject those norms from which the principle of strict liability is derived: what can be done also by reinterpreting the provisions from which it is extracted.

The reformulation of the system makes it possible to understand more clearly the choice between two alternative sets which have as their basic principles the standards we have just mentioned.

10.5 The Formal Features of the Normative Basis

In the formal analysis of the formal defects of normative systems, commonly an abstraction is made regarding interpretive questions. If one removes such an abstraction, one can notice that the formal properties of a system depend, to a great extent, on the ascription of meaning to the provisions which constitute the sentential basis identified by the jurist.

[40]The normative system can be developed as follows (taking into account the fact that this system also contains what we have called the "norm of closure of liability"): [NCL] ~Dx → ~ORx):

Cases/Norms	[1] Dx → ORx	[5] Dx & ~ Fx → ~ORx	[NCL] ~Dx → ~ORx
Dx & Fx	OR		
Dx & ~Fx	OR	~ORx	
~Dx & Fx			~ORx
~Dx & ~Fx			~ORx

To make the system consistent, one has to eliminate one of the two inconsistent norms. The elimination of each of the two norms brings about two alternative systems: the system of liability based on negligence and the system of strict liability.

In an interesting case discussed before the European Court of Justice (ECJ),[41] the relationship of priority between two Directives was debated. The first one was the *Doorstep Selling Directive*, the second one was the *Consumer Credit Directive*. Both directives provided two incompatible solutions for the same generic case, i.e. the right to cancel a consumer's loan secured by charge. While the *Consumer Credit Directive* did not allow for such a cancellation (providing, at section 2.1(a), the exclusion of the applicability of the Directive to such a case),[42] the *Doorstep Selling Directive* recognized it, within certain limits, at section 5.1. Finding itself in front of such an antinomy, the Court (re)interpreted section 2.1 of the *Consumer Credit Directive* as not applicable to the case at hand.[43]

Interpretation is, inter alia, the operation by means of which the jurist (or the judge) builds up a normative basis, starting from a sentential basis. Once having selected, more or less discretionally, the provisions composing the sentential basis, the jurist deals with the possible semantic options which it admits in order to build up a normative basis.

Indeed, in this passage from the sentential basis to the normative basis, the jurist makes choices that will have repercussions on the formal properties of the normative set. She can interpret provisions, in fact, so that gaps or antinomies are produced or ruled out.[44]

The system of liability based on negligence must be reformulated as follows (the addition of [7], of course, is required by the expulsion of [1], which provided that a compensation was due in the case "Dx & ~Fx"):

Cases/Norms	[7] Dx & Fx → ORx	[5] Dx & ~Fx → ~ORx	[NCL] ~Dx → ~ORx
Dx & Fx	ORx		
Dx & ~Fx		~ORx	
~Dx & Fx			~ORx
~Dx & ~Fx			~ORx

The system of strict liability should be so reformulated:

Casi/Norme	[1] Dx → ORx	[NCR] ~Dx → ~ORx
D	OR	
~D		~ORx

[41] ECJ, *Heininger and another v. Bayerische Hypo und Vereinsbank AG*, January 24, 2002, 9945, in "All England Law Reports", 2004, European Cases, pp. 1 ff.

[42] Section 2.1 (a) provides that: "This Directive shall not apply to: (a) credit agreements or agreements promising to grant credit: – intended primarily for the purpose of acquiring or retaining property rights in land or in an existing or projected building".

[43] ECJ, *Heininger and another v. Bayerische Hypo und Vereinsbank AG*, p. 11: "To inquire as to a relationship of precedence between the two directives presupposes that they both apply to the case. But that is not the position".

[44] Guastini (2004, pp. 231–237, 248–249).

It is important to recall here the distinction, previously introduced, between first and second interpretation. First interpretation is the operation by means of which jurists, dealing with some of the sentences of the legal sources, attach a first, tentative, meaning – which usually consists in what is called "current legal meaning", i.e. the meaning which is widespread within the legal community, on the basis of settled doctrinal and judicial theses.

In approaching a certain set of legal materials, the jurists use some doctrinal or judicial theses, which lead them to spot some formal features which we can call prima facie, in analogy to the interpretation which produces them. Such formal features are then re-elaborated during the process of reinterpretation, so that it is possible to maintain that a first "systematization" is carried out at the interpretive level.

Such systematization responds to the regulative ideal that law, as a product of doctrinal interpretation, *must* have a systematic nature. However, if law must have a systematic nature, and if jurists may carry out several operations on pre-interpreted materials, then a more detailed analysis of such operations is needed in order to reconstruct the methods by means of which such a nature is attributed or denied. In the next section, we shall deal with the operations which are used to deny or assert that law is incomplete, while in the following sections we shall examine those operations which are designed to affirm or deny that law is inconsistent.

10.6 The Identification of Gaps

The traditional account of normative gaps understand them as "data of experience", which jurists cannot but ascertain.[45]

This is not the case: on the one hand, expressed norms are the product of a complex interpretive process, which in any of its phases involves interpretive choices and is influenced, at every step, by dogmatic theses. On the other hand, unexpressed norms are derived from expressed norms by means of a variety of inferential ways, the choice among which is also influenced by doctrinal theses regarding interpretation and logical development.

Hence, if norms are the product of such a complex interpretive and "expansive" process, and gaps are regarded as the lack of a norm, the presence or the absence of a gap in a certain normative system depends upon a series of *lato sensu* interpretive, constructive, and systematizing operations carried out by jurists.

In facing the problem of gaps, then, it is important to call to mind some basic concepts, such as those of:

(1) "Normative provision", by which we understand any sentence of the legal sources;

[45] Chiassoni (2001, p. 45).

(2) "Expressed norm", by which we understand the meaning-content of a certain normative provision, assigned to it by an act of interpretation (i.e. meaning-ascription)
(3) "Unexpressed norm", by which we understand a norm derived, by means of several kinds of inferences, from an expressed norm.

Moreover, it will be useful to remind the distinction between first (or prima facie) interpretation and second interpretation (or reinterpretation), understanding the former as an attribution of a tentative meaning, product of a first "intuitive" approach to the sources to be interpreted, and the latter as the final meaning, product of a "all-things-considered" investigation on the elements which are relevant for attaching a certain set of meanings to a certain sentential basis.

The distinction between first and second interpretation makes it possible to refine the conceptual analysis of the operations carried out by jurists in order to "ascertain" the incompleteness of a certain system of norms.

As we have noticed, interpretation may rule out or create gaps, but it cannot fill them up: the filling-up of gaps is something which occurs when interpretation has already been carried out.[46]

But it is also true that, in jurists' works, the cases in which a gap is expressly admitted are relatively rare. The construction of normative materials usually is carried out in a way that it gives the impression that the law is always complete, at least in the sense that it contains no implicit gap.[47] In other words, the jurist, when recognizing an explicit gap regarding a certain system, tends not to admit that the law does not provide any solution at all for a certain generic case. There is always the possibility, for instance, that a principle can be developed in a way that it allows one to find a solution for such a case, or that the analogical application of a norm, prima facie not taken into consideration, can provide the normative problem with a solution regarded as satisfactory or reasonable by the jurist.

Let us consider the following example. In order to avoid responsibility, some enterprises assign some risky activities to other enterprises (so-called "satellite enterprises"), which are often constituted with small capitals, and hence are barely capable of bearing the economic burden of repairing damages. On a first interpretation, Italian law provides nothing on the joint responsibility of both enterprises. Only the enterprise which materially carries out the activity (i.e. "the satellite enterprise") ought to restore the damaged subjects. Obviously, this involves some great difficulties regarding the safeguard of damaged people and the distribution of the risk in carrying out the dangerous activity: there is indeed a high probability that the

[46]Cf. Guastini (2013b).

[47]Here I am referring to the interesting distinction between explicit and implicit gaps provided by Chiassoni (2001, p. 46). By the phrase "explicit gap" Chiassoni means the lack, in relation to a certain set of legal materials LM and a normative question Q, of an explicit norm which provides for the legally relevant case C. By the phrase "implicit gap" he means the lack, in relation to a certain set of legal materials LM and a normative question Q, of an implicit norm which provides for the legally relevant case C.

damaged subject will be unable to receive compensation. In order to avoid such an undesired effect and fill up the gap regarding the responsibility of the contractors, Italian jurists have analogically extended, to the case at hand, section 2049 of the Italian Civil Code (which provides that "The owners and the clients are responsible for damages caused by the unlawful acts of their workers and clerks in the performance of duties to which they are put"), and so regarded the contractor enterprise liable for damages (of course, jointly with the contracting "satellite enterprise").[48]

The identification of a gap is only the last, possible, stage of a composite reconstructive process. More precisely, one can distinguish at least six operations carried out by jurists in order to prevent or create gaps, and that allow the jurist, respectively, to avoid or carry out the integration of a certain normative micro-system[49]: (1) prima facie negative ascertainment, (2) prima facie positive ascertainment, (3) creation, (4) prevention, (5) pondered weak ascertainment, and (6) pondered strong ascertainment.

Some qualifications are in order here.

(1) Prima facie negative ascertainment consists in denying, at the stage of first interpretation, and on the basis of legal scholarship's common opinion (if any), the existence of a gap regarding a certain conduct. This kind of ascertainment depends on the selection of legal materials, on the interpretation of such materials, and on the rules of inference used by the jurist in developing the content of such a normative set. In many cases, this negative ascertainment is implicit in the argument of the jurist. However, it happens sometimes that it is made explicit, mostly when considering scholars' disagreements on the "gappiness" of a case, the evolution of a certain set of legal regulations, or judicial attempts to fill in a pre-existing gap.
(2) Prima facie positive ascertainment consists in affirming, at the stage of first interpretation, and on the basis of legal scholarship's common opinion (if any), the existence of a normative gap regarding a certain conduct.

In other words, the jurist approaches a certain normative system, according to the most widespread interpretive and doctrinal theses, regarding it as a gappy system, which does not connect any normative solution to a generic case. This happens often, since the systems built-up by different jurists for different aims hardly overlap. This is to say that a certain jurist singles out a specific set of provisions and extracts from it a certain normative system which is considered, in ordinary doctrinal reconstruction, as incomplete. However, it is often the case that, subsequently, the gap is filled-up by different legal scholars in diverging ways.

For instance, by denying that section 156.1 of the Italian Civil Code[50] – providing on the maintenance of separated spouses – can be extensively or analogically

[48] Bessone (1987, pp. 354–355).

[49] Chiassoni (1999c, pp. 294 ff.), (2007, pp. 203 ff.).

[50] Section 156.1 of the Italian Civil Code provides that "In pronouncing the separation, the judge provides that the spouse, to whom the separation cannot be charged, is entitled to receive what is necessary for his or her maintenance, if he or she does not have adequate incomes of his or her own".

applied, one creates a gap regarding the case of maintenance of the former unmarried partner. Since this is the common view among Italian scholars, the positive ascertainment is the "natural move" in order to begin the reconstruction of the normative system bearing upon the obligations of unmarried partners after they split up.

When the jurists carries out a negative ascertainment, and so denies the existence of a gap within the portion of a legal system she takes into consideration, she can confirm or reject, at the stage of second interpretation, the result of her first ascertainment. In the former case (i.e. confirmation), the system the system will conform, from the very beginning, to the ideal of completeness that usually guides the activities of scholars. In the latter case (i.e. rejection), she creates a gap probably in order to fill it up later on, and so modifies the normative system (by adding new materials, by changing the interpretations of the legal materials previously identified, or by admitting new rules of inference).

(3) There is creation of a gap when the jurist, at the second interpretation stage, creates a gap which *did not exist* at the first interpretation stage. For instance, this is the case of those who defend the view that section 48 of the Italian Constitution contains a gap regarding the right to vote of foreign people, whereas the most common reading (the "current legal reading") is that foreign people have no right to vote in Italy (except for resident UE citizens in administrative elections).

(4) There is prevention of a gap when the jurist cancels, at the second interpretation stage, a gap which existed at the first interpretation stage. According to Italian legal scholarship, for instance, there is no rule which, prima facie, provides strict liability for assuming the risk upon those who carry out a dangerous activity.[51] However, a different reading of section 2050 of the Civil Code makes it possible to fill up this gap and to eliminate the relevance of negligence. This is made clear by the following passage[52]:

> Is it possible to say that there are no rules of the [Italian] Civil Code in which cases of strict liability are identifiable? [...] At a first reading of the rules, only two of them seem designed to regulate forms of faultless liability [ie: section 2049 and 2054 of the Civil Code]. However, if one deepens the analysis of the other rules where, in various ways, a *relative* presumption of fault is introduced, and therefore the opportunity to offer discharging evidence is given to the responsible person, it is easy to identify other rules of strict liability. The formulas from time to time endeavored to indicate the content of discharging evidence (according to section 2050, the responsible must prove that "[she has] taken all the appropriate measures to avoid the damage" [...]) are in fact many expressions of directives of strict liability.

(5) We are in front of a weak ascertainment when the jurist *does not* cancel, at the second interpretation stage, a gap which existed at the first interpretation stage, even though it was argumentatively easy to do so.

[51] According to the theory of normative systems, the qualification of finer cases does not reach less fine cases. It is not possible to infer from the norm "$(Dx \& Fx) \rightarrow ORx$" the other norm "$Dx \rightarrow ORx$". The case consisting in damages, but not also in the negligence of the liable person (a case which corresponds, roughly, to the case of strict liability) lacks any normative solution.

[52] Bessone (1987, pp. 351–352).

Going back to an example we used before: a weak ascertainment of a gap is made by someone who, approaching section 48 of the Italian Constitution, reads it, at first, as expressing a incomplete set of norms regarding the vote of foreign people in Italy, and, at a later stage, *does not* fill in such a gap, though she could easily do it by means of the a contrario canon "Expressio unius est exclusio alterius".

(6) We are in front of a strong ascertainment when the jurist confirms the existence of a gap, already identified by first interpretation, since it is difficult, if not hardly possible, to justify another interpretive result.[53]

This happens for example in the case of the recovery of damages for infringement of the right to privacy when the fact is not a criminal offense. The Italian scholar Cosimo Mazzoni observes[54]:

> The protection of the right to privacy requires that the legal system has a serious impediment in the lack of compensability of the damages that do not have a patrimonial character, established by section 2059 of the [Italian] Civil Code. The matter of confidentiality is among those most affected by the inadequacy of the rule, which now several parties have urged to review, or even to repeal. The damage caused by the violation of the right to privacy is mostly a damage of a moral nature, such as pain, discomfort, embarrassment, irritation, anger, hurt on the injured party because of the means used in the aggression of her own sphere of intimacy and for the dissemination of news or pictures offered to the curiosity of the public. Legal scholars have begun to use the phrase *existential damage*. Well, unlike what happens in other countries, and in particular in the Anglo-Saxon systems, where this type of damage does not differ for the purposes of recoverability from the damage of a patrimonial nature, in our country it is recognized to it a very limited scope of protection: in particular, the damage is compensable according to the criteria of the financial loss only when the action constitutes a crime, according to the rule laid down by section 185 of the Criminal Code.

In all those situations where we are in the presence of a gap (whether it is the result of creation or ascertainment), there is the need to integrate the law, if we want to confer to it the formal feature of completeness. Now, the legal gap regarding the right to privacy has generally been filled by means of a variety of techniques, by jurists and judges, who in doing so mainly referred to section 32 of the Italian Constitution.

10.7 The Identification of Inconsistencies

The notions we have just sketched with regard to legal gaps can be profitably used, *mutatis mutandis*, in relation to the analysis of the doctrinal operations prior to the possible solution of inconsistencies. We have to distinguish, in this case too, six

---

[53] Chiassoni (1999c, p. 295).

[54] Mazzoni (2003, p. 71).

different operations[55]: (1) prima facie negative ascertainment, (2) prima facie positive ascertainment, (3) creation, (4) prevention, (5) weak ascertainment, and (6) strong ascertainment.

Let me elaborate.

(1) Prima facie negative ascertainment consists in denying that two sentences belonging to the same micro-system, understood in their literal meaning or current legal meaning, express two (partially or totally) incompatible norms.[56] This kind of ascertainment is usually an implicit one.
(2) Prima facie positive ascertainment consists in affirming, at the stage of first interpretation, and on the basis of legal scholarship's common opinion (if any), the existence of a situation of incompatibility between two norms derived from the same sentential basis. In other words, the jurist approaches a certain normative micro-system that, according to the common view among scholars, attaches two conflicting solutions to the same generic case. According to the prevalent view in Italian legal scholarship, for example, there is a hardly solvable conflict between the freedom of the press and the right to privacy, both derivable from constitutional provisions.[57]

In the same way as for gaps, the jurist may confirm or reject the prima facie ascertainment, whether it was a negative or a positive one, at the second interpretation stage.

(3) We have the creation of an inconsistency whenever the interpreter, in the second interpretation stage, brings about a contradiction that did not seem to exist at the stage of first interpretation. This happens, for example, when an interpretation-product prima facie is reinterpreted broadly, so as to overlap and conflict with an interpretation-product of opposite sign.
(4) There is the prevention of an inconsistency whenever the interpreter eliminates, in the second interpretation stage, an inconsistency whose existence was positively ascertained in the first interpretation stage.

This is the case of the principle-oriented interpretation section 2043 of the Italian Civil Code advocated by the Constitutional Court.[58] If such a section is read according to the prevalent view, it provides that damages other than patrimonial damages and so-called "moral damages" cannot be restored. This interpretation creates an inconsistency – the Court argues[59] – between the statutory rule and sections 3, 24,

[55] Here I follow closely Chiassoni (1999b, c, pp. 297 ff.), (2007, pp. 277 ff.).

[56] On the concept of (total or partial) inconsistency between norms, see Ross (1958, pp. 128 ff.) and Chiassoni (2007, pp 262 ff.).

[57] Alpa (1986, p. 174).

[58] Alpa (1985, pp. 213–214, 216–217).

[59] Italian Constitutional Court, decision 88/1976.

and 32 of the Italian Constitution, respectively stating the principles of equality, of the legal protection of subjective rights, and the right to health. Such an inconsistency disappears (or is prevented) if one understands section 2043 as admitting the restoration of other kinds of damages.

(5) We are in front of a weak ascertainment when the jurist *does not* cancel, at the second interpretation stage, an inconsistency which existed at the first interpretation stage, even though it was argumentatively easy to do so.

An example of weak ascertainment concerns the crime of creation of constituting subversive associations (section 270 of the Italian Criminal Code).[60] This section is generally considered by many commentators (who carry out a weak ascertainment) as a rule suspect of unconstitutionality with respect to various parameters, namely for alleged violation of the right to freedom of thought (Section 21 of the Constitution), of the right of association (Section 18 of the Constitution), and the right of association in political parties to concur by means of democratic methods to determining national policy (Section 49 of the Constitution) and, finally, for being allegedly contrary to the principle of offensiveness which generally characterizes criminal offenses. Another line of thought, avoiding weak ascertainment and carrying out prevention, would resolve the antinomy by arguing that section 270, far from sanctioning an association for the sole reason of supporting a subversive program, rather represses the "violent means" that the association intends to use in order to achieve the desired objective: from this point of view, the contested provision would be perfectly compatible with both sections 18 and 49, provided that the rights inherent to freedom of association are limited by the prohibition to pursue purposes which are forbidden by criminal law (and the use of violence would fall precisely within the aforesaid prohibition).

(6) Finally, we have a strong ascertainment when a jurist confirms the existence of an inconsistency, which is the outcome of a positive prima facie ascertainment, since it is difficult, or hardly possible, to justify a different result.

A hardly solvable conflict in the Italian legal order, for instance, is that between the crime of criminal apology and the right to free expression of thought. As one may gather from the following passage, a prevention of such an inconsistency is carried out (wrongly, according to the authors, who favor a strong ascertainment) by the Italian Constitutional Court[61]:

> With regard to the relationship between criminal "apology" (or propaganda) and free expression of thought, the jurisprudential view, that tries to tends to reduce apology to a simple favorable opinion regarding a particular fact or episode [constituting a crime], is certainly unacceptable. So interpreted, apology is in fact a form of expression certainly protected by section 21 of the Constitution. In order to make compatible the indictment of the facts of apology or propaganda with section 21 of the Constitution, the Constitutional Court, in the decision n. 65/70, laid down the principle that the punishable apology "is not

[60] Fiandaca and Musco (1988, pp. 31–32).

[61] Fiandaca and Musco (1988, pp. 65–66).

the pure and simple manifestation of thought, but a manifestation of thought which constitutes a behavior in fact capable of causing the commission of crimes". In so doing, however, the features of apologetic conduct are surreptitiously distorted, because the subject of the indictment is now the so-called "indirect incitement", with the result that the incrimination of apology results in an unnecessary duplication of the criminalization of incitement. The Court has clearly reached a compromise solution, due in all probability to the desire to avoid alleged gaps in protection. [...] Therefore, it would have been preferable to openly acknowledge that the incrimination of merely apologetic facts creates in our system an irreconcilable conflict with constitutional principles.

10.8 The Solution of Inconsistencies and the Ordering of Legal Materials

After having identified an inconsistency, in one of the ways previously exposed, the jurist can chose among different procedures in order to solve it.

The traditional criteria used by jurists are, as everybody knows, *lex superior* (i.e. superiority), *lex posterior* (chronology), and *lex specialis* (specificity).

The last of these criteria is used to resolve contradictions eminently through interpretation: in other words, it enables one to change the connections between cases and solutions established by the rules of the system, by changing the rules that can be derived from the sentential basis.

The jurist – notes Jemolo[62] – must identify the lawgiver's idea regarding the various institutes, without being able to add or take away. However, what will happen in subsequent legislation if the legislature does not remain faithful to that which had been its original idea of a certain institution? In this case, the lawgiver commits a sin against legal logic, by enacting two incompatible rules: the remedy is given by the institution of implied repeal of the earlier measures.

This is the modus operandi of the criterion of *lex posterior*. From the passage, however, one cannot derive the "dual nature" of this criterion (dual nature that it shares with the principle of *lex superior*). Both criteria may in fact affect, in turn, the sentential basis, by repealing the provision that expresses the contradictory rule, or the normative basis, expelling the norm without affecting the formulation of the provision.

By bringing the system back to its founding principles, the jurist may also carry out balancing or, alternatively, reconciliation. Both techniques, however, are generally considered unsuitable for resolving contradictions *in abstracto*: they would act only in specific cases, for which it is possible to determine the "weight" of each principle involved in the process of balancing.[63]

Finally, the jurist can proceed to systematize the elements of the system, by ordering them.

[62] Jemolo (2004, pp. 129–130).

[63] Cf. Guastini (2004, pp. 219–221). Regarding the differences between balancing and conciliating, see id., p. 219, fn. 60.

The ordering of legal materials is the last, merely possible, operation which systematization in the broad sense (i.e. the building-up of a complete and consistent system of norms) is made of. Obviously, this is a logical sequence, not a chronological or a psychological one. One cannot order materials that have not been, at least, previously interpreted and logically developed.

Ordering consists in putting the norms of the system in a certain order, with the result that certain norms serve as general rules and other rules as norms of detail, with the effect of expunging from the system those norms that are incompatible with its "axioms".

In this sense, ordering is similar to repealing: by changing the order of the norms, and the relationships of "preference" among them, the solution which a normative system connects to the relevant generic cases also changes.

Indeed, ordering is also configurable – in partial antithesis with balancing (which brings about an axiological hierarchy which varies from case to case) – as a fixed axiological hierarchy. Its solutions are conceived as abstract ones, so that they are, in general, applicable to infinity of cases. Once the issue of liability is traced back to the principles of faultless damage and strict liability, then the norms which do not conform with them are "expelled", and this operation brings about potentially durable results (to be sure, the effects of such an ordering can be more durable than some legislative derogations).

It often happens that the jurist confers the status of a principle to a norm, expressed or unexpressed, and structures the normative set on its basis. In other words, by using the ideal of system, the jurist creates normative hierarchies in favor of some general norms, which later elevates to the rank of principles.

Introduced into a system elaborated by the jurist, principles, so understood, are used to carry out three main functions: explication, integration, and "preparation". First, they are used to build a sort of explicative theory of existing legislative materials.[64] Secondly, they are used to fill in possible gaps of the normative basis. Finally, they are employed to reduce the system to its ultimate elements, among which, in case of conflict, an ordering is made.

Principles are used to understand a system not as a simple set of norms, but as an ordered set of norms.[65] Their function consists in orienting the explication and the integration of law towards a systematic ideal: they are instrumental to attributing, to all the operations carried out on legal norms, the rationality one can find in a system. As has been said, "when the interpreter builds-up a principle she "is creating" the system".[66]

Ordering – we have said – is the last of the scholars' operations of systematization of a certain normative set.

However, in the actual formulation of scholarly works, ordering appears not at the end, but at the beginning of the inquiry. In other words, the work of the jurist shows the results of the inquiry by expounding a certain ordering hypothesis.

---

[64] Guastini (1986).

[65] Atienza and Ruiz Manero (2012).

[66] Prieto Sanchís (1992, p. 182).

Examples of ordering are legion, but a very clear one is provided by the aforementioned division between the system of fault liability and the system of strict liability.[67]

By recognizing the existence of a system of strict liability alongside a system of fault-based liability, many of the cases, previously subsumed under the fault-based liability and hence allowing a much easier release from liability, can now be traced back to the principle of strict liability which provides a much harder release for risky activities. The construction of the principle of strict liability makes it possible to change the system of civil liability, by propitiating the reinterpretation of the irreconcilable provisions, filling up legislative gaps, and extending the liability to pay compensation to ever new cases.

For instance, in the beginning of one of his works devoted to strict liability,[68] which we referred to above,[69] the famous Italian jurist Pietro Trimarchi sets out to build a system based on the principle of strict liability for business risk. The entire work is based on this ordering hypothesis. Yet there is insufficient evidence to suggest that this presumption is the final element of the whole reconstruction of the author. On closer inspection, indeed, he moves from the identification of a few statutory sentences; gives them prima facie meaning following the interpretation which is found in the prevailing doctrine; it provides a new interpretation that rejects the results of the first interpretation; builds a normative basis; draws its implications; induces its "structural" principles, from which he draws additional rules to fill in the statutory gaps; identifies conflicting standards; where it is possible he tries a re-interpretation of the provisions from which they are extracted; resolves residual conflicts ousting the rules do not accord with the apical principles of the system.

If all the above is correct, the model developed in this contribution can aspire to be a proper explanation of the activities commonly carried out by jurists in order to make the law, or at least some of its subsets, a systematic whole.

Acknowledgements I would like to thank Thomas Bustamante, Pierluigi Chiassoni, Andrea Dolcetti and Riccardo Guastini for very helpful comments on a previous draft of this contribution.

References

Aarnio, Aulis. 1977. *On legal reasoning*. Turku: Turun Yliopisto.

Aarnio, Aulis. 1986. On changes in the systematics of law. In *Vernunft und Enfahrung im Rechtsdenken der Gegenwart*, Rechtstheorie, Beiheft 10, ed. Torstein Eckhoff, Lawrence Friedman, and Jirky Uusitalo, 161–170. Berlin: Duncker und Humblot.

Aarnio, Aulis. 2011. *Essays on the doctrinal study of law*. Dordrecht: Springer.

Alchourrón, Carlos Eduardo. 1986. Systematization and change in the science of law. In *Vernunft und Enfahrung im Rechtsdenken der Gegenwart*, Rechtstheorie, Beiheft 10, ed. Torstein Eckhoff, Lawrence Friedman, and Jirky Uusitalo, 171–184. Berlin: Duncker und Humblot.

[67] Trimarchi (1961, p. 39).

[68] Trimarchi (1961, pp. 1–6).

[69] See, *supra*, section 2.1.

Alchourrón, Carlos Eduardo. 2012. On law and logic (1996). In *The logic of legal requirements. Essays on defeasibility*, ed. J. Ferrer Beltrán and Giovanni Battista Ratti, 39–52. Oxford: Oxford University Press.

Alchourrón, Carlos Eduardo, and Eugenio Bulygin. 1971. *Normative systems*. Wien/New York: Springer.

Alpa, Guido. 1986. *L'arte di giudicare*. Bari: Laterza.

Alpa, Guido. 1985. *Compendio del nuovo diritto privato*. Torino: Utet.

Atienza, Manuel, and Juan Ruiz Manero. 2012. Rules, principles, and defeasibility. In *The logic of legal requirements. Essays on defeasibility*, ed. J. Ferrer Beltrán and Giovanni Battista Ratti, 238–253. Oxford: Oxford University Press.

Bessone, Mario. 1987. *Casi e questioni di diritto privato, III, Obbligazioni e contratti – Responsabilità civile*. Milan: Giuffrè.

Bobbio, Norberto. 1994. *Contributi ad un dizionario giuridico*. Turin: Giappichelli.

Bowers, Frederick. 1989. *Linguistic aspects of legislative expression*. Vancouver: University of British Columbia Press.

Bulygin, Eugenio. 1982. Time and validity. In *Deontic logic, computational linguistics, and legal information systems*, vol. II, ed. Antonio A. Martino, 65–81. Amsterdam: North Holland.

Bulygin, Eugenio. 1986. Legal dogmatics and systematization of law. In *Vernunft und Enfahrung im Rechtsdenken der Gegenwart*, Rechtstheorie, Beiheft 10, ed. Torstein Eckhoff, Lawrence Friedman, and Jirky Uusitalo, 193–210. Berlin: Duncker und Humblot.

Chiassoni, Pierluigi. 1999a. Interpreting games: Statutory construction through Gricean eyes. In *Analisi e diritto 1999. Ricerche di giurisprudenza analitica*, ed. P. Comanducci and R. Guastini, 79–99. Turin: Giappichelli.

Chiassoni, Pierluigi. 1999b. Interpretazione dei documenti normativi. In *Interpretazione e diritto giurisprudenziale, I. Regole, metodi, modelli*, ed. M. Bessone, 21–45. Turin: Giappichelli.

Chiassoni, Pierluigi. 1999c. *La giurisprudenza civile. Metodi d'interpretazione e tecniche argumentative*. Milan: Giuffrè.

Chiassoni, Pierluigi. 2001. Lacune nel diritto. Appunti per una tipologia realistica. In *Prassi giuridica e controllo di razionalità*, ed. Lucia Triolo, 37–89. Turin: Giappichelli.

Chiassoni, Pierluigi. 2007. *Tecnica dell'interpretazione giuridica*. Bologna: Il Mulino.

Fiandaca, Giovanni, and Enzo Musco. 1988. *Diritto penale, Parte speciale*, vol. I. Bologna: Il Mulino.

Guastini, Riccardo. 1986. Production of rules by means of rules. *Rechtstheorie* 17: 295–309.

Guastini, Riccardo. 2004. *L'interpretazione dei documenti normativi*. Milan: Giuffrè.

Guastini, Riccardo. 2011. *Interpretare e argomentare*. Milan: Giuffrè.

Guastini, Riccardo. 2013a. *Distinguendo ancora*. Madrid: Marcial Pons.

Guastini, Riccardo. 2013b. Juristenrecht: Inventing rights, wrongs, and powers. In *Neutrality and theory of law*, ed. Jordi Ferrer Beltrán, José Juan Moreso, and Diego M. Papayannis, 147–159. Dordrecht: Springer.

Jemolo, Arturo Carlo. 2004. Ancora sui concetti giuridici. In *La polemica sui concetti giuridici*, ed. Natalino Irti, 101–148. Milan: Giuffrè.

Jori, Mario. 1985. *Saggi di metagiurisprudenza*. Milan: Giuffrè.

Mazzoni, Cosimo. 2003. Diritti della personalità. In *Lineamenti di diritto privato*, ed. Mario Bessone, 65–71. Milan: Giuffrè.

Minale Costa, Enrica. 2004. *Percorsi giurisprudenziali nel diritto del lavoro*. Turin: Giappichelli.

Musy, Alberto M. 1997. Responsabilità precontrattuale (culpa in contrahendo). In *Digesto delle discipline privatistiche. Sezione civile*, Vol. XVII, 354–398. Torino: Utet.

Navarro, Pablo Eugenio, and Jorge Luís Rodríguez. 2014. *Deontic logic and legal systems*. Cambridge: Cambridge University Press.

Niiniluoto, Ilkka. 1981. On truth and argumentation in legal dogmatics. In *Methodologie und Erkenntnistheorie der juristischen Argumentation*, Rechtstheorie, Beiheft 2, ed. Aulis Aarnio, Ilkka Niiniluoto, and Jirk Uusitalo, 53–76. Berlin: Duncker und Humblot.

Parodi, Gianpaolo. 1996. Lacune e norme inespresse nella giurisprudenza costituzionale. In *Struttura e dinamica dei sistemi giuridici*, ed. P. Comanducci and R. Guastini, 87–115. Turin: Giappichelli.

Prieto Sanchís, Luis. 1992. *Sobre principios y normas. Problemas del razonamiento jurídico*. Madrid: Centro de estudios constitucionales.

Ratti, Giovanni Battista. 2014. Consistencia, completitud y coherencia de los sistemas normativos. In *Analisi e diritto*, 309–317. Madrid: Marcial Pons.

Rodríguez, Jorge Luis. 2014. *Teoria del diritto e analisi logica*. Madrid: Marcial Pons.

Ross, Alf. 1958. *On Law and Justice*. London: Stevens & Sons.

Sacco, Rodolfo. 1988. *Introduzione al diritto comparato*. Turin: Giappichelli.

Trimarchi, Pietro. 1961. *Rischio e responsabilità oggettiva*. Milan: Giuffrè.

Van Hoecke, Mark. 1986. La Systématisation dans la Dogmatique Juridique. In *Vernunft und Enfahrung im Rechtsdenken der Gegenwart*, Rechtstheorie, Beiheft 10, ed. Torstein Eckhoff, Lawrence Friedman, and Jirky Uusitalo, 217–230. Berlin: Duncker und Humblot.

Chapter 11
Argumentation from Reasonableness in the Justification of Judicial Decisions

Eveline T. Feteris

Abstract In legal decision-making reasonableness plays an important role. In the literature, generally speaking, there is a consensus that reasonableness as a norm for judges in the application of law implies that they take into account a combination of different considerations of a normative and factual nature with the aim of reconciling the requirements of abstract formal justice and justice and fairness in the concrete case. Although reasonableness is considered to be an important reason for making an exception to a legal rule, in the legal literature little attention has been paid to the kind of arguments that can constitute a sound justification of such a decision.

The central question I answer in this contribution is what an adequate justification based on argumentation from reasonableness with the function of correcting a legal rule for the concrete case exactly amounts to. My aim is to develop an argumentation model for the rational reconstruction that enables the analyst to make explicit the different considerations underlying a decision that is based on reasonableness so that they can be submitted to rational critique. To do justice to the context-dependency of the concept of reasonableness in the context of legal justification, I will concentrate on the role of reasonableness in a specific domain, civil law in the Netherlands. In civil law in the Netherlands reasonableness plays a central role as a mechanism for the correction of outcomes that would be unacceptable from the perspective of justice in a concrete case.

In this contribution I proceed as follows. First, in (2), I discuss the role of arguments from reasonableness in legal justification: I go into the nature of the argument and I will discuss the content and structure of the complex argumentation underlying a justification based on the correction of a legal rule referring to reasonableness. Then, in (3), I develop an argumentation model for the rational reconstruction of legal arguments from reasonableness. I explain the conditions under which arguments from reasonableness can be correctly used in legal justification. In (4) I concentrate on the role of reasonableness in Dutch Civil Law where it is recognized explicitly as a reason for making an exception. To demonstrate how the argumentation model can be used in the rational reconstruction, in (5) I apply it to an example

E.T. Feteris (✉)
Department of Speech Communication, Argumentation Theory and Rhetoric,
University of Amsterdam, Spuistraat 134, 1012 VB Amsterdam, The Netherlands
e-mail: e.t.feteris@uva.nl

© Springer International Publishing Switzerland 2015

T. Bustamante, C. Dahlman (eds.), *Argument Types and Fallacies in Legal Argumentation*, Law and Philosophy Library 112,
DOI 10.1007/978-3-319-16148-8_11

from Dutch civil law in which this form of argumentation is used. On the basis of an exemplary analysis I explain how the model can be used to establish in what respects argumentation from reasonableness used in this case can be considered as an acceptable contribution to a rational legal discussion.

11.1 Introduction

In legal decision-making reasonableness plays an important role. In the literature, generally speaking, there is a consensus that reasonableness as a norm for judges in the application of law implies that they take into account a combination of *different considerations* of a *normative* and *factual* nature with the aim of reconciling the requirements of abstract formal justice and justice and fairness in the concrete case. As Bongiovanni et al. (2009: xi) state in their introduction to the volume *Reasonablenss and Law*, reasonableness can be conceived as 'a quest for a *practical equilibrium*, in an attempt to bring into balance different normative possibilities, measures and arguments in relation to different circumstances'.

Normally judges do not refer explicitly to reasonableness when giving a decision. However, in certain hard cases where there is a need for corrective justice, judges sometimes explicitly refer to reasonableness when they are of the opinion that the law has to be corrected in order to evade a manifest unacceptable, unjust or absurd result. In such cases they decide not to apply a rule whose conditions for application are fulfilled, because application would lead to an unacceptable result. They may argue that reasonableness requires that they make an exception for the case at hand because a rational legislator cannot have intended that application of the rule in the concrete case would lead to results that would be unacceptable from the perspective of reasonableness.

An example of such an argument from reasonableness is used in the famous Dutch case of the 'Unworthy Spouse' (Hoge Raad, NJ 1991/593 07-12-1990).[1] In this case a male nurse, L., had taken care of a 72 year old lady, mrs. van Wylick, which he had married. Five weeks after the marriage he killed her for which he was convicted and imprisoned for 12 years. On the basis of article 1:100 of the Dutch Civil Code L. claimed his right to his share in the community of matrimonial property. However the other inheritors, the children of Mrs. van Wylick, contested this right. All courts, the district court, the court of appeals and the Supreme Court were of the opinion that L. could not exercise this right. The courts made an exception to article 1:100 of the Dutch Civil Code on the basis of reasonableness, although this article does not contain the norm of reasonableness. They justified this correction of article 1:100, stating that 'the claims of L. must be considered as so unreasonable and unfair, in the aforementioned circumstances of this case and also in light of the

[1] For the relevant parts of the decisions in this case see A at the end of this contribution. For an analysis of the argumentation in this case see Feteris (2012).

mentioned legal principles (E.F. that can be summarized as 'Crime does not pay') that the exertion of the claimed rights must be denied to him completely' (Court of Appeals, NJ 1989/369, 24-11-1989).

In this case we see that the courts are confronted with the problem of reconciling the requirement of certainty to apply the law if the conditions for application of a legal rule are fulfilled and the requirement of reasonableness and fairness to evade a result that would be unacceptable from the perspective of justice. In this case, the courts try to find an equilibrium by applying the criterion of reasonableness and make an exception on the basis of a combination of different considerations of a normative and factual nature: they apply the legal principles in light of the exceptional circumstances of the a-typical case.

Such argumentation from reasonableness in which it is claimed that an exception should be made to a legal rule because strict application would lead to an unacceptable result, can be considered as exemplary for the way in which judges try to solve the problem of the tension between *legal certainty* and *predictability* of legal decisions on the one hand and *justice in the concrete situation* on the other. When a judge decides that an exception should be made on the basis of reasonableness he tries to reconcile the requirement of *formal* justice to treat like cases alike by applying abstract norms to similar cases, and the requirement of *substantial* justice by making an exception in an a-typical case.

Although judges have a discretion in adapting the law to new circumstances, the way in which argumentation from reasonableness is used in practice is sometimes the object of discussion. On the one hand arguments from reasonableness are considered as an important instrument for a dynamic interpretation of the law with the aim of adapting the law to new developments in society and promoting an acceptable result in concrete cases. However, argumentation from reasonableness is also considered as a 'cover' of activities of the judge that should be presented explicitly as the creation of new law. Judges are hesitant to acknowledge that in certain hard cases they need to create a new rule, because the new rule would lack the legitimacy guaranteed by rules formulated by the legislator. To hide the fact that they create a new rule, judges may use the 'cover' of the exception on the basis of reasonableness that would allow them to depart from a rule, instead of explicitly acknowledging that they are creating new law.[2]

Although reasonableness is considered to be an important reason for making an exception to a legal rule, in the legal literature little attention has been paid to the kind of arguments that can constitute a sound justification of such a decision. On the one hand reasonableness is considered to have a conceptual core, but on the other hand, as Bongiovanni et al. (2009: xiii) state, 'problems emerge when it comes to specifying exactly what these demands and criteria are and how they should properly be balanced against one another. In fact, this is the most problematic part of the

[2] See for example Hesselink (1999: 410–411) who discusses the strategic use of reasonableness as a cover for the creation of new law. See also Adinolfi (2009: 383) who points at the fact that argumentation from reasonableness is often used to cover a solution that has been chosen for other reasons that judges do not want to make explicit. See also MacCormick (2005: 170–171) about the question whether the judge acts as a standin-legislator when he creates new law.

reasonable, from a theoretical standpoint as well as from the standpoint of the practice of law'. Insight into the standards for argumentation based on reasonableness is important from the perspective of the rationality of the application of law, because only on the basis of such standards it can be established whether the judge has used his discretionary power in an acceptable way. The central question I will answer in this contribution is what an adequate justification based on argumentation from reasonableness with the function of correcting a legal rule for the concrete case exactly amounts to. My aim is to develop an argumentation model for the rational reconstruction that enables the analyst to make explicit the different considerations underlying a decision that is based on reasonableness so that they can be submitted to rational critique. To do justice to the context-dependency of the concept of reasonableness in the context of legal justification, I will concentrate on the role of reasonableness in a specific domain, civil law in the Netherlands. In civil law in the Netherlands reasonableness plays a central role as a mechanism for the correction of outcomes that would be unacceptable from the perspective of justice in a concrete case.

In this contribution I proceed as follows. First, in (2), I discuss the role of arguments from reasonableness in legal justification: I go into the nature of the argument and I will discuss the content and structure of the complex argumentation underlying a justification based on the correction of a legal rule referring to reasonableness. Then, in (3), I develop an argumentation model for the rational reconstruction of legal arguments from reasonableness. I explain the conditions under which arguments from reasonableness can be correctly used in legal justification. In (4) I concentrate on the role of reasonableness in Dutch Civil Law where it is recognized explicitly as a reason for making an exception. To demonstrate how the argumentation model can be used in the rational reconstruction, in (5) I apply it to an example from Dutch civil law in which this form of argumentation is used. On the basis of an exemplary analysis I explain how the model can be used to establish in what respects argumentation from reasonableness used in this case can be considered as an acceptable contribution to a rational legal discussion.

11.2 The Role of Argumentation from Reasonableness in Legal Justification

11.2.1 Contexts in Which Argumentation from Reasonableness Is Used

In most legal systems it is allowed to make an exception to a legal rule on the basis of reasonableness if application would yield an unacceptable result.[3] The need for an argument from reasonableness for this purpose has already been discussed by

[3] See Hesselink (1999) for an overview of the use of reasonableness and fairness in European Law. See Bongiovanni et al. (2009) for a discussion of different aspects of the norm of reasonableness in the law.

Aristotle.[4] In his view, a judge is allowed to correct the law on the basis of 'equity' if it would be unjust because of its generality. According to Aristotle, in such cases equity amounts to justice to correct the injustice that would be caused by strict application of a universal rule in a concrete case.

Normally a judge can comply with the requirements of formal and substantive justice by checking whether the conditions of a general legal rule are fulfilled. If the conditions are fulfilled he can apply the legal consequence specified in the rule. However, since legal rules are abstract, general formulations of the conditions for applying a legal consequence in a particular situation, a case may occur in which it would be reasonable to not apply the legal consequence to the a-typical facts of the specific circumstances. The question to be answered is what a judge must do when the conditions of a legal rule are fulfilled but he is of the opinion that application of the rule would be unreasonable and unfair in the circumstances of the given case.[5] When a judge is of the opinion that application would be unacceptable from the perspective of reasonableness, he can correct the rule by making an exception to the rule that limits the range of application in light of the circumstances of the given case.[6] When correcting the rule, the judge at the same time tries to do justice to the requirement of formal justice that like cases should be treated alike, as to the requirement of fairness that the circumstances of the concrete case should be taken into consideration.

From the perspective of the Rule of Law that requires certainty and predictability, and from the perspective of the separation of powers that puts a certain limit to the discretionary power of judges to create new law, the problem, however, is under what circumstances it is allowed to make an exception on the basis of reasonableness and fairness and how such an exception can be justified. Other than in cases in which the judge limits or extends the range of application of a legal rule by analogy by referring to other rules of the relevant branch of law or the legal system, in cases in which the judge makes an exception on the basis of reasonableness and fairness he cannot refer to another rule to justify the exception, but he will have to refer to other factors such as general legal principles and values in relation to the circumstances of the given case. In what follows I will explain what considerations should be taken into account when making an exception on the basis of reasonableness and how the exception should be justified.

---

[4] See Aristotle (1980), *Ethica Nicomachea* (Book V, x). See also Perelman (1979) who argues that the requirement of reasonableness is a requirement for the judge to apply the law in a just way, that is the requirement to treat like cases alike and unlike cases differently.

[5] As Hesselink (1999: 59) states, there is a limit to the exertion of a legal right, he who comes to court should have 'clean hands', which implies that in certain circumstances it can be reasonable not to apply a rule if the exertion would be unreasonable.

[6] Another context where reasonableness is applied is when the conditions of a legal rule are not fulfilled but the judge is of the opinion that not-applying the rule would be unacceptable from the perspective of reasonableness. In such a case he can 'supplement' the rule by making an exception that extends the range of application of the rule for the circumstances of the concrete case. This form of using arguments from reasonableness is less problematic from the perspective of legal certainty and predictability because the judge does not limit but extends a particular right. For a discussion of such arguments see Feteris (2005).

11.2.2 Considerations Underlying the Application of Reasonableness in the Context of Legal Decision-Making and Legal Justification

In the legal literature 'reasonableness' is considered as a normative concept that refers to what is reasonable to do or not to do in a given context.[7] The concept of reasonableness is used in such different contexts as civil law where it refers to the acts of a 'reasonable man', 'the foresight of the reasonable person', of 'reasonable care' in cases of negligence and 'unreasonable conduct' in divorce cases. It is used in criminal law where the standard of evidence is 'beyond reasonable doubt'. It is also used in administrative cases where the 'reasonableness' of administrative decisions is questioned. And in European law, for example in the decisions by the European Court of Human Rights, reasonableness is a criterion in the application of article 14 of the ECHR that states that differential treatment is discriminatory if it has 'no objective and reasonable justification'.

Although the concept of 'reasonableness' is considered to have a 'conceptual core' implying that it is a standard of 'normal behaviour', it does not translate into any fixed set of requisites or hard-and-fast rules.[8] For various fields of law, the factors that have to be considered and addressed in a given situation to judge the reasonableness of an act or an omission to act in a concrete situation differ. A value like 'reasonable' is very context-sensitive and the judgement what reasonableness amounts to in a concrete context has to be made on the basis of an evaluation of different considerations of a normative as well as a factual nature.

One of the central problems in the application of the norm of 'reasonableness' is that it is not a rule that can be applied by subsuming the facts of the case under the conditions formulated by the legislator for the legal consequences to follow.[9] The reason is that the facts that justify applying the norm of reasonableness cannot be formulated *a priori*. Reasonableness can be considered as an *open norm* of which the content cannot be established in an abstract way but must be established in light of the circumstances of the given case.[10] It is left to the discretion of the judge to decide what reasonableness amounts to, all the relevant circumstances being considered.

The legislator uses the open norm of 'reasonableness' in certain contexts to make the development of law and adaptation of the law to changing developments in society possible. A norm like 'reasonableness' makes the law flexible in contexts where this is required. By using such open norms in a codification the legislator makes it

[7] See for example Alexy (2009: 2007), Bongiovanni et al. (2009: xi–xiv), MacCormick (2005: 162ff).

[8] See for example Bongiovanni et al. (2009: xi).

[9] See for example Hesselink (1999: 37). See also Alexy (2009).

[10] There are also authors who contend that reasonableness is also a principle in its own right, an autonomous principle, that carries its own legal import or status. See for example della Cananea (2009: 306–307).

possible to take into account the circumstances of a-typical cases when applying an abstract statutory norm. In this way he leaves space for the courts to develop the law for certain cases.

When applying legal rules with a norm referring to reasonableness, judges must give an interpretation of what the open norm of reasonableness amounts to in the given situation. Often statutes that prescribe a standard of reasonableness explicitly indicate relevant factors that should be taken into account such as general legal principles and generally accepted values in a particular society.[11] In these cases the legislator gives explicit but non-exclusive guidance by specifying the normative factors which are relevant to a judgement of reasonableness with regard to a specific legal situation.

Apart from the cases in which a judge must apply a legal rule that contains the norm of reasonableness, there are also cases in which the judge is of the opinion that the requirement of reasonableness should be applied to correct a legal rule by making an exception for the concrete case, without the existence of a legal norm that specifies the relevant factors. An example of such a case is the decision in the case of the Unworthy Spouse I discussed where the courts were of the opinion that an exception should be made to article 1:100 of the Dutch Civil Code on the basis of reasonableness, although this article does not contain the norm of reasonableness.

In all these cases, for the concrete situation, it is the task of the judge to formulate in an *objective* and clear way the considerations that have played a role in his decision to correct the legal rule for the a-typical situation.

As various authors such as Alexy (2009: 7–8), Bongiovanni et al. (2009: xi–xiv) and MacCormick (2005: 173, 181, 185–186) stress, 'reasonableness' is an evaluative concept that requires that a plurality of considerations be considered and that these considerations be put in the correct relation to each other in order to justify the judgement that provides the answer. The way in which these considerations are put together in relation to each other is by some authors characterized as a form of 'weighing and balancing'.[12] This weighing and balancing involves on a meta-level a decision about certain values and circumstances that are considered to be decisive. For the justification of the weighing and balancing this implies that the judge must make explicit these considerations in order to justify his decision.[13]

The decision not to apply a rule but to make an exception implies according to some authors that it is claimed that the rule should be reformulated for certain a-typical cases with an exception, of which the concrete case can be considered as

---

[11] See for example article 3:12 of the Dutch Civil Code that will be discussed in Sect. 11.4 of this contribution.

[12] For a discussion of the balancing of arguments in relation to reasonableness see Alexy (2009) and MacCormick (2005: 178–188).

[13] As MacCormick (2005: 178–179) argues, reasonableness itself is not a first order value, but a higher-order value which we exemplify in considering a balance of first order, or anyway lower-order values and coming to a conclusion about their application. The task of interpretation of reasonableness in a given context is that of identifying values, interests and the like that are relevant to the given focus of attention. This in turn depends on the types of situation or relationship that are in issue, and on a view of the governing principle or rationale of the branch of law concerned.

an instantiation. According to Hesselink (1999: 416 ff) this decision on a meta-level could be characterized as a '*rule of exception*' that is created in an attempt to generalize the circumstances of the concrete case in light of the relevant general legal principles and values.[14] From the perspective of certainty and predictability it is important that the judge specifies as precise as possible the circumstances that have been decisive in correcting or supplementing the rule on the basis of reasonableness. In Hesselink's view (1999: 400–401) a decision would be unpredictable if the judge would not mention any concrete circumstances that can be considered as decisive for his decision. It is the function of legal principles to justify the decision by referring to the specific circumstances of the concrete case in light of certain legal principles and values as a reason for supplementing or correcting a legal rule if the existing rules do not provide a solution. In his view (1999: 414) judges should try to formulate the 'rule' that underlies the exception for the concrete case. The application of reasonableness as a reason for making an exception to a general rule for a concrete case implies in his view that a general exception to a rule is accepted for the concrete case.[15]

11.2.3 The Content and Structure of the Complex Argumentation Based on the Application of Reasonableness

As I indicated, argumentation from reasonableness is used in a context in which application of a legal rule would lead to an unacceptable result. In order to justify that an exception should be made by limiting the range of application for the concrete case, the judge is required to give a justification that consists of different considerations. This implies that argumentation from reasonableness is not what can be called a 'single argument', but that it amounts to a complex form of argumentation consisting of different types of argument that are weighed and balanced in relation to each other. To explain what these arguments exactly are and what the relation between these arguments is, in what follows I will go deeper into the nature of argumentation from reasonableness and into the relation between the different considerations that together constitute what is characterized as the 'weighing and balancing of a plurality of different considerations'.

Argumentation in which it is claimed that application of a particular legal rule in an exceptional situation would lead to certain unacceptable consequences and that

[14] In the German legal literature such rules of exception are considered as 'Fallgruppen' that constitute groups of cases that can be considered as specifications of the open norm, and as such, can function as examples for similar cases. See Hesselink (1999: 48).

[15] See also Alexy's (1989: pp. 223 ff.) principle of universalizability with respect to legal argumentation as expressed in the rules J.2.1 (At least one universal norm must be adduced in the justification of a legal judgement), J.2.2 (whenever it is open to doubt whether a is a T or an Mi, a rule must be put forward which settles this question).

for this reason the rule should be corrected for the concrete case, can be considered as a specific form of *an argument from unacceptable consequences*, or as a specific form of an *argument from absurdity*. The argument refers to the unacceptable or absurd consequences of strict application of the rule and states that application of the rule with an exception for the concrete case would lead to an acceptable result.[16] The unacceptability or absurdity of the result is justified by referring to the fact that it is incompatible with certain values that constitute a particular implementation of 'reasonableness' in the concrete case that 'outweighs' the requirement of legal certainty that would oblige the judge to apply the law as it is formulated by the legislator. The judge argues that, given the unacceptable consequences of application of the rule in its accepted meaning, it would be reasonable to 'amend' the rule for the circumstances of the specific case by formulating what could be called a 'new rule with an exception' that implies that subsumption of the concrete case under this rule would lead to an acceptable result.

With respect to argumentation that is based on the unacceptable, unjust or absurd consequences of a strict application of a legal rule, in their international research project on the use of various forms of interpretative arguments in different legal systems, MacCormick and Summers (1991) conclude that in all legal systems discussed in this project it is acknowledged that there can be a conflict between application of a legal rule in its literal interpretation and the observation that application in this interpretation in the concrete case would lead to an absurd or manifestly unjust result.[17] This type of argument takes on different forms in various legal systems. Sometimes it is formulated in terms of a presumption or presupposition to the effect that the legislature does not intend absurd or manifestly unjust outcomes. In other cases it is constitutionalized, and is thus formulated as an argument that invalidates the absurd or manifestly unjust result.

The common aspect of these forms of argumentation is that the judge refers to the consequences of application of the rule in its (literal) standard interpretation and gives a negative evaluation of these consequences. This negative evaluation is based on the consideration that this outcome is incompatible with the intentions of a rational legislator. The presumption is that a rational legislator cannot have intended that a rule should be applied in a concrete case if application would lead to an absurd or unjust outcome that is incompatible with certain fundamental principles and values. Various authors consider the argument from absurdity as a specific form of *objective-teleological* argumentation in which the objective purpose, the rational ends or values that a statute is considered to have, the rational intention of the legislator, the

[16] Cf. MacCormick (2005: 176) who contends that arguments from reasonableness can be considered as an example of consequentialist reasoning in which consequentialist grounds for an interpretation are given. The consequentialist grounds imply that the judge points to the inexpedient and unjust consequences of adopting a particular standard. These consequentialist arguments can be backed up by arguments from coherence and consistency.

[17] See various authors in MacCormick and Summers (1991) for different countries: Aarnio (1991: 152–163) for Finland, La Torre et al. (1991: 221–222) for Italy, Bankowski and MacCormick (1991: 371–373) for the UK and Peczenik and Bergholz (1991: 312) for Sweden.

so-called *ratio legis*, is reconstructed.[18] The rational intention is not the intention of the historical legislator but the intention of a rational legislator who is supposed to intend a rule to have reasonable results. The intention of the legislator can be reconstructed by referring to the goals and values implemented in the general legal principles that are underlying the branch of law in question.[19]

In the research project of MacCormick and Summers (1991) they describe a hierarchy of interpretation methods in which they classify arguments from reasonableness and other forms of arguments referring to unacceptable consequences as a form of *teleological- evaluative* argumentation, that is argumentation that is based on the goals and values a rule is intended to realize. From the perspective of the hierarchy of interpretation methods, if a judge uses an argument that belongs to the category of teleological-evaluative argumentation, he must justify his decision by showing why other arguments that are higher in the hierarchy such as linguistic and systematic arguments (which are supposed to reflect the intention of the historical legislator), would lead to an undesirable result. In terms of MacCormick and Summers (1991) a judge must explain why the argument from reasonableness 'cancels' or 'outweighs' the reasons for applying the rule in its standard interpretation.[20] For arguments from reasonableness this implies that a judge must show that, in light of the circumstances of the concrete case, strict application of the rule would have unacceptable consequences from the perspective of the goals and values the rule is intended to realize and he must explain why the application of the rule with an exception would have acceptable consequences.

On the basis of the discussion of the ideas about arguments from reasonableness it has now become clear that:

- The norm of reasonableness creates a possibility to correct the law by making an exception to a legal rule where strict application would lead to unacceptable consequences in light of the facts of the concrete case.
- Reasonableness as explicit part of a legal rule is an *open norm* which is intentionally left open by the legislator to create a possibility for the judge to implement the norm and in this way to adapt the law to concrete circumstances.
- To account for the discretionary power to implement the norm, the judge must explain how he has implemented reasonableness in the concrete case by specifying in an objective and clear way the normative considerations (legal principles,

[18] For a discussion of the use of a reference to the *ratio legis* in legal argumentation see Canale and Tuzet (2009).

[19] See MacCormick (2005: 114) about the role of values as the grounds for evaluating judicial consequences.

[20] See MacCormick and Summers (1991: 537 ff.) for the different argumentation structures involved in the use of the different forms of argument. Legal systems differ with respect to the question which arguments can be independent fundamental grounds of argumentation or grounds which are dependent upon explicit or implicit principles of a system. See also Alexy (2009: 7–11) about the relation between reasonableness and the weighing of diverse criteria. See also MacCormick (2005: 132 ff.) and MacCormick and Summers (1991: 524 ff.) about the role of objective-teleological arguments and their function in cancelling other arguments. For a more detailed description of the requirements of a justification in the context of teleological-evaluative arguments see Feteris (2007).

legal values) and factual considerations (exceptional a-typical circumstances of the case) that justify the 'rule of exception' for the specific case.

- The argumentation based on the application of reasonableness is a complex form of argumentation referring to the different considerations that specify what reasonableness amounts to in the circumstances of the concrete case.

In order to establish the interrelations between the different considerations specifying what reasonableness amounts to it must be determined how the argument referring to the absurd, unacceptable consequences functions as an argument that cancels the reasons for applying the rule in its literal standard interpretation.

11.3 An Argumentation Model for the Rational Reconstruction of Argumentation from Reasonableness

On the basis of the results of the previous discussion about the role of arguments from reasonableness, I will explain how an argumentation model for the rational reconstruction of arguments from reasonableness can be used for the analysis.[21] The aim of the model is to make explicit the argumentative burden of a judge who uses argumentation from reasonableness by specifying the necessary elements of his argumentation and the interrelations between these arguments so that his decision can be submitted to rational critique. To this end, I will make use of the conceptual distinctions from the pragma-dialectical argumentation theory developed by van Eemeren and Grootendorst (1992) to enable a systematic rational reconstruction of arguments from reasonableness as they occur in actual legal practice.

A judge who argues that application of a rule with an exception in the concrete case would be reasonable because application without an exception would have unacceptable consequences does this in the context of what can be called a 'mixed dispute' in which one party argues that the rule R must be applied in the accepted standard meaning R′ (that can be based on a linguistic or systematic interpretation of the rule), and the other party argues that in the context of the concrete case the rule R must not be applied in the meaning R′ but in the amended meaning R″ with an exception E, so that the rule is not applicable to the concrete case. This implies that the standpoint can be reconstructed as a *complex standpoint* that consists of two components: a component **1a** that consists of a preference for the amended meaning R″ with an exception and a component **1b** that consists of a rejection of application in the standard meaning R′ without an exception:

1a Application of rule R in the amended meaning R″ with the exception E for the concrete situation is reasonable

and

1b Application of rule R in the literal standard meaning R′ without the exception E for the concrete situation is unreasonable

[21] For a discussion of the rational reconstruction of different forms of legal argumentation see MacCormick and Summers (1991, chapter 13).

1a Application of rule R in the amended meaning R″ with the exception E for the concrete situation is reasonable

  1a.1 Application of rule R in the amended meaning R″ leads to the acceptable result (S″) in the exceptional circumstances of the concrete case (C)

    1a.1.1 In light of the values (V) and the legal principles (LP) the result (S″) is acceptable in the exceptional circumstances of the concrete case (C)

      1a.1.1.1a Specification of the values (V) and/or the legal principles (LP) the rule is intended to realize

      1a.1.1.1b Specification of the exceptional circumstances of the concrete case (C)

and

1b Application of rule R in the literal standard meaning R′ without the exception E for the concrete situation is unreasonable

  1b.1 Application of rule R in the literal standard meaning R′ leads to the unacceptable result (S′) in the exceptional circumstances of the concrete case (C)

    1b.1.1 In light of the values (V) and the legal principles (LP) the result (S′) is unacceptable in the exceptional circumstances of the concrete case (C)

      1b.1.1.1a Specification of the values (V) and/or the legal principles (LP) the rule is intended to realize

      1b.1.1.1b Specification of the exceptional circumstances of the concrete case (C)

Fig. 11.1 Argumentation model for the rational reconstruction of argumentation from reasonableness

For the argumentative burden of the judge who wants to make an exception, this implies that he has to justify why in the concrete case the rule R must be made more precise by adding an exception E which implies that the rule should not be applied in the concrete case. The argumentation supporting these two components consists, in its turn, of a complex *coordinative* argumentation that accounts for the choice between the components 1a and 1b of the standpoint. The reconstruction of this argumentation is shown in the argumentation model in Fig. 11.1.

The first line of argumentation justifies the preference for standpoint 1a and the second line of argumentation justifies the rejection of standpoint 1b.

The argumentation is complex also in other respects because the argumentation must consist of different levels of *subordinate* argumentation that support each other.

On the first level (consisting of argument 1a.1 and 1b.1) the judge must justify that the preferred version of the rule (R″) leads to the acceptable result (S″) and the rejected version (R′) to the unacceptable result (S′). These arguments constitute a specific implementation of an argument from (acceptable and) unacceptable consequences/an argument from absurdity.

The argumentation of the *second level* (consisting of the argument 1a.1.1 and 1b.1.1) must justify the acceptability of result (S″) and the unacceptability of the result (S′) in relation to the relevant legal principles (LP) and values (V) and the exceptional circumstances of the case C.

The argumentation of the *third level* (consisting of 1a.1.1.1a and 1a.1.1.1b etc.) must specify the sources of the legal principles (LP) and values (V) as well as the exceptional circumstances of the concrete case C.

The argumentation on the second and third level forms the reconstruction of the intention of a rational legislator by specifying the principles and values that justify the exception in light of the circumstances of the a-typical case C.

This reconstruction of the argumentative obligations of a judge who uses an argument from reasonableness into an argumentation model clarifies his argumentative obligations. In this way the model serves as a heuristic tool for reconstructing the commitments of the judge that have been characterized in the literature as the 'plurality of normative and factual considerations'. I have tried to implement the 'reconstruction of the intention of a rational legislator/ratio legis' in terms of a specific implementation of an argument from absurdity and I have translated what is in the literature called the 'cancelling' or 'weighing and balancing' into elements of an argumentation model that account for the preference for rule R″ with an exception to rule R′ without an exception for the concrete case. It serves as a critical tool also for assessing the quality of the argumentation by checking whether the necessary elements of the argumentation are represented and whether they can be considered acceptable from a legal point of view. Whether the arguments are acceptable from the material perspective depends on the criteria of acceptability in a specific field of law. In section (4) I give a specification of the implementation of the concept of 'reasonableness' in Dutch civil law and on the basis of this, in (5), I use the model to give an analysis of an example of the use of an argument from reasonableness and fairness in Dutch civil law.

11.4 The Use of Arguments from Reasonableness and Fairness in Dutch Civil Law

To do justice to the context-dependency of the concept of reasonableness in the context of legal justification, I concentrate on the role of reasonableness in a specific domain, civil law in the Netherlands. In civil law in the Netherlands reasonableness plays a central role as a mechanism for the correction of outcomes that would be unacceptable from the perspective of justice in a concrete case. First, in 4.1, I explain the relevant rules with respect to the use of norm of reasonableness. Then. in 4.2, I discuss a decision of the Dutch Supreme Court in which the criterion of reasonableness as a reason for making an exception is implemented for a specific case.

11.4.1 The 'Derogating' Function of Reasonableness in Dutch Civil Law

In Dutch civil law, in some cases an argument from reasonableness and fairness is an argument that is explicitly recognized as an acceptable argument by the legislator. On the basis of article 6:248, 2 of the Dutch Civil Code the judge has the authority to make an exception to a contractual provision on the basis of reasonableness and fairness if application of the provision would be unacceptable in the concrete circumstances:

> 2. A contractual provision that is valid between the creditor and the debtor on the basis of the law, a custom or a legal act, does not apply if this would be unacceptable from the perspective of the standards of reasonableness and fairness.

In book 3 of the Dutch Civil Code in the general article 12 the legislator specifies the factors that play a role in determining what can be considered as reasonable and fair:

> When determining what reasonableness and fairness require, generally accepted legal principles, legal convictions that are generally accepted in the Netherlands, and social and personal interests in the concrete case, should be taken into account.

These articles specify when a judge is allowed to make an exception to a legal rule on the basis of reasonableness and fairness and they specify the considerations that are necessary to justify an exception to a legal rule.

In Dutch law, such a use of reasonableness and fairness is called the 'derogating function' of reasonableness and fairness because reasonableness is considered as a criterion that 'derogates' other considerations that would normally justify applying the rule if the conditions of application are fulfilled.

In Dutch law, in other cases a judge can make an exception also to a rule but he has a heavier 'argumentative burden' which is in line with the obligations I have described in the argumentation model in Sect. 11.3. He must explain why a strict application would lead to an unacceptable result by specifying why a strict application would be incompatible with certain legal principles and values underlying the relevant branch of law and why the circumstances of the concrete case are exceptional so that they justify an exception on the basis of these principles and values.

11.4.2 The Implementation of Reasonableness and Fairness in the Context of the Application of Article 248 Book 6 in a Concrete Case

After the introduction of article 6:248, 2 of the Dutch Civil Code the first case in which the Dutch Supreme Court gave a fundamental decision about the way in which reasonableness should be implemented for the circumstances of a specific case was in the context of a dispute in which the question was whether the relatives of victims of asbestos cancer (mesothelioma) have a claim against the employer when the legal limitation period of 30 years (as specified in article 3:310, 2 of the Dutch Civil Code) has lapsed, since this form of cancer manifests itself only after 20 years and results in death within a year.[22]

The decision was in the case against the Nederlandse Scheldegroep (Supreme Court, HR 28 April 2000, NJ 2000, 430). The Supreme Court ruled that an exception to the limitation period on the basis of reasonableness and fairness is, in principle, acceptable in exceptional cases.[23] The court did not give a clear rule but formulated the 'points of view' that should be taken into account when evaluating the unacceptability of the limitation period of 30 years. According to the court, these are requirements that weigh heavy. The Supreme Court sent the case back to the Court of Appeals to give a decision on the basis of these points of view.

This is the only case in which the Supreme Court explicitly made an exception on the basis of reasonableness and fairness. In the two cases that followed this case (Eternit and Hertel), the Supreme Court gave a different decision. In the Eternit case because the limitation period had not yet lapsed so that article 3:310,2 was not applicable, in the Hertel case the Supreme Court sent the case back to the Court of Appeals that had to investigate the unacceptability of the term of limitation on the basis of the points of view.

In the first case of the Scheldegroup the Supreme Court specifies for a particular category of cases which conditions should be fulfilled in order to make an exception on the basis of reasonableness and fairness of article 6:2. In this way the Supreme Court implements the open norm: for cases in which the death of the employee is caused by the work with asbestos, on the basis of reasonableness and fairness it is justified to depart from the general rule about the limitation of 30 years. The Supreme Court formulates this implementation of the open norm of reasonableness as follows:

3.3.3 Whether, in cases as the present one, application of the limitation period of 30 years after the event on which the liability rests, is indeed unacceptable according to standards of reasonableness and fairness, should be evaluated by taking into account the circumstances of the concrete case. As points of view that should be mentioned by the judge in his evaluation the following can be mentioned:

---

[22] According to the annotator, ARB (A.R. Bloembergen) the decisions about the term of limitation of which this decision forms part constitute the most important application of article 6:2, 2. According to him this decision is a clear example of the fact that the Dutch Supreme Court wants to limit autonomous elements in the judicial application of law. For an overview of the law regarding the consequences of asbestos cancer in other countries see http://en.wikipedia.org/wiki/Asbestos_and_the_law.

[23] This case of the Scheldegroep differs from other examples (of the Unworthy Spouse I discussed in the introduction and the Unworthy Grandson that I will discuss in the next section). In this case the Supreme Court does not refer to the goal of the rule or the intention of the legislator to justify an exception: from the legislative history it is clear that the legislator explicitly wanted to include also asbestos cases in the legal rules regarding the term of limitation.

(a) whether it concerns the compensation for an injury/damage of property or for a disadvantage that does not concern an injury/damage of property, and
(b) to what extent the victim or his relatives have recourse to a payment (uitkering) with respect to the injury/damage from another source;
(c) the extent to which the defendant is responsible for the event;
(d) to what extent the defendant, before the limitation period has lapsed, has taken into account or should have taken into account the possibility that he would be responsible for the damage;
(e) whether the defendant still has the possibility to defend himself against the claim;
(f) whether the liability is covered by an insurance;
(g) whether, after the damage has been discovered, the plaintiff has made his claim about the liability within a reasonable term and whether a legal action has been started.

(Supreme Court, HR 28 April 2000, NJ 2000, 430) See also Supreme Court, HR 28 April 2000, NJ 2000, 431 and HR 20-10-2000, NJ 2001, 268

In this case the Supreme Court specified the points of view that should be taken into account when implementing the derogating function of 'reasonableness and fairness' in the context of article 6:248, 2 for cases that concern the limitation period for liability for the consequences of asbestos cancer. As became clear, the Supreme Court wanted to limit the criteria for application of article 6:248, 2 to this type of cases and did not want to commit itself to a more general formulation of criteria.

11.5 An Exemplary Analysis of Argumentation from Reasonableness in the Case of the 'Unworthy Grandson'

To illustrate how the argumentation model can be used for the analysis, I will discuss a representative example of the way in which Dutch courts use the argument from reasonableness to justify the decision to correct the law in a specific case on the basis of reasonableness and fairness.

In the case that is called the 'Unworthy Grandson', the district court of Haarlem uses an argument from reasonableness and fairness to justify that in the case in which a grandson had killed his father, an exception should be made to the legal rule of article 4:889 of the Dutch Civil Code about the right of a heir to his legal part of the inheritance.[24] The 'unworthy grandson' who had killed his father and the wife of his father (for which he has been convicted and imprisoned in Australia) claims his share in the inheritance of his grandmother. He claims to have a right to his share on

[24] For the relevant parts of the decision of the District Court of Haarlem see B at the end of this contribution. For the relevant articles of the Dutch Civil Code see C at the end of this contribution.

the basis of article 4:889 of the Dutch Civil Code that gives a child as a substitute a right to the legal part of the inheritance of a deceased parent. However, the other inheritors contest this right. The district court of Haarlem rules that the grandson is not entitled to his father's share in the inheritance. As a justification the court refers to the derogating function of reasonableness and fairness stating that 'in light of the legal principle that someone should not profit from the intentionally caused death of someone else, the right of the grandson to exercise his right to his legal share of the inheritance on the basis of article 4:889 of the Dutch Civil Code would, according to the standards of reasonableness and fairness in the circumstances of this concrete case, lead to an unacceptable result'.[25]

The district court decides that article 4:889 of the Dutch Civil Code that gives a child as a substitute a right to the legal part of the inheritance of a deceased parent, is not applicable in the concrete case because it would lead to an unacceptable result from the perspective of the underlying principle regarding unworthiness in the law of inheritance.[26] By making an exception on the basis of reasonableness, the court applies article 6:248, 2, referring to the decision of the Supreme Court in the case of the 'Unworthy Spouse' I discussed at the beginning, in which the court applied article 6:248 also to an a-typical case in the field of inheritance.

I will now discuss the analysis of the relevant parts of the decision on the basis of the argumentation model. You find the analysis in Fig. 11.2.

On the *first level* (reconstructed as argument 1a.1) the court justifies that the preferred version of the rule R″ with the exception E for the concrete situation, implying that the rule of article 4:889 is not applicable to a person who has murdered his father, leads to the acceptable result (S″) in the concrete case that the son who has murdered his father cannot exercise his right to his legal share of the inheritance.

On the *second and third level* the court explains why result S″ is acceptable by explaining the evaluation of the results in light of the legal principle (LP) that someone should not profit from the intentionally caused death of someone else in relation to the exceptional circumstances of the concrete case (C) where the son has murdered his father, leads to the acceptable result (S″).

The argumentation on the second level (consisting of 1a.1.1), justifies the acceptability of the result S″ by specifying that the result can be considered acceptable in light of the legal principle (LP) and the exceptional circumstances of the concrete case (C) . The argumentation on the third level (consisting of 1a.1.1.1a and 1a.1.1.1b) justifies the existence of the legal principle by referring to the decision of the Dutch Supreme Court in the case of the 'Unworthy Spouse' and specifies the exceptional circumstances of the concrete situation C that form the a-typical

[25] In appeal, the Court of Appeals (Court of Appeals Amsterdam, August 15, 2002, nr. 1304/01, NJ 2003, 53) rejects the appeal and confirms the decision of the district court. The Court of Appeals adds in 4.3 that the district court, all the more so because the grandson would inherit his father's part in the inheritance by way of replacement because he has killed his father, is of the opinion that it would be an unacceptable legal consequence that the grandson would have a right to the inheritance according to the standards of reasonableness and fairness.

[26] In 2003 the Dutch law of inheritance has been changed, now the relevant articles are 4.3 and 4.12 of the Dutch Civil Code.

circumstances that justify the exception E. This argumentation on the second and third level forms the reconstruction of the intention of a rational legislator by specifying the principles and values that justify the exception in light of the circumstance of the a-typical case.

For the other line of argumentation (in defence of the second part of the standpoint 1b that application of rule R in the meaning R′ leads to the unacceptable result S′) a similar argumentation structure can be reconstructed.

The analysis makes clear that in legal decisions only part of the complex standpoint and argumentation is made explicit. The standpoint that a particular exception E to the rule R is necessary (part 1a of the standpoint) is defended by means of the argumentation line 1.1b etcetera that should be reconstructed as a justification of part 1b of the standpoint. For a complete rational reconstruction, however, the whole complex argumentation must be reconstructed to make the underlying arguments explicit so that they can be submitted to critique.

The analysis of the argumentation demonstrates that the court, from the formal perspective, lives up to its argumentative burden as specified in the argumentation

1a Application of article 4:889 in the amended meaning R″, with the exception E for the concrete situation, implying that the rule is not applicable to a person who has murdered his father, is reasonable

1a.1 Application of rule R in the amended meaning R″ in the concrete case (C) where the son has murdered his father leads to the acceptable result (S″)that the ‘grandson’ cannot exercise his right to his legal share of the inheritance

1a.1.1 In light of the legal principle (LP), that someone should not profit from the intentionally caused death of someone else, the result (S″) that the son who has murdered his father cannot exercise his right to his legal share of the inheritance, is acceptable in the exceptional circumstances of the concrete case (C) where the son has murdered his father

1a.1.1.1a This principle is formulated by the Supreme Court in his decision of December 7 1990 (the ‘Unworthy spouse’)

1a.1.1.1b Application of rule R in the amended meaning R″ is compatible with the personal interests of the parties involved in the concrete case (C) where the son has murdered his father, implying that it is in the present circumstances compatible with the sense of justice that the will of the testatrix is obeyed because the testatrix, who had suffered a great deal from what the grandson had done to her, had explicitly stated in her will that she did not want that the grandson would get a share of her inheritance

Fig. 11.2 Analysis of the argumentation in the case of the ‘Unworthy Grandson’

1b Application of article 4:889 in the meaning R′, without the exception E for the concrete situation, implying that the rule is applicable to a person who has murdered his father, is unreasonable

1b.1 Application of rule R in the amended meaning R′ in the concrete case (C) where the son has murdered his father leads to the unacceptable result (S′) that the 'grandson' cannot exercise his right to his legal share of the inheritance

1b.1.1 In light of the legal principle (LP), that someone should not profit from the intentionally caused death of someone else, the result (S′) that the son who has murdered his father can exercise his right to his legal share of the inheritance, is unacceptable in the exceptional circumstances of the concrete case (C) where the son has murdered his father

1b.1.1.1a This principle is formulated by the Supreme Court in his decision of December 7 1990 (the 'Unworthy spouse')

1b.1.1.1b Application of rule R in the amended meaning R′ is incompatible with the personal interests of the parties involved in the concrete case (C) where the son has murdered his father, implying that it is in the present circumstances incompatible with the sense of justice that the will of the testatrix is obeyed because the testatrix, who had suffered a great deal from what the grandson had done to her, had explicitly stated in her will that she did not want that the grandson would get a share of her inheritance

Fig. 11.2 (continued)

model. The exception is justified by three levels of argumentation specifying that the rule with the exception leads to an acceptable result, is in accordance with the law and with the personal interests of the persons involved in the concrete case, which is in line with the requirements of the article 3:12 of the Dutch Civil Code.

Whether the justification is acceptable from the material perspective depends on the question whether the support of the argumentation is acceptable. In this case, relevant considerations in this respect are that the argumentation is defended by a decision of the Supreme Court in the case of the 'Unworthy spouse' in which the legal principle (LP) is formulated. It is also supported by an argument in which it is specified that the history of the case makes clear that the personal interests of the testatrix are indeed in accordance with the decision to deny the grandson his right to his legal share.

In a similar way, the other line of argumentation supporting the claim that application in the strict meaning R′ would be unreasonable and unfair can be evaluated.

11.6 Conclusion

In this contribution I have analyzed the role of argumentation from reasonableness in the justification of judicial opinions. I have clarified the complex argumentation structure of this form of argumentation and the types of argument that constitute this complex argumentation. I have explained that arguments from reasonableness can be an acceptable way of justifying a judicial opinion if certain conditions are fulfilled. I have explained that, from a legal perspective, 'reasonableness' is not necessarily a subjective criterion that is not open for discussion. By referring to the acceptability of the preferred solution and the unacceptability of the rejected outcome, a judge can explicitly account for the balancing of a legally desirable and a legally undesirable solution. In doing so, he has the obligation to refer to objective goals intended by the legislator and to the principles and values underlying these goals. By explicitly referring to these legal considerations, he opens his argumentation to rational critique and intersubjective testing. By explicitly mentioning the a-typical circumstances of the case he explains what kind of factual considerations can form relevant considerations for applying a rule of exception in certain cases. In this way, courts contribute to the development of law by specifying the relevant criteria for the application of a 'rule of exception' in cases that have not been foreseen by the historical legislator but should be applied from the perspective of a rational legislator.

A. The Case of the 'Unworthy Spouse'

DECISION OF THE COURT OF APPEALS NJ 1989/369, 24-11-1989

(…)

5.13 Since the district court has assumed that Mrs. van Wylick intended with the marriage - that also according to L was a marriage of convenience- a financial benefit for L, the district court has rightly stressed that to the factual situation described in the foregoing the general legal principle is applicable that he, who has deliberately caused the death of someone else, who has favoured him, should not profit from the this favour.

(…)

5.16 In this context it is also important to mention that the aforementioned legal principle is closely related to another legal principle, i.e. that one should not profit form the deliberately caused death of someone else, which principle has among others been expressed in article 885 under 1 book 3 CC. (…)

5.17 Application of the mentioned legal principles leads under the aforementioned facts and circumstances to the conclusion that L is not entitled to the benefit that is the consequence of the community of property created by the marriage without a marriage settlement with mrs. van Wylick.

5.18 Also an examination of the claims of L in light of the requirements of reasonableness and fairness according to which he is supposed to behave in the community of property that is created by the marriage, as is stated by Brouwers c.s., leads to the conclusion that L should not profit from the marital community of property. In this case the court applies a strict standard because the appeal to reasonableness and fairness is aimed at preventing the claims of L completely. Also **when applying such a strict standard the court is of the opinion that the claims of L must be considered as so unreasonable and unfair, in the aforementioned special circumstances of this case and also considered in light of the mentioned general legal principles, that the exertion of the claimed rights must be denied to him completely**.

B. Articles from the Dutch Civil Code Applied in the Case of the Unworthy Spouse

Article 1:100 of the Old Dutch Civil Code

1. The spouses have an equal share in this divided community of property, unless a different division is established by means of a marriage settlement (…).

Article 4.3 of the New Dutch Civil Code (introduced after 1990)

1. Legally unworthy to profit from an inheritance are: He who has been condemned irrevocably because he has killed the deceased, he who has tried to kill the deceased or he who has prepared to kill the deceased or has participated in preparing to kill the deceased.

Article 6:248, 2 of the Dutch Civil Code

An arrangement that is valid between the creditor and the debtor on the basis of the law, a custom or a legal act, does not apply if this is unacceptable from the perspective of the standards of reasonableness and fairness.

Article 3:12 of the Dutch Civil Code

When establishing what reasonableness and fairness require, generally accepted legal principles, legal convictions that are generally accepted in the Netherlands, and social and personal interests in a particular case, should be taken into account.

C. The Case of the 'Unworthy Grandson'

District Court Haarlem, July 24, 2001, nr. 68989

5.7 The exceptional situation of this case has not been foreseen by the legislator. But even if it would have been foreseen, this does not exclude that in certain circumstances the judge can appeal to the 'derogating' function of reasonableness and fairness if application of the law would lead to an unacceptable result.

5.8 The Court is of the opinion that in this case such circumstances obtain. The Court holds that the defendant acts in this special case as inheritor and statutory heir of his grandmother because he has killed his father, the inheritor in the first line.

(…)

5.10 The rules regarding unworthiness in the law of inheritance make explicit the underlying general legal principle to which the decision of the Supreme Court of December 7 1990 also refers, i.e. that someone should not profit form the intentionally caused death of someone else. **In the light of this principle the right of the defendant to exercise his right to his legal share of the inheritance on the basis of clause 4:889 of the Dutch Civil Code would, according to the standards of reasonableness and fairness in the circumstances of this concrete case, lead to an unacceptable result.**

5.11 The Court holds that in the present circumstances it is important also that the testatrix, who had suffered a great deal from what the grandson had done to her, had explicitly stated in her will that she did not want that the grandson would get a share of her inheritance. Although it is true that a testator cannot disinherit someone from his legitimate share to the inheritance, the right to the legitimate share is not absolute. In the present circumstances disobeying the will of the testatrix would conflict with the sense of justice in such a serious way that exertion of this right cannot be accepted.

D. Relevant Articles Used in the Case of the Unworthy Grandson

Article 4:889 of the Dutch Civil Code (now article 4.12):

1. Replacement in the direct downward line takes place infinitively.

Article 4:885 of the Dutch Civil Coce (now article 4.3):

The following persons can considered to be unworthy to be an inheritor and can, for this reason be excluded from the inheritance:

1. He who has been convicted of killing of trying to kill the deceased;

References

Aarnio, A. 1991. Statutory interpretation in Finland. In *Interpreting statutes. A comparative study*, ed. N. MacCormick and R.S. Summers, 123–170. Aldershot: Dartmouth.

Adinolfi, A. 2009. The principle of reasonableness in European Union Law. In *Reasonableness and law*, ed. G. Bongiovanni, G. Sartor, and C. Valentini, 383–404. Dordrecht/Heidelberg: Springer.

Alexy, R. 1989. *A theory of legal argumentation. The theory of rational discourse as theory of legal justification*. Oxford: Clarendon Press.

Alexy, R. 2009. The reasonableness of law. In *Reasonableness and law*, ed. G. Bongiovanni, G. Sartor, and C. Valentini, 5–16. Dordrecht/Heidelberg: Springer.

Aristotle. 1980. *The Nicomachean ethics*. Translated with an introduction by David Ross. Revised by J.L. Ackrill and J.O. Urmson. Oxford etc.: Oxford University Press. (Edition of 1980).

Bankowski, Z., and N. MacCormick. 1991. Statutory interpretation in the United Kingdom. In *Interpreting statutes. A comparative study*, ed. N. MacCormick and R.S. Summers, 359–406. Aldershot: Dartmouth.

Bongiovanni, G., G. Sartor, and C. Valentini (eds.). 2009. *Reasonableness and law*. Dordrecht/Heidelberg: Springer.

Canale, D., and G. Tuzet. 2009. Inferring the ratio: Commitments and constraints. In *Argumentation and the application of legal rules*, ed. E.T. Feteris, H. Kloosterhuis, and H.J. Plug, 15–34. Amsterdam: Rozenberg.

della Cananea, G. 2009. Reasonableness in administrative law. In *Reasonableness and law*, ed. G. Bongiovanni, G. Sartor, and C. Valentini, 295–310. Dordrecht/Heidelberg: Springer.

Feteris, E.T. 2005. The rational reconstruction of argumentation referring to consequences and purposes in the application of legal rules: A pragma-dialectical perspective. *Argumentation* 19(4): 459–470.

Feteris, E.T. 2007. The rational reconstruction of teleological-evaluative arguments. In *Logic, argumentation and interpretation*, ed. J. Aguiló-Regla, Proceedings of the 22nd IVR World Congress Granada 2005. *ARSP Beiheft 110*, 57–67. Stuttgart: Franz Steiner Verlag.

Feteris, E.T. 2012. Strategic maneuvering in the case of the 'Unworthy spouse'. In *Exploring argumentative contexts*, ed. F.H. van Eemeren and Bart Garssen, 149–164. Amsterdam: John Benjamins.

Hesselink, M.W. 1999. *De Redelijkheid en Billijkheid in het Europese Privaatrecht*. (Reasonableness and fairness in European Private Law). Dissertation Amsterdam. Dordrecht: Kluwer.

MacCormick, N. 2005. *Rhetoric and the rule of law. A theory of legal reasoning*. Oxford: Oxford University Press.

MacCormick, N., and R.S. Summers (eds.). 1991. *Interpreting statutes. A comparative study*. Aldershot: Dartmouth.

Peczenik, A., and G. Bergholz. 1991. Statutory interpretation in Sweden. In *Interpreting statutes. A comparative study*, ed. N. MacCormick and R.S. Summers, 311–358. Aldershot: Dartmouth.

Perelman, Ch. 1979. *The new rhetoric and the humanities. Essays on rhetoric and its applications*. Dordrecht etc.: Reidel.

van Eemeren, F.H., and R. Grootendorst. 1992. *Argumentation, communication and Fallacies*. Mahwah: Erlbaum.

Chapter 12
Legal Argumentation and Theories of Adjudication in the U.S. Legal Tradition: A Critical View of Cass Sunstein's Minimalism, Richard Posner's Pragmatism and Ronald Dworkin's Advocacy of Integrity

Bernardo Gonçalves Fernandes

Abstract This chapter aims at studying the theories of adjudication in U.S. law, beginning with a criticism against the old "justifying dichotomy" between interpretivism and non-interpretivism, which is still present in U.S. legal thinking. In a second moment, I will analyze alternatives to this gap envisioned by Cass Sunstein's judicial minimalism, by pragmatism, by Richard Posner's anti-theoretical movement and by Ronald Dworkin's Theory of Integrity. Finally, I will take a stand on this debate and provide an answer as to which of these theories is equipped with the best resources for the reaching adequate and correct legal judgments.

12.1 Introduction

Theories of legal argumentation usually work within different fields where legal arguments are at stake, of which two unquestionable examples can be mentioned: the legislative process and the enforcement of rules for the resolution of specific cases.

Legal theorists, particularly after the second half of the twentieth century, have been largely concerned with the discourses of adjudication, in a clear move to "strengthen" the role of the judiciary in resolving conflicts and "reasonable disagreements" existing in contemporary societies. The recurrent use of the expression

B.G. Fernandes (✉)
Law Faculty, Federal University of Minas Gerais (Universidade Federal de Minas Gerais), Belo Horizonte, Brazil
e-mail: bernardogaf@yahoo.com.br

© Springer International Publishing Switzerland 2015

T. Bustamante, C. Dahlman (eds.), *Argument Types and Fallacies in Legal Argumentation*, Law and Philosophy Library 112,
DOI 10.1007/978-3-319-16148-8_12

"everything pours into the judiciary", or at least "almost everything", is no casualty either in Civil Law or in Common Law legal traditions.[1]

In this context, one can notice an increasing need not only to explain how decisions are formed, but also to justify them.

Theories of legal argumentation seek to unveil all the relevant aspects concerning the rational use of arguments to justify judicial decisions. Semiotics, legal logic, legal axiology, philosophy of language, rhetoric and theories of interpretation are some of the tools developed for this analysis (Bustamante and Maia 2008, p. 361).

But if modern theories of legal argumentation are largely characterized both by an explanation of the "use of arguments" and a normative account to determine the "value of these arguments" in the discourses that seek to justify a judicial decision and to make that decision rationally acceptable, how can we conceive this assertion in a tradition in which judicial decisions have long been justified according to the dichotomy "interpretivism versus non-interpretivism"?

This chapter aims at studying the theories of adjudication in U.S. law, beginning with a criticism against the old "justifying dichotomy" between interpretivism and non-interpretivism, which have been largely present in U.S. legal thinking.[2] In a second moment, I will analyze the alternatives to this gap envisioned by Cass Sunstein's judicial minimalism, Richard Posner's anti-theoretical pragmatism, and Ronald Dworkin's conception of "Law as Integrity". Finally, I will take a stand on this debate and provide an answer as to which of these theories is equipped with the best resources for the reaching adequate legal judgments.

12.2 The Dichotomy Between Interpretivism and Non-interpretivism

Until recently, American judges used to justify their decisions and have their arguments studied according to either "interpretive" or "non-interpretive premises". A magistrate or even a counsellor was classified on the basis of this duality. Let us analyse how those interpretive perspectives account for legal argumentation.

Interpretivists, on the one hand, advocate a conservative position – advanced by great exponents like Judge Robert Bork and Justice Antonin Scalia – according to which the interpreter, especially in constitutional adjudication, shall be limited to grasping the meaning of the explicit precepts or at least the meaning perceived as clearly implicit in the text, i.e. within its semantic texture. While interpreting the Constitution, one should have his eyes on the constitutional text that lies ahead, having as his farthest limit an opening to search for the original intention of the founders. They claim that taking a step beyond the frame of the text would subvert the principle of the Rule of Law, distorting it in the form of a judge-made law. This prudential attitude would prove essential in the judicial review of legislative acts,

[1] For a criticism of these opinions that strengthen the judiciary at the expense of Parliament, see the works of Jeremy Waldron, especially: Law and Disagreement (2009).

[2] For a straightforward characterization of this basic dichotomy, with a critical stance, see Ely (1980, pp. 43–72) and Dworkin (1985, pp. 34–38).

which should be limited by the constitutional framework, under the assumption that a decision which employs other methods would be in violation of the democratic principle, inasmuch as the laws under the surveillance of judicial review are enacted with the support of a majority of the members of a political community.

The non-interpretivist account, on the other hand, is more sympathetic to judicial adjudication of the rights enshrined in the Constitution, and is not satisfied with a formalistic or originalist interpretation, despite the great constellation of internal divergences within the advocates of this approach to interpretation. Principles such as justice, freedom and equality should speak louder composing the constitutional project of a self-respecting democratic society, rather than a blunt and strict subservience to the semantic reading the constitutional text. Thus, while interpretivists say that the constitutionally adequate solution to dilemmas and conflicts arising in the legal arena should be found in the lawmakers' opinion, non-interpretivists seek for answers in values (and traditions) arising from society itself.

Here, the criticisms of John Hart Ely, during the 1980s, are particularly appealing because they constitute a strong benchmark against something that was naturalized in U.S. legal doctrine until then.

As to interpretivism, which adopts a restricted notion adjudication, Ely acknowledges that strict adherence to the text of the Constitution itself requires a respect for the will of the majority expressed and interpreted in accordance with the law. Nonetheless, in spite of the fact that the majoritarian premise is at the centre of the American democracy, it is not, and should not be made, absolute. In this sense, he argued that minorities need to be protected against abuses that might occur in a representative democracy. Moreover, attachment to the wording of the Constitution is also problematic in the sense that the text is neither a closed framework nor a perfect product that can cover all of the possible situations of application (Ely 1980, pp. 07–52).

Non-interpretivism, on the other hand, has to face the problem of determining what modes of integration and complementation of the Constitution should be made available for judges. In other words, they must answer which sources of arguments may be deployed to supplement the constitution. Would it be from the natural law tradition, reason, consensus, principles or moral digressions? If any of these suggestions is accepted, the parliament borne democratic element (which stems from the principle of democratic representation) could be shaken, since legal judgments would depend on the subjectivity or even arbitrariness of judges that rely on criteria which are provided with certainty and security (Ely 1980, pp. 07–52).

From there comes the need for new theoretical conceptions that aim to overcome the old dichotomy between interpretivism and non-intepretivism. Ely himself was one of the first authors to develop a theory to overcome this gap (Ely 1980).

As Dworkin has argued, the scheme of classification underlying this dichotomy is a poor one, since "any recognizable theory of judicial review is interpretive in the sense that it aims to provide an interpretation of the Constitution as an original, foundational legal document, and also aims to integrate the Constitution into our constitutional and legal practice as a whole" (Dworkin 1985, pp. 34). Any sensible real-world theory of interpretation, therefore, needs to overcome the limits of this dichotomic approach to constitutional argumentation.

In the present chapter, I will work with three of the contemporary theories that go beyond "interpretivism" and "non-interpretivism" in the American landscape.

12.3 Cass Sunstein's Judicial Minimalism

Cass R. Sunstein is one of the exponents of an interpretive approach known as "judicial minimalism", the purpose of which is to re-interpret the role that courts should play in a constitutional democracy.

Minimalists are suspicious about constitutional theory and judicial review, even when these are deployed with emancipatory purposes. For this reason, they are reluctant to accept a social protagonism on the part of judges, who should rather focus on the specific solution of the case under their auspices.

Sunstein's basic idea is that judges, in constitutional adjudication, must leave many questions open, having no hurry to introduce substantive and conclusive answers – or even brilliant academic theses – to their constituency. It is rather explicit the preference for a type of legal practice in which judges must move away from "theoretical" arguments in their decisions.

He believes that the U.S. Congress understands the democratic dimension much better than the Supreme Court, and therefore is more entitled to give final answers on most of the legal issues. In consequence of this, there would be a "greater promotion of democracy" if judicial interference in the political process decreased. Thus, a minimalist decision has the merit of leaving a space for future reflections on the matter, at national, state and local levels.[3]

In order for that to happen, magistrates must understand that there is not the slightest need – or legitimacy – for them to decide questions which cannot be regarded as essential to the resolution of the case at hand. Therefore, the assessment of complex cases that have not yet reached a level of maturity in the course of decisions in society should be avoided by simply denying the *certiorari*.[4]

Sunstein argues that a minimalist decision shall normally have two features: superficiality and narrowness or restriction (Sunstein 1999, p. 10). Hence, the Court objectively decides on the case at hand, rather than making an attempt to establish rules for application in other similar or future cases.[5]

---

[3] Michael Dorf (1998) prefers to refer to this judicial stance as legal experimentalism, since this complementary space, for both the Legislative and the state Courts, allows a greater reflection on the problem to be discussed by the entire society at various levels (pluralism favoring).

[4] Here we have a reduced burden of legal decisions and decreased risk of a mistaken decision: with this, it is possible to avoid overloading judicial decisions tasks, so that eventual errors of the courts become less frequent and less damaging. As it is widely known, judicial resolutions of issues that are highly complex from the technical standpoint and politically controversial can generate political and economic side effects (Sunstein 1999).

[5] An example is the judgment on gender discrimination at the Virginia Military Institute, in 1995. By adopting a minimalist understanding of the decision, the Supreme Court did not attempt to establish a general rule that could put an end to the discussion about the constitutionality of the gender discrimination practiced by the U.S. military schools that only accepted male students, ruling instead in the strict case of the State of Virginia. (United States v. Virginia, 518 U.S. 515, 1996).

Therefore, decisions must be "narrow rather than broad" and "shallow rather than deep". In these terms, "decisions should be narrow to the extent that the court should simply decide on that case, without anticipating how similar (or analogous) cases would be solved. And should be shallow to the extent that they should not try to justify the decision for reasons involving basic constitutional principles."[6]

In these terms, the minimalist approach would have the power to: "a) not have courts deciding on issues unnecessary to the resolution of a case; b) have courts refusing to decide cases that are not yet mature and ready for decision; c) have courts avoiding the discussion on constitutional issues; d) have courts respecting their own precedents, e) not have courts issuing advisory opinions, f) have courts following the previous legal precedents but not necessarily following personal opinions expressed in votes that have no binding force; g) have courts exercising passive virtues associated with maintaining silence about the big day-to-day issues" (Sunstein 1999, pp. 04–05).

With this, we have in Sunstein's theory a relevant space for the constructive use of silence. That would be "a trivial and correct measure for the activity of judicial institutions", either because it allows the court to "buy time" while the appropriate political forums do not solve the problem, or because judges have "little democratic legitimacy to provide wide public evidence over certain matters".[7]

But despite taking the minimalist approach, Sunstein also spells out what he means by maximalism. For him maximalism requires judicial decisions that establish "general rules for the future" as well as "ambitious theoretical justifications". These decisions will be "deep" and "wide". Under certain contexts and circumstances, they will be necessary (minimalism does not always prevail, because it is not absolute, as no interpretive theory could be, as a matter of fact, in the words of Sunstein). In these terms, there is a minimalism favourable assumption though it can be overcome, in certain specific (contextual) situations, by law enforcement.

So the idea is, if the "limited" and "superficial" nature of the decisions is an assumption rather than a dogma, how could it be possible for one to know when it is desirable to frankly adopt a more "proactive" stance? Certainly, it would not be possible to find an answer that definitively resolves this problem, although for Sunstein, some general considerations can be advanced.

In this vein, according to Sunstein, there are a few cases in which it may be recommended to construct arguments supported by broader and more abstract principles, especially in the following cases: (i) When a wider solution can reduce the cost of the uncertainty of the decision for both the court itself and the litigants; when it is necessary to establish conditions for a prior planning, able to provide legal certainty and predictability to actors in society in general; where the lack of clear decisions may deprive citizens from a solid support to act democratically. Moreover, it is also admissible (ii) when a more activist approach promotes democratic goals,

[6] For Sunstein, a judge must decide "one case at a time" and limited to what the case requires as to avoid taking position on moral or political controversies which are not indispensable to the solution of the particular problem (Sunstein 1999, pp. 10–11).

[7] In law, as everywhere, what is said is not necessarily more important than what is not said. This is especially so when the acceptance of a controversial theory can increase the risk of assessment mistakes, errors that judges and courts are not often in a good position to evaluate.

enabling essential prerequisites to the functioning of deliberative democracy. The decision of the U.S. Court in *Brown v. Board of Education*[8] is certainly the most suitable example (Sunstein 1999, pp. 56–57).

On the other hand, the features that make a more modest approach recommended in turn are: (i) when the situation in which the court must decide generates great uncertainty about fundamental aspects of the rules, especially constitutional ones, or in case of rapid social changes and instability; (ii) when any broader solution seems to entail great uncertainty for future cases; (iii) when there is no urgent need to establish safe public planning criteria for the future; (iv) when the preconditions of democratic deliberation are not in play and democratic goals are unlikely to be promoted by a bolder judgment (Sunstein 1999, pp. 56–57).

As mentioned above, Sunstein's main concern is not with the decision itself, or its internal and external justification, but with the "consequences" of that decision. He moves away from the search for legitimacy, correctness or suitability of the decision rendered. The "arguments of principle" are overridden by "political arguments". Here, in an extremely instrumental way, what really matters are the impacts of the decision. As a matter of fact, the decision will only be appropriate when in accordance with its strategic effects in concrete situations, in a given time span (the "adequate" cannot be "adequate" in a given instance for a political reason), so even "theoretical arguments" should be eschewed in favour of "practical arguments" and the empirical perspective (empirical research on attitudes and practices of judges and courts) prevails over any theoretical construction (based on interpretative theories).[9]

12.4 Pragmatism and the Anti-theoretical Trend Against the Backdrop of Richard Posner's Law and Economics

The works of Richard Posner have been highly discussed in several countries, and their contribution, which will be analyzed here, concerns the so-called "law and economics" as well as the debate on pragmatism and the anti-theoretical movement in legal discourse.

Starting with "law and economics", its milestone dates back to a book published in the early 70s of the last century, in Chicago (Posner 2003b). This work was divided into seven (7) parts, involving topics such as corporate and financial markets law, the distribution of wealth and tax revenues, the American legal procedure and the profile of the legal economic arguments (Economic Legal Reasoning) (Posner 2003b).

The core of such theory lays on the assumption that law is an instrument for accomplishing social ends, and with that, its ultimate goal would be economic effi-

[8] *Brown* v. *Board of Education of Topeka* – 347 U.S. 483 (1954).

[9] For an empirical institutional analysis of judicial practice, which advances this perspective, see: (Vermeule 2006) and (Vermeule 2009).

ciency. For such a task, Posner considers economics as the science of rational choices *par excellence*, stating in his digressions that economy guides the making of the law and that people are the rational maximizers of their satisfactions. Therefore, all persons (except for small children and the mentally retarded) throughout all activities (except under the influence of psychosis or mental disorders caused by drug or alcohol abuse) work with choices and should maximize them (Posner 2003b).[10]

The thesis of law and economics could then be synthesized from the utilitarian perspective (although it is not the "traditional utilitarianism" or "pure utilitarianism" which aims to maximize the "wellness", "pleasure" or "happiness"), in which the decision of a judge must be guided by a cost-benefit ratio. Thus, the duty is perspectival when it promotes the maximization of economic relations, and the maximization of wealth (wealth maximization) should guide the involvement of judges (Posner 2003a, b).

We draw attention here to the so-called North-American legal pragmatism, from a "realistic matrix", which sees legal reasoning by an exogenous (external) logic which searches for the best "practical" and, consequentially, strongest results. Law then inexorably stands as a *strategic* and indefinite instrument, which suffers from a legitimation deficit and lacks any commitment to the idea of "rightness" or correctness.

As to legal pragmatism, it is advisable to clarify that although there are many different approaches to this philosophical traditions, there seem to be three general characteristics that define this concept, namely: contextualism, consequentialism and anti-foundationalism.

Contextualism implies that any proposition is judged on the basis of its compliance with human and social needs. Consequentialism, in turn, requires that any proposition to be tested by anticipating its consequences and possible outcomes. Finally, anti-foundationalism is the rejection of any kind of metaphysical entities, abstract concepts, *a priori* categories, perpetual principles, past instances, transcendental entities and dogmas, among other possible foundations to thinking.

Hence, when Posner postulates that legal judgments should be evaluated according to a cost-benefit ratio which seeks wealth maximization, he provides a place for the judicial system to ensure dogmas (i.e., private property, contracts, etc.) that shift the standards of legitimacy of judicial decisions from law to economic parameters. Legal decisions lose their deontological nature if guided by a ratio of costs and economic impacts interconnected by the logic of efficiency. That is, we have here a strand of the "strong consequentialism", which holds that judicial decisions must be made not with the eyes in the past (following an interpretive bias, for instance), but always with an eye to the future (the prospective), with a view to choosing among

[10]Thus, according to Posner, the Chicago School clearly supports the application of microeconomic analysis in law based on three assumptions: (a) individuals are rational maximizers of their satisfactions with behaviors both out and inside the market; (b) individuals respond to price incentives with behaviors both in and out of the market, (c) rules and legal actions can be evaluated based on efficiency, since legal decisions should promote efficiency.

the options one that brings greater advantage from the economic perspective. Posner, who is a Federal Judge, will be heavily criticized for many of his opinions. One of those criticisms comes from Posner's defence of the correctness of the U.S. Supreme Court in its decision concerning the *Bush X Gore* election,[11] in which the original outcome was maintained (with the Bush victory) in spite of the fact that the election has been knowingly forged in the State of Florida.[12] According to Posner, the decision contrary to the recount (even if it was legally consistent because of the possible fraud) would cause a huge loss to the institutions of the country, let alone an excessive instability in not making a decision about who would be the future President during the election reanalysis period.

We point out that the assessment of the consequences of the decision, rather than its strict "legality", becomes increasingly more important for Posner. Yet, this consequentialist approach faces some important objections. If market imperatives are driving the judicial conduct, Law becomes colonized by another system with a different logic, replacing law's binary statements of "legal" and "illegal" by a reasoning based on "profit and losses", with a tendency towards the disappearance of Law and giving way to obvious risks to the legitimacy and stability of a democratic society.

Another important point to be noticed is that Posner's pragmatism frontally attacks most of the scholarly theories of law (*legal scholars*).[13]

That means this is part of what is called an anti-theoretical populist movement, which holds that no moral theory can provide a solid basis for moral judgments (no moral theory that can convince a person, for example, a judge, to accept a moral judgment he initially rejects).[14] Moreover, Posner also argues that whatever the force that a moral theory may have in ordinary life, or even in politics, judges should ignore it because magistrates have better resources to defend their objectives and decisions (Dworkin 2006, p. 117).

The central argument is that judges are not faced with moral questions in their cases, and more, are not interested and should not be interested in issues of justice.

[11] Bush v. Gore – 531 U.S. 98 (2000).

[12] As Dworkin states "by far the best known defense of the Supreme Court decision in Bush X Gore is the assertion that the court spared the country from a new, and perhaps prolonged, period of legal and political battles, not to mention the uncertainty about who would be the new US President. From this point of view, the five conservative judges knew it was impossible to justify their decision on legal grounds, but heroically decided to pay the price of having their reputation as law officials scratched in order to save the nation from all these difficulties: as is sometimes said, they have burned themselves to preserve us. In a book of which I was the organizer, Richard Posner, with his usual vigor and niggardliness, presents a favorable argument to this view more clearly than anyone else ever did". (Dworkin 2006, p. 133).

[13] Those somehow establish a connection between the philosophy of law and moral philosophy, or better yet, insert legal theory into moral theory. Posner's prime targets (legal scholars) are: Ronald Dworkin, Charles Fried, Anthony Kronman, John Noonan and Martha Nussbaum.

[14] (Dworkin 2006, p. 117) Here the author does not advocate a moral nihilism (i.e.: nothing is morally right or wrong), but a moral relativism in which there are valid moral claims, namely those which are derived from a local perspective, i.e., related to a moral code of a particular culture.

According to Posner, when faced with challenging cases where a simple answer cannot be drawn from ordinary sources of guidance (Constitution, precedents, laws), judges "can do nothing but resort to notions derived from the management of public affairs, professional and personal values, intuition and their own opinion". (Posner 1999, p. 08)

More important than making the judge aware the moral content during her decision making process, (i.e., the value of democracy within a society, what is the meaning of the clause of mutual respect, or if a law prohibiting physician-assisted suicide is compatible with the Constitution), is to have her (the magistrate) mastering the knowledge of all economic, social and political issues involved in the matter. She must have control, with the highest possible predictability, over of the consequences generated by her decision, always taking the adoption of the measure that will bring greater benefit or an improvement to the general conditions observed by those involved in the case as his guiding framework.

12.5 Ronald Dworkin's Theory of Integrity: The Defence of "Theoretical Argument" Against "Practical Arguments"

For the north-american jurist and philosopher Ronald Dworkin law must be read as part of a collective enterprise shared by the whole society. Rights would then be creatures of history and morality, to the extent that they have a historical-institutional construction for sharing within the same society the same set of principles and recognition of equal rights and freedoms to all subjective members (communal principles).[15] This involves recognizing that all who belong to the same society necessarily share a common set of basic rights and duties, including the right to participate in the construction and attribution of meaning to these rights, whether in the field of the Legislative or the Judiciary Power.

Therefore, magistrates neither would be free to exercise strong discretion while deciding concrete cases brought to the courts, nor could base their decisions in the pursuit of collective goals (which benefit only a portion of society over another branch) if individual rights (embodied by legal principles) are under question, because – as wildcards in a game of cards – they hold primacy over the first (collective goals), given their universal character – being valid for all members of that given society (Dworkin 1986).

The view that the adjudication is not produced in the vacuum, but rather in a constant dialogue with history, bears the influence of Gadamer's hermeneutics. Nevertheless, Dworkin goes beyond Gadamer and advocates a constructive inter-

[15] The "Communal principles" becomes the fundamental idea in the Dworkian theory, for it is the condition of possibility for the metaphors of Judge Hercules and the "Chain Novel".

pretation[16] and, therefore, a critical hermeneutic theory in which the decision of a case produces the "growth" a particular tradition. Moreover, the construction of the decision of a case and, consequently, of its constitutional interpretation, shows itself as something undertaken collectively and open to constant evolution and – why not – review.

Dworkin devises a metaphor (the chain novel) in which each judge is regarded as merely the author of a chapter in a long collective work about the proper interpretation of a legal system. Each judge is, therefore, not only bound to the past, but also is committed to continue the work of her predecessors and to preserve the integrity of the legal practice by constructing the best possible theoretical scheme of the principles recognized by the community in which she is inserted (Dworkin 1986).

To summarize the argument: the political value of integrity denies that the legal statements are either mere factual reports geared to the past, as argued by conventionalist positivism, or instrumental programs geared towards the future, as held by pragmatism and its predecessors from American Legal Realism. For Law as integrity, legal assertions are interpretive positions aimed both at the past and the future.

A society which accepts integrity as a virtue becomes, according to Dworkin, a special type of community that promotes its moral authority in order to take over and mobilize the monopoly of coercive force. Therefore, Dworkin's theory brings us at least four (4) points worthy of emphasis, since they are relevant to this discussion: (1) the denial of judicial discretion (in the strong sense), (2) the opposition against judicial decisions based on political guidelines, (3) the importance of the concept of due process to the dimension of integrity, and (4) the notion of integrity itself, which raises the requirement that each case be understood as part of a linked history; therefore, not to be dismissed without a reason based on coherent principles (Dworkin 1986).

So for Dworkin, the judge, according to the theory of integrity, should identify among the principles accepted by society one that justifies the decision in his case, conceiving law as part of a linked history and thus developing a constructive interpretation based on the coherence of these principles.

The judge must act with his or her gaze facing the past and looking forward to the future, building a coherent theory with a view to justifying the way by which the community of principles embodies social practices. These communal principles form what Dworkin sees as the "political morality" of a given community, which should provide the basis for identifying the associative purposes of such community and the key standard about how the practice of law should be constructed.

This so-called political morality that serves as a substrate for coherent decisions can be explained by the principles of equality and freedom, which are fundamental

[16]A social practice such as law or courtesy is interpreted in a "constructive" way when the interpreter does two things: (1) First, he acknowledges that this practice is not merely a brute social fact, but rather has a purpose or a "point" that makes it valuable to him/her and to those who join the practice. (2) Second, he interprets this practice in a constructive way because he regards the practice as "sensitive" to this point and strives to make this practice the best it can be from the point of view of its very point. (Dworkin 1986).

to the theory of Dworkin. A real political community must accept that its members are governed by common principles and not only by rules created from a common political compromise. According to Dworkin, law as integrity is no longer just a guiding theory for the magistrates' activities, but rather revealed as a "commitment to people" towards equal respect and concern for all individuals, so that no group is excluded, guiding in this way the realization of the project of a political community (Dworkin 1986).

A society that accepts integrity as a political virtue becomes, according to Dworkin, a special type of community that promotes its morals and overcomes an account of legal authority based merely on coercive force.

For that matter, Dworkin's theory, as already explained, shows us the requirement of integrity, according to which each case must be understood as a link of the chained story and cannot be dismissed without a reason based on consistent principles. This is, indeed, the key ***argumentative obligation*** imposed upon legal reasoners who accept Dworkin's model of Law as Integrity.

Integrity, therefore, becomes a necessary element, rather than an option, to the democratic rule of law that appears endowed with legitimacy, allowing legal decisions to be made by the same "collective body", i.e., by this community of principles that even in face of a reasonable disagreement (pluralism of lifestyles and dignified living options) demands equal respect and concern for all citizens. In other words, Dworkin argues that judges, regardless of their personal and moral convictions, must be endowed with the responsibility (stemming from "political morality") to make the best decision for each case that arises as a unique and unrepeatable event (Dworkin 1986).

But how can such a construction be achieved? What would be the proper way of reasoning about the enforcement of law? For Dworkin, there are two answers to the question of knowing what the appropriate way of thinking about the truthfulness of legal allegations is. The first, called "theoretical approach", involves the application of a network of legal principles of political morality to specific legal problems. A second response, called "practical approach", sustains that a judicial decision is a political event that should be achieved by analyzing the consequences of different responses according to an economic assessment, not being mandatory the use of a "library of political philosophy" for such purpose (Dworkin 2006, pp. 72–73).

The practical approach has been developed by numerous supporters and seems to be more sensible and tuned to the North-American way of thinking, although Dworkin, in his philosophical endeavours, has objectively demonstrated the shortcomings of this approach, making it patent that the "theoretical approach" may be more appropriate, and even necessary, for the application of law to be done with integrity.

The theoretical approach assumes that issues about the truth of legal claims is an interpretive matter, which must be justified by principles that best reflect the legal practice in the case at hand and put the case to its best light. It is seen as interpretive, since any legal argument is subject to "justificatory ascent": when we move our eyes away from the particular case toward a more general examination of the issues embedded in it, we must determine whether the principle with which we want to justify our decision is inconsistent or not in line with the principle that justifies another broader sphere of law[17] (Dworkin 2006, p. 76). The "justificatory ascent" to Dworkin would be provided by the metaphor of Judge Hercules, who, as a judge of extraordinary powers, does not expresses his arguments from the inside out, as do most lawyers, but from the outside in, trying to grasp the more abstract issues and finally decide the case. In these terms, Dworkin argues that

> Before judging his first case, he could develop an all-encompassing, gigantic and broad scope theory, appropriate to all situations. He could decide all the key issues of metaphysics, epistemology, and ethics, as well as moral, including political morality. He could decide about what exists in the universe and why it is justifiable to think that is what exists, of what justice and impartiality require, about what it means to have a well understood freedom of expression, and whether and why it is particularly worthy of protecting, and about when and why it is correct to require damages to be awarded to persons whose activity is linked to the loss of others. He could combine all that and other things to form an architecturally wonderful system. When a new case arises, he would be very well prepared. Starting from outside in – starting perhaps in intergalactic dimensions of his wonderful intellectual creation – he could quietly lean on the problem at hand: finding the best possible justification for law in general, for the American legal and constitutional practice as a branch of law, for constitutional interpretation, for liability and then finally to the poor woman who took pills in excess and the enraged man who set fire to the flag (Dworkin 2006, p. 79).

In a dialogue engaged on with a number of interlocutors, Dworkin summarizes what he calls "the three major criticisms" directed at the "theoretical approach" by the advocates of the "practical approach".

The first criticism, metaphysical in nature, is based on the idea that there are no objectively correct answers to legal questions or objective truth about the political morality that can be discovered by lawyers. To such criticism, all our beliefs are simple creations of our language games, so that language creates our moral universe instead of expressing it.[18]

A second critical perspective of the theoretical approach is called professional critique and departs from the premise that we are just lawyers and not philosophers, and then we cannot get our legal reasoning based on the grounds of the typical arguments of philosophical investigations.

Finally, we have the pragmatic critique, directly linked to authors such as Richard Posner, that states that his views on judicial decision are independent, since they only focus in an economic perspective, analysing and choosing the best conse-

[17] In Dworkin's example, where there is the right to claim that a person who suffers harm as a result of the use of a medication deserves to win or lose his cause, we can see that principle X is not compatible with principle Y, that applies to tort cases.

[18] In *Justice for Hedgehogs* (2011), Dworkin defends the idea that there is truth in morals, either against those who hold what can be called as internal skepticism, i.e., the skepticism inherent to substantive moral judgments, or against those who hold the external skepticism, which is based on external, 'second-order' claims on morality. The internal skeptics use moral as the foundation to denigrate the moral, stating, for example, that if God does not exist, it removes any basis for morality, or that morality is empty because all human behavior is causally determined by events that go beyond the control of any person; external skeptics judge moral from outside and reject any possibility of moral knowledge, stating, for example, that moral judgments are neither true nor false, but the simple expression of feelings (Dworkin 2011, pp. 31–34).

quences for the specific case. Such an analysis would be "progressive", once linked to consequential and deontological arguments not because the deontologist could take a result that, in certain situations, manages the worst consequences, while the pragmatists (so-called "progressives") would always be stuck in searching for the maximum welfare in the decision.

It turns out that the theory of integrity, defended by Dworkin, has a diverse consequentialist concern than the one raised by Posner, for it always aims at a general objective which is a structure of law and a community that ensures equal respect and consideration at all. I.e., consequentialism should indeed exist, but cannot be taken to the last consequences, as to break the necessary limit with the "integrity of the decision". A consequentialism that "takes law seriously" can only be defended on "weak" terms. As Dworkin poses: "It is consequential in the details: each interpretive legal argument is intended to safeguard a state of things which, according to the principles embodied in our practice, is superior to the alternatives. It is therefore impossible to consider an objection to the theoretical approach the assertion that it is not sufficiently progressive, in case progressive means consequential". (Dworkin 2006, p. 89)

Dworkin will also question the use of the concept of welfare to search for correct answers as a plausible argument. A utilitarian would claim that a legal decision would only make a certain situation better off in case it would bring improvements to the discussion, either in absolute or average terms. This type of utilitarianism, of Posnerian matrix, however, could not serve as a guide to judicial decisions because in Dworkin's opinion constitutional rights presuppose the principles of equality and freedom that will oppose, in certain situations, to the argument of the best result for the majority. By detaching from the lawful/unlawful code, utilitarianism would only be concerned about what works or what might be best for the greatest number of individuals, leaving aside what may be the truth, according to the moral principles embraced by our society.

12.6 Conclusion

It is with some confidence that one can say it is not usual to find theories of legal argumentation in the North-American legal system as those developed in Roman-Germanic tradition (by authors such as Viehweg, Perelman, Alexy, Aarnio, Günther) and the UK legal system (in particular by MacCormick 2005, p. 23). It is an interesting argument as to why American jurists not bend over a methodological study on rules (and procedures) to the discourses of justification of judicial decisions.

Notwithstanding the strong attachment to legal realism since the early twentieth century, the American theoretical tradition, given a series of characteristics, sought to justify the Supreme Court decisions regarding the interpretation of Constitution, by taking into consideration, up until very recently, the dichotomy of "interpretivism versus non-interpretivism". Of course each of these positions has internal differences, but they keep common traits that were exposed along this chapter. That is, at the end of the day, finding an interpretivist or non-interpretivist judge or lawyer has never been a great challenge.

Sunstein's minimalism, Posner's pragmatism and Dworkin's theory of Integrity are attempts to break the above mentioned dichotomy, in order to better operate the foundations for the interpretation and application of legal decisions.

Among these attempts, we chose to support Dworkin's opinion in the current chapter, since contrary to minimalism (that advocates the need for vague and superficial decisions), we understand that: (1) the "arguments of principle" should override the arguments of "policy" or "political", which stand at the root of minimalism. According to my position, minimalist decisions underestimate the need for equal respect and consideration in the light of political morality advocated by Dworkin, (2) minimalism, following the "anti-theoretical" stream, moves away from the proposed use of "theoretical arguments" in the application of law, producing thereby a clear deficit of legitimacy in judicial decisions; (3) the minimalist proposal is actually covered by a type of utilitarianism with an extremely instrumentalist bias (adaptation of means to ends) that "does not take law seriously", (4) for the advocates of minimalism, what matters in the end is not the decision itself, and its bases built on the principles of rationality of equal respect and consideration, but rather the effects of the decision and its impact, i.e., merely the consequences of that decision. Here, although we are facing a weaker consequentialism if compared to Posner's (in so far as a "valuable theory" for interpretation is acceptable) there is a consequentialism stronger than Dworkin's (to the extent that the use of a "theory of the value" is relativized on "controversial cases"). In Sunstein's account of legal adjudication, the theoretical premises that are necessary to provide a justification for a legal decision may remain bracketed or pushed to the background on the basis of a compromise or an incompletely theorized agreement, without any power to influence the outcome of a legal decision (Vermeule 2006).

Against Posner's "pragmatic" anti-theoretical movement (which advocates a strong consequentialism and maintains that no moral theory can provide a basis for the judges to decide cases), I argue that: (1) Dworkin's account of legal argumentation is not drawn solely from a tangle of abstract moral and legal concepts; (2) in these terms, the moral argument which provide the basis for a legal decision is not built by judges only in borderline cases of "difficult" decisions. In fact, any legal interpretation requires a moral argument; (3) concepts such as democracy, freedom, equality, due process of law, among others, are legal concepts that are impregnated by political morality and that, whenever challenged in court, necessarily will be interpreted; (4) for all that, those who interpret the law must do so with a view to constructing arguments that provide the best possible justification for the legal practices of the political community. To that extent, the theoretical approach argues that there are principles so embedded in our legal practice that when we apply them to a case at hand they transfer (or not) the right to the claiming party; (5) we justify legal claims as we demonstrate that the principles that underpin them also offer the best justification for a more general legal practice in the field of law involving the case;

(6) constitutional law presupposes the principles of equality and freedom that will preclude the majority, in certain situations, from adopting a particular political directive; (7) for sure, there will be disagreement concerning which set of principles offers the best solution to the case. But this disagreement, rather than leading to the rejection of the thesis, is by itself what makes it more attractive; in this perspective, the controversy over this set of principles – that is a moral issue – will be resolved by means of the comparison of the various arguments deployed to solve the case, and the one to prevail, shall be that which demonstrates more responsibly the best fit to the legal practices; (8) the claim that no moral theory can provide a solid basis for a legal judgment is contradictory because it is based on an implicit moral theory to vindicate this claim, (9) in other words, Posner's proposal, despite all its seeming indifference to moral issues, ends up being the holder of a certain conception of morality: one that, in our view, is seen in utilitarianism; (10) in reality, as Dworkin would say, the debate about the moral content of legal concepts is inescapable. Just as it is the theoretical reflection, because everyone who is committed to some ambition of equality and democracy will have better success if he or she blazes the trails of theory, (11) just as the use of theory should not replace empiricism, empiricism (which is currently of great importance to the analysis the process of adjudication by courts) cannot "annihilate" the use of theoretical arguments; (12) with all that, we can see that moving away from theory and the "practical reason" inherent to it, amounts to distancing ourselves from the world, something impossible given our human condition, unless we can lie to ourselves (self-deception). Accordingly, the anti-theoretical movement is nothing but a contradiction in terms.

References

Bustamante, Thomas, and Antônio Maia. 2008. Argumentação como justificação. In: *Teoria do Direito e da Decisão Racional*. Rio de Janeiro: Ed. Renovar.

Dorf, Michael. 1998. The Supreme Court 1997 term – the limits of socratic deliberation. *Harvard Law Review* 4. Cambridge: Harvard University.

Dworkin, Ronald. 1985. *A matter of principle*. Cambridge, MA: Belknap.

Dworkin, Ronald. 1986. *Law's empire*. Cambridge, MA: Belknap.

Dworkin, Ronald. 2006. *Justice in robes*. Cambridge, MA: Belknap.

Dworkin, Ronald. 2011. *Justice for hedgehogs*. Cambridge, MA: Belknap.

Ely, John Hart. 1980. *Democracy and distrust: A theory of judicial review*. Cambridge: Harvard University Press.

MacCormick, Neil. 2005. *Rhetoric and the rule of law*. Oxford: Oxford University Press.

Posner, Richard. 1999. *The problematics of moral and legal theory*. Cambridge, MA: Harvard University Press.

Posner, Richard. 2003a. *Law, pragmatism and democracy*. Cambridge, MA: Harvard University Press.

Posner, Richard. 2003b. *Economic analysis of law*, 6th ed. New York: Aspen.

Sunstein, Cass. 1999. *One case at a time – Judicial minimalism on the Supreme Court*. Cambridge, MA: Harvard University Press.

Vermeule, Adrian. 2006. *Judging under uncertainty – An institutional theory of legal interpretation.* Cambridge, MA: Harvard University Press.
Vermeule, Adrian. 2009. *Law and the limits of reason.* Oxford: Oxford University Press.
Waldron, Jeremy. 2009. *Law and disagreement.* Cambridge: Cambridge University Press.

Index

© Springer International Publishing Switzerland 2015
T. Bustamante, C. Dahlman (eds.), *Argument Types and Fallacies in Legal Argumentation*, Law and Philosophy Library 112,
DOI 10.1007/978-3-319-16148-8

MIX
Papier aus verantwortungsvollen Quellen
Paper from responsible sources
FSC® C105338

If you have any concerns about our products,
you can contact us on
ProductSafety@springernature.com

In case Publisher is established outside the EU,
the EU authorized representative is:
Springer Nature Customer Service Center GmbH
Europaplatz 3, 69115 Heidelberg, Germany

Printed by Libri Plureos GmbH
in Hamburg, Germany